RESTORING
DEMOCRACY

RESTORING DEMOCRACY

IN AN AGE OF
POPULISTS & PESTILENCE

JONATHAN MANTHORPE

Cormorant Books

The publisher gratefully acknowledges the support of the Canada Council for the Arts
and the Ontario Arts Council for its publishing program. We acknowledge
the financial support of the Government of Canada through the Canada Book Fund (CBF)
for our publishing activities, and the Government of Ontario through
Ontario Creates, an agency of the Ontario Ministry of Culture,
and the Ontario Book Publishing Tax Credit Program.

LIBRARY AND ARCHIVES CANADA CATALOGUING IN PUBLICATION

Title: Restoring democracy in an age of populists and pestilence / Jonathan Manthorpe.
Names: Manthorpe, Jonathan, author.

Identifiers: Canadiana (print) 201902406IX | Canadiana (ebook) 20190237295 |
ISBN 9781770865822
(softcover) | ISBN 9781770865839 (HTML)
Subjects: LCSH: Democracy. | LCSH: Populism.
Classification: LCC JC423.M36 2020 | DDC 321.8—dc23

Cover photo and design: angeljohnguerra.com
Interior text design: Tannice Goddard, tannicegdesigns.ca
Printer: Friesens

Printed and bound in Canada.

CORMORANT BOOKS INC.
260 SPADINA AVENUE, SUITE 502, TORONTO, ON, M5T 2E4
www.cormorantbooks.com

While writing this book I always kept in mind my three
grandsons, Edmund, Hereward, and Fen Manthorpe.
It is their generation that will have to confront and resolve the
issues I have raised here, and doubtless many more besides.
Apart from the thoughts and observations in this book,
all I can offer them is the benediction in Mashonaland
for someone setting out on a journey —
Mufambe Zvakanaka: Travel Well.

Contents

Introduction

THIS IS GOING to be a fast gallop over heavy ground. In a few thousand words and a handful of chapters, I am going to set out what I think has gone wrong with liberal democracy in the last forty years. But this is not a book about failure. It is a book about hope. The threats to democracy can be beaten off and reversed.

Because they seek to respond to the views and expectations of their citizens, liberal democratic societies are inherently adaptable and resilient. But some of them have drifted, and some are now drifting; they risk tipping into the ditch of despotism or worse. They can and must be refashioned to function and thrive in the new age that has been thrust upon us. There will not be one uniform solution. Each nation is going to have to find salvation built upon the foundation of its individual history, culture, and aspirations, as well as how it has come out of the pandemic socially and economically. COVID-19 has changed the rules of many games, but it is also a reminder of what is of value in human communities, what is essential to making them flourish, and what is mere frippery. The timing of the pandemic and the insights it has provided ought to enliven the quest to restore democracy. It is a challenge that must be embraced with excitement and exhilaration. It is an adventure that should be approached with an entirely open mind for the almost infinite possibilities available for the construction and protection of modern democratic frameworks. This exploration will require courage, perseverance, and a clear understanding of what has gone wrong in the last four decades.

The factors I consider important in the erosion of democracies are my own selections, based on my fifty-five years in journalism. My experience in North America, Europe, Africa, and Asia has given me the opportunity to see up close how democracies are created, what sustains them, why some fail to survive, and the tricks despots use to destroy them. I make no claim that the events I've written about are exhaustive or the best ones to illustrate the situation. They do, however, illuminate my concerns. I have chosen to focus on the challenges to democracy in the countries of Europe and North America. My purpose is two-fold. Taking into account the widely differing cultural contexts in other democracies threatened by populism, such as Brazil, India, or the Philippines, would widen the lens too much, and the narrative would lose focus. Examples of the kinds of threats to democracy evident worldwide are to be found throughout the North Atlantic. In my career as a journalist and, more pertinently, as a foreign correspondent and international affairs columnist since 1979 in Europe, Africa, Asia, and North America, I have been in the front row as many of the events described in this book unfolded. My judgments and selections may be open to criticism, but they were come by honestly.

One of humanity's less attractive traits is a passion for gloom and doom. All too often, people see the cloud on the horizon and not the otherwise flawless blue sky above. The tendency to focus only on the negative is a real danger in these times of political turmoil and uncertainty. Paranoia can become self-fulfilling. We face an unceasing barrage from talking heads and political strategists warning us that democracy and its accompanying virtues of liberalism, tolerance, and communal cohesion are under immediate threat from the forces of authoritarianism, hatred, and tribalism. There are indeed threats to modern democratic liberalism from within and without, just as there have always been since it emerged out of Western Europe's Age of Enlightenment three and a half centuries ago. There is, however, nothing inevitable about the victory of populists, despots, and demagogues, no matter how fertile the ground may be for them. Far from it.

The concept of liberal democracy has always contained contradictions and fundamental differences of opinion about its philosophy, even among its most avid supporters. During most of the twentieth century, those contradictions were sidelined by the greater battles between democratic liberalism and first fascism and then communism. But with the end of the Cold War and the collapse of the Soviet Union, the fallibility and conflicts within liberal democracy have not only bubbled to the surface, they are threatening to erode the whole structure of what I think of as North Atlantic culture. The threats include the emergence of intellectually detached and socially isolated ruling classes that span politics, government, business, academia, and the media. Accompanying that isolation are gross disparities of wealth. This has produced entire communities beached by technological advances and changing patterns of commerce while, according to Oxfam, 1 percent of the world's population — 75 million people — holds half the world's wealth, making them richer than the other 7.4 billion people.

Arising from the insecurity fostered by economic stagnation are fundamental changes in the concept of the nation-state. For many people, especially in the North Atlantic countries, their culturally familiar and homogenous communities are changing or disappearing as foreigners migrate to their countries in search of work or freedom from fear and war. These migrants bring cultural and social changes with them. When a community's identity and self-confidence is already under stress from economic uncertainty, the arrival of foreign influences is not always welcome. For some liberal democracies, especially nations built by immigration, such as Canada, cultural, social, and racial diversity remains a virtue and a goal. But even in immigrant societies like Canada and Australia, and among some European countries with welcoming refugee policies, there are resentful minorities who feel their culture is being changed or diluted. These people must not be ignored.

The volume and intensity of the debate over these conflicts and contradictions is ratcheted up by confusion over what constitutes fantasy, truth, and lies. The cacophony created by the torrent of instantaneous digital communication and chaotic social media is unlike anything with which humans have had to contend before.

Singly and in combination, these threats provide fodder for those who would undermine and overthrow democracy. Some of the adversaries come from within. These are the populist flim-flam artists and those darker beings who believe in the power of destruction. They see the buffeting of democracy as an opportunity to indulge their own personality disorders and extremist notions.

There are fundamental differences between the populist uprisings in Eastern Europe, the United Kingdom, and the United States. Poland and Hungary are countries transitioning to democracy from long histories of authoritarian rule; they are moving from the grip of one empire, the Soviet Union, into that of another, the European Union. These difficult and scary progressions deserve a lot more careful attention than they are currently receiving. It was a populist movement, perhaps even a revolution, that led to the UK's departure from the EU at the end of January 2020. But what stands out is that the three years of apparent chaos between the referendum and "getting Brexit done" were so difficult because those involved were determined to play by the rules of parliamentary democracy. The same cannot be said of populism in the United States. The unholy alliance of Tea Party libertarians and fundamentalist Christian evangelicals that has propelled American populism is bent on destroying the national institutions that stand between them and their vision of paradise. Donald Trump is the chosen and willing agent of this agenda. In his first term, he has already done much to undermine the rule of law — always the first target of would-be despots — and to continue the already well-entrenched perversion of the US political system.

The attacks from outside the US are principally from the Russian Federation and the People's Republic of China. Russian leader Vladimir Putin is intent on buttressing his country against domination by the West and regaining something of Moscow's global stature, lost in the collapse of the Soviet Union. China sees within its grasp a return to its position as the world's pre-eminent nation, as it was through most of recorded human history. The "humiliation" of China by the semi-colonial incursions of the industrialized nations in the last two hundred years is an angst not yet buried by the country's extraordinary economic, military, and political revival, which began in the 1980s. To these ends, China and Russia seek, in some cases with success, to turn democracy's strengths against it. One of the most difficult questions for democracies to address is that their virtues of transparency, the rule of law, and constitutionally guaranteed freedoms of speech and of association are all open doors to the kind of national home invasions being mounted by Moscow and Beijing. Somehow, democracies have to find ways of fighting off the autocrats without setting aside, in the process, the very freedoms that define their societies.

THIS BOOK TAKES as its foundation the belief that democracy is the most effective and philosophically defensible method of governing human affairs that has been devised so far. It is generally accepted that there are four cardinal principles to a fully democratic society. The first is that the government should be a faithful representation of choices made by citizens in free and fair elections. The second is that all citizens, including the head of state, should be subject to the rule of law administered by an independent judiciary. The third is that those laws and that judiciary must also be required to protect the liberties and the human and civil rights of the citizens. Finally, and possibly most importantly in a successful democracy, society as a whole must promote and enable its citizens to participate in the democratic process and the functioning of society.

Remarkably few countries have achieved complete democracy under those fundamental principles. An annual assessment published by the Economist Intelligence Unit (EIU) lists only twenty-two countries as complete democracies in 2019. The list starts with Norway, runs through Iceland, Sweden, New Zealand, Finland, and Ireland, puts Canada equally at seventh with Denmark, places Australia, Switzerland, and the Netherlands at ninth, tenth, and eleventh, swings down through Luxembourg and

Germany, picks up the United Kingdom, gathers up Uruguay, Austria, Spain, and Mauritius, and then concludes with Costa Rica, France, Chile, and Portugal. The US is twenty-fifth on the list, sandwiched between Japan and Malta among fifty-four "flawed democracies."

American democracy has been on a downward slide for well over a decade. Its faults, according to the EIU's ranking, include low scores for political participation, political culture, and civil liberties. The US shares these deficits with France, Italy, Belgium, and several other countries often considered top-tier democracies. The reality that even many countries commonly considered democracies — such as the former Soviet-dominated states, now members of the European Union — have yet to achieve that goal is an important and sometimes crucial matter when assessing the assaults they face.

The EIU report tabulated a general decline in democratic values among Western democracies for several years, the evidence for which is:

- An increasing emphasis on elite/expert governance rather than popular participatory democracy;
- A growing influence of unelected, unaccountable institutions and expert bodies;
- The removal of substantive issues of national importance from the political arena to be decided by politicians, experts, or supranational bodies behind closed doors;
- A widening gap between political elites and parties on the one hand and national electorates on the other; and
- A decline in civil liberties, including media freedom and freedom of speech.

"In the mature democracies the result was an unsustainable political status quo: the increasing vacuity of national politics and the retreat of political elites and parties from engagement with their electorates resulted in falling levels of popular trust in political institutions and parties, declining political engagement, and a growing resentment among electorates at the lack of political representation," the EIU report states. "Eventually the alienation of people from the 21st-century body politic gave rise to populist movements, which repudiated the mainstream political parties and demanded a new political contract between the people and their elected representatives."

A complicating factor is that there is no universal agreement on what liberal democracy means. Democracy and liberalism grew out of the Enlightenment — the rediscovery and embellishment of the political, communal, and artistic philosophies of ancient Greece and Rome in the seventeenth and eighteenth centuries in Western Europe. That revival blossomed on roots nurtured by the Protestant Reformation, the withering of feudalism, and the emergence of a politically active and demanding merchant and commercial class. This ended the dominance of the Catholic Church and fostered unrestricted thinking on religious matters, which in turn encouraged intellectual curiosity. The downside of intellectual freedom, of course, was the rise of contesting religious certainties and several hundred years of persecution and warfare.

Over the past four hundred years, two major conventions have emerged when defining liberalism: those who put personal rights and freedoms as the paramount elements of liberal democracy and those who think communal responsibilities and duties should dominate. Usually, in the politics of North Atlantic culture in the last one hundred years, these differences have manifested themselves as support for left-leaning or right-leaning political parties. The parties of the left can be full-blown socialist operations managing nationalized industries or, more usually, social democratic parties blending free market economics with welfare state social services. Right-of-centre parties are mirror images of this. Centrist conservative parties tend to put more emphasis on the efficient use of tax revenues and user-pay elements in state-provided education, health, and other social services. Parties further to the right often advocate the privatization of social services and even responsibilities stemming from a government's duty to preserve the security of the state, such as the management of prisons. Where right-wing parties contain strands of social conservatism —

frequently born of strong religious elements in the political party — this may produce lack of empathy or interest in minority groups and, in extreme cases, disdain and contempt.

These definitions are not hard and fast, as two examples of Christian-based parties show. While the puritanical, conservative beliefs of the evangelical Christian right have been the main influence on the anti-social policies of the Trump administration in the US, the same is not true of Angela Merkel's right-of-centre Christian Democratic Union in Germany. Indeed, it was Merkel and her CDU who spearheaded the European efforts to receive and assimilate the estimated 1.5 million refugees seeking asylum in Europe after the 2011 Arab Spring revolutions and civil wars. Under Merkel's administration, Germany alone received more than a million refugees, mostly from Syria.

DEMOCRACY'S TRAGEDY OVER the last thirty years is the erosion of the centre as political parties and establishment classes have, to one degree or another, lost touch with large segments of their societies. Socialism and communism have attracted surprisingly few of these abandoned voters, which is what previously happened over much of the twentieth century. Some have opted for special interests, such as the Green parties, but for the most part, disenchanted citizens have turned to the right, seeking solace with nationalist, religious, and populist solutions for their grievances. This spirit of grievance fed the campaign for the UK to leave the EU, ostensibly to regain control over its own affairs. It has sustained the rule of Viktor Orbán, whose politics were unexceptional when he was prime minister of Hungary from 1998 to 2004 but who has drifted to the far right since returning to power in 2010. Almost all European parliaments now have members from far-right parties, and in some they form part of governing coalitions.

Outside of Europe, Canada, New Zealand, and Australia have all seen rising popularity for the hard right. In democracies elsewhere, there have been similar movements. Indian Prime Minister Narendra Modi's

Bharatiya Janata Party is avowedly Hindu and nationalist. After he was first elected in 2014, there was much anxiety among India's more than two hundred million Muslims that his government would favour the country's one billion Hindus and that it might even turn to persecution. Those fears were heightened after Modi and the BJP won re-election in 2019 and soon afterwards ended the autonomy of the predominantly Muslim region of Kashmir. He has gone on to introduce a refugee policy that appears to bar the entry into India of Muslims fleeing persecution.

Public yearning for solutions to complex social problems has lured voters in the Philippines and Brazil to the easy remedies prescribed by Rodrigo Duterte and Jair Bolsonaro.

YET WHILE THERE have been shifts to the political or nationalist right in several countries, there has not been a direct and conclusive overthrow of democracy or democratic institutions.

As I write in May 2020, some established democracies are tottering on the brink, and the COVID-19 pandemic has played into the hands of several leaders, allowing populists to become would-be despots. Democracies across the North Atlantic have invoked state-of-emergency laws in order to be able to confront the pandemic with the necessary agility and control. But, as will be described, there is widespread concern that once the crisis is over, some leaders will hesitate to relinquish their absolute power or will keep in place some of the most useful elements, such as editorial control over the media. There are reasonable grounds for these suspicions.

In Turkey, President Recep Tayyip Erdoğan has conspired and connived for nearly twenty years to remove the institutional checks and balances of the judiciary, political opposition, the military, and the media. He has had considerable success in gathering power that is not easily challenged. It is not clear yet, however, whether he has conclusively demolished Turkey's pillars of democracy, which, in truth, were not firmly founded to begin with.

In the US, President Donald Trump has worked hard to override the checks and balances built into that country's political system. He has tried to run government with the same kind of domineering performance he brought to his starring role in the reality television show *The Apprentice*. After three years in office, he appears to have managed to intensify the anti-government feelings among his supporters, who were already philosophically suspicious of the Washington establishment in all its manifestations. On December 18, 2019, the constitutional machinery of reaction to any attempts to rule autocratically ground into gear, and Trump was impeached by the House of Representatives. On January 16, 2020, articles of impeachment were drawn up and sent to the Senate for trial. But Trump is a master bully. The tactics he learned in business — loudly and persistently denying the truth, hitting back hard when challenged, and quickly diverting attention to some other, even more outlandish, action — have proved useful for politics. His cowing of the Republican Party into simpering subservience is extraordinary. There was never any doubt that the Republican-controlled Senate would ignore the substantial evidence of Trump's abuse of office and throw out the charges against him. Like all would-be despots coming to power in democracies, Trump recognized that the rule of law and an independent judiciary were the greatest threats to his ambitions. Aping the examples of Robert Mugabe in Zimbabwe and Erdoğan in Turkey, Trump has neutered the Department of Justice and waged a persistent campaign to vilify law agencies such as the Federal Bureau of Investigation.

Of all the democracies of the North Atlantic, I am most pessimistic about the ability of the United States to reform and revive its institutions. It is already going through a calamitous civic and political crisis, but there are as yet no signs of any political party, group, or individual who fully grasps the danger the country is in, let alone possesses a vision of how to reverse it. This is because, as I shall describe, I see Trump as a product of deep and irreconcilable divisions within American society. These divisions are easy fodder for merchants of fear, hatred, and violence, of which the US has more than its fair share. The US is approaching a moment when it will have to recognize that the structure of politics and government the Founding Fathers dreamed up at the end of the eighteenth century is no longer fit for purpose. If democracy is to survive in America, radical reform and reconstruction is necessary.

THE ARRIVAL OF 2020 and the new decade was set to be the year when the contest for the survival of liberal democracy in the North Atlantic countries would enter a more intense phase. In Europe, the battlefield was the aftermath of the UK's withdrawal from the EU — Brexit — and all the questions that raised about the survival of the community. In North America, the issue was the looming campaign for the re-election of Donald Trump to the US presidency, the prospect of ever-deepening partisan intolerance, and the fate of America as the pre-eminent world power.

Then, in mid-November, a person in the central Chinese city of Wuhan died of a particularly virulent pneumonia of unknown origin. Sometime between that event and December 30, when the Chinese government notified the World Health Organization (WHO), the coronavirus called SARS-COV-2 evolved into the highly contagious and deadly disease COVID-19, which has been designated the first pandemic of the twenty-first century. The virus likely originated in a bat or other mammal sold for food in the Chinese "wet markets," as they are known. These markets, which sell live animals of unusual or exotic species such as pangolins, civets, and bats, have been incubators before for diseases that have spread worldwide. The severe acute respiratory syndrome (SARS) epidemic came out of just such a market in southern China in 2003. It killed nearly eight hundred people before it was done. But the new version of a similar coronavirus has proved to be a threat of an entirely different order. COVID-19 does not kill as many people who get infected as did SARS, but is far more contagious among humans. It swiftly moved around the world by air and sea with the aid of human carriers who did not know they were infected and infectious. By March 11, when the World Health Organization declared a global pandemic, COVID-19 was already infecting thousands of people a day in

Europe and Asia, and killing hundreds.

At the same time, COVID-19 made itself the central player in the story of the political, economic, and social pressures threatening democracy. At the political level, the pandemic is a vivid reminder that a fundamental reason why humans created governments in the city states of Mesopotamia seven thousand years ago was for the protection and regulation of communal life. Among the essential responsibilities the authorities were expected to fulfil was maintenance of public health. That has remained a core duty and expectation of government. This has flummoxed the populist libertarians of today's political stage, especially Donald Trump and Boris Johnson. Their reluctance to abandon their own agendas and take up the ancient responsibilities of rulers led to the death and infection tolls in the US and UK being much higher than they need have been.

Eventually, all but a handful of European and North American countries shut down their economies in order to encourage people to stay at home and inhibit the spread of the disease. A good deal of public discussion has begun about using this time as an opportunity to refashion the structure of North Atlantic economies to try to address inequities that have become embedded.

The isolation imposed on people to curb COVID-19 has raised many practical and intellectual questions about the nature of community and family. In particular, the ease with which many people adopted virtual platforms for both their work and social lives has accelerated the revolution in human contact that was already underway.

Yet, by and large, the coronavirus and its fallout has underlined the lesson of the last forty years. While democracy can be vulnerable if left untended, the power of the four principles of democracy is that they can evolve and adapt as the demands of society change. Adaptability is one of democracy's greatest strengths. But the people who live in democracies have to work for these changes. They have to manipulate the machinery of their society to protect it and to direct it where they want to go. Democracy is well able to see off the challenges it faces now, and there are some signs that the counterattack is already underway. The response needs a good deal more energy and direction than is currently evident. With that in mind, the current chorus of people, many of them eminent analysts and commentators, singing out warnings of the imminent death of democracy is strange to see. Viewed from a few steps back, this pessimism had its birth forty years ago. It is, ironically, a result of the conclusive victory of democracy in the long and tedious Cold War between the West and the Communist nations of the Soviet Union and China. The end of the Cold War came with the 1989 convulsions within the Soviet Union, leading to its dismemberment in 1991, and the abandonment of pure Marxist economics by China in favour of a hybrid form of state-managed market economy. But those victories bred unhealthy triumphalism among the democracies, an insouciant mood that allowed dangerous and divisive internal social ructions to remain unaddressed until they became destructive. Those attitudes sprang from political and social machinations that had been grinding and churning since the Second World War, particularly through the 1970s and 1980s. But the widespread perception is that it was 1989 that changed the world, so it is there that this story will begin.

Victoria, British Columbia, May 2020

CHAPTER ONE

—

Brave
New World

THE MAJOR STRANDS of global life at the opening of the third decade of the twenty-first century lead back to one extraordinary year: 1989. That year managed to cram more seminal changes to modern human life into twelve short months than any other in recent memory. The tectonic shifts in global politics, economics, and culture sparked by the events of 1989 were so profound that we are living with the aftershocks today — and will continue to do so for the foreseeable future.

Initially, 1989 was believed to herald an era of peace and plenty. It was the year the Cold War ended as the Soviet Union imploded. From a few steps further back, 1989 can be seen as the year when the chain of wars and conflicts generated by the First and Second World Wars finally subsided into silence. The mistakes and ambitions that had fashioned the flawed peace at the end of the First World War helped to create the incendiary pressures that ignited the second. And the Second World War flowed seamlessly into the Cold War after 1945 as Soviet and Allied troops divided up Eastern and Central Europe into occupied territories and spheres of influence.

UK Prime Minister Winston Churchill had just been defeated in the first postwar election when, in a speech at Fulton, Missouri, on March

5, 1946, he said, "From Stettin in the Baltic to Trieste in the Adriatic, an iron curtain has descended across the Continent." That image was made into reality just over ten years later when Moscow and the East German authorities decided to block the escape of about two thousand people a day over the border into West Germany. On the night of August 12, 1961, East German troops put down more than thirty kilometres of barbed wire fencing along the dividing line in Berlin. Two days later, they began building what would become the Berlin Wall, the most potent symbol of the political and economic divisions inherent in the Cold War.

It was a cold war only in the sense that the two major protagonists, the United States and the Soviet Union, did not come to blows directly or use their massive arsenals of nuclear weapons, the threat of which haunted the age. Even at the time, the certainty of mutually assured destruction was a mad way of organizing international security. There were, however, countless wars fought by surrogates and proxies, armed and trained by Moscow or Washington. Some were under the guise of wars of liberation against colonial masters in Asia, Africa, and Latin America. Others were armed resistance to attempted takeovers by communist insurgents. Still others were the overthrow of duly elected but left-wing governments, such as those of Salvador Allende in Chile and Patrice Lumumba in Congo. Others were the destruction of duly elected governments. All too often, these fighters against the horrors of the Red Menace were petty despots of one sort or another, dressed up as heroic defenders of democracy by their backers in Washington. All these wars had as their political and philosophical inspiration the contest between the closed and highly regulated economy of communism and the free market of democracy that had been the core rift of the Cold War.

Throughout 1989, however, the Soviet Union and its component parts buckled and cracked under the pressures of its internal contradictions. That process had begun a few years earlier with the death in November 1982 of Leonid Brezhnev, who had been general secretary of the Central Committee of the Soviet Communist Party since 1962. Brezhnev's death precipitated an extraordinary and almost laughable cavalcade of new

leaders who were on their deathbeds when they came to power. For those watching from outside the Iron Curtain, it became a pub game to bet on how long the latest ashen-faced grey suit would last. Brezhnev was succeeded by Yuri Andropov, the sixty-seven-year-old chairman of the KGB. But he lasted only fifteen months before dying of renal failure. Next in line was seventy-two-year-old senior Politburo member Konstantin Chernenko. He survived a mere thirteen months in office, dying in March 1985 after months of failing health.

Inevitably, this parade of elderly men who were already near death when they took office created the image of a Soviet Union that was also in deathly decline. So, when the Politburo picked the relatively sprightly Mikhail Gorbachev, aged only fifty-four and apparently in good health, to be the next general secretary, it seemed to be a moment of rejuvenation. These chimes of generational change in Moscow had an especially cheerful tone because Ronald Reagan, already into his second term in the Oval Office, was seventy-four years old and of the same generation as the Kremlin's just departed geriatric ninepins. It seemed the Soviet Union might have stolen a march on the United States. Gorbachev was a breath of fresh air who looked and sounded like a vigorous reformer. That, indeed, was his intention. Gorbachev's first imperative was to revive the Soviet economy, but he quickly realized he could not do that without reforming the basic political and social structures of Russia and its federation, a fundamental truth that thirty years later, in 2020, the Chinese Communist Party (CCP) has yet to accept. Gorbachev saw that Moscow could no longer withstand the pressures of popular discontent in Russia and nationalism in the satellite states. There was also the unavoidable realization that the Soviet Union could not sustain its military parity with the North Atlantic Treaty Organization (NATO) in the face of the clear superiority of the American economy. Soon after taking power, Gorbachev launched a campaign of political and economic reform under the banner of *perestroika*. That was followed a few months later by a commitment to *glasnost* (transparency and openness).

There are few more difficult political conjuring tricks than managing

the transition from an autocracy to some form of open, liberal society. When the restraints are lifted, even tentatively, off a repressed society, the compulsion is to blow the lid. That is what happened in the Soviet Union, and Gorbachev, largely because of his humanity, was not the man to effectively control and guide the tide of change. In 1986, the Baltic states of Latvia, Estonia, and Lithuania, which had been forcibly incorporated into the Soviet Union in 1944, began demonstrating for liberation. Later the same year, the quest for liberation and self-determination overflowed in a series of riots and clashes with police and military troops across the Soviet states of Central Asia. In 1987, the shock waves reached down into the Caucasus. By 1988, much of Russia's empire in Europe, Central Asia, and the northern fringes of the Middle East was in turmoil and beyond retrieval.

From the start of 1989, there were portents that it was to be a year of unusual change. On January 7, Japanese Emperor Hirohito died. He was the national symbol for Japan's military imperialism in the 1930s and 1940s, and he was the last surviving national leader of the Second World War. George H.W. Bush, who had been Ronald Reagan's vice-president, was sworn in as US president on January 20, blessed with the gift of low expectations. The year shifted into high gear on February 2, with Moscow's ignominious retreat from its nine-year occupation of Afghanistan. This occupation had become increasingly untenable as the United States turned up the pressure by supplying the insurgent mujahedeen with sophisticated weapons, especially Stinger missiles capable of downing Soviet helicopters. Democratic Texas Congressman Charlie Wilson mounted an efficient and effective lobby to persuade the Central Intelligence Agency (CIA) to finance and arm the mujahedeen resistance to the Soviet invasion. The CIA's Operation Cyclone convinced Moscow it could never win the guerrilla war against the Afghan insurgents. It was best to declare victory and quit with as much grace as possible. But elements of "Charlie Wilson's War" came back to haunt the US. In particular, encouraging Saudi Arabia to fund and motivate young male Afghan exiles in Pakistan and elsewhere by sending fundamentalist clerics to run schools among the refugees; this created a groundswell of Islamic militancy. One of the groups training

and supplying the mujahedeen was al Qaeda — "the Base" — founded in 1988 with a young Saudi militant, Osama bin Laden, as *emir*, or leader. He had a long-term vision to purge Islam of modernity and return it to what he and other Sunni fundamentalists saw as its clean, puritan roots. To that end, bin Laden believed it essential to drive the US away from supporting the Saudi royal family and other Middle Eastern rulers. Sometime in 1989 — the exact date is unknown — al Qaeda established its first cell in New York City and began to make plans. On February 26, 1993, Ramzi Yousef, a Gulf Arab born in either Kuwait or the United Arab Emirates, and a Jordanian friend, Eyad Ismoil, drove a yellow van carrying a bomb into Lower Manhattan and pulled into the public parking garage beneath the World Trade Center at around noon. The six-hundred-kilogram bomb, made from fertilizer, was intended to knock the North Tower into the South Tower, bringing both towers down and killing thousands of people. It failed, but it still killed 6 civilians and injured 1,042 other people, including 919 civilians, 88 firefighters, and 35 police officers. Other al Qaeda attacks were the almost simultaneous truck bomb attacks on US embassies in Kenya and Tanzania in 1998, which killed over two hundred people. In another, a suicide attacker in a bomb-laden speedboat blew a hole in the guided missile destroyer USS *Cole* in the harbour of Aden, Yemen, in 2000. Seventeen sailors died in that attack. These, however, were only preludes to the brutally successful attacks on the World Trade Center in New York and the Pentagon in Washington on September 11, 2001, using hijacked civilian aircraft. In response, US President George W. Bush and his coterie of military-minded advisers lashed out blindly. Their "War Against Terror" started with the invasion of Afghanistan and was followed eighteen months later by the invasion of Iraq. These diverted and misdirected Washington's attention at a time when it should have been paying equal attention to the gathering threats to democracy from other directions.

Back in 1989, the Communist regime in Poland gave up trying to deny the political legitimacy of its opposition, the trade union–based Solidarity movement. This had formed as an independent trade union in 1980 and grown as a political force with much quiet support from the "Polish Pope," John Paul II. After some back and forth, the Warsaw regime agreed to multi-party elections. The crumbling of one-party states even spread to Russia, where parliamentary elections were held in March, and the Communists lost seats.

The physical Iron Curtain between Eastern and Western Europe had grown more porous as the Cold War dragged on. Throughout the late 1980s, persecuted ethnic Hungarian minorities from Transylvania in Romania found it relatively easy to make their way to Austria by crossing Hungary with the quiet help of Hungarian officials. By May 1989, Hungary gave up pretending it was still a loyal part of the Eastern Bloc and dismantled 240 kilometres of fencing along its border with Austria. In June, Solidarity won the elections in Poland, prompting a visit from US President George H.W. Bush the following month. He went on to Hungary, promising economic aid and investment to both countries.

Revolution took a short respite over high summer, but then gathered pace again in late August when two million people in the Soviet-occupied Baltic states of Estonia, Latvia, and Lithuania formed a six-hundred-kilometre-long human chain to demand independence. The scales began to tip more precariously in mid-September, when the Hungarian government formally opened another border to allow refugees from East Germany to flee into Western Europe. Later that month, the Czech government did the same; by the end of the first week of October, there were mass demonstrations in East Germany against the communist regime. Within ten days, the East German leader, Erich Honecker, was forced to step aside. The same day, Hungary's National Assembly voted to reinstate multi-party democracy, something the country had not enjoyed since before the Second World War.

The last days of October were a tumultuous time throughout Eastern Europe, especially in East Germany, which had been riven by mass demonstrations and thousands of people pouring over the borders to get to the West. On November 7, the communist government of East Germany resigned, leaving a power vacuum. It was a vacuum quickly filled by a few lowly East German border guards. Two days later, they opened the checkpoints in the Berlin Wall and, in effect, ended the Cold War.

Before November was out, the Communist Party in neighbouring Czechoslovakia announced it would give up its monopoly on power. In December, Romania joined the list of Soviet satellite states where the communist regimes were collapsing. On Christmas Day, Romanian leader Nicolae Ceausescu and his wife, Elena, were shot by firing squad after having been captured while trying to escape the country two days before. Two weeks later, January 7, 1990, the new government of Romania abolished capital punishment.

THE COLLAPSE OF the Berlin Wall and the East German regime was watched closely by a middle-rank KGB officer stationed in East Germany's second city, Dresden. Vladimir Putin was trying to rebuild a career damaged by a drunken brawl with some friends while he was on a training course in Moscow. Even though he was fluent in German, because of this blot on his copybook, when he was posted in 1985 it was not to West Germany, where he would have had the opportunity to become a spymaster, but to the relative backwater of Dresden in the east. Putin's main responsibilities involved liaising with the East German secret police, the Stasi, whose headquarters were just over the road from his own office at 4 Angelikstrasse. Ironically, because censorship survived in East Germany while it was withering in Russia, Putin missed Gorbachev's "glasnost" revolution of criticism of Soviet Russia. Even so, Putin has said since that he saw reflected in the collapse of East Germany many of the weaknesses in the Soviet system. His response was to observe the strengths of West Germany, of which he became and remains a big fan.

By the end of 1989, the Soviet Union was convulsed in its death throes, and most states of what had been the Russian empire were trying to assemble functional democracies out of the chaos.

One place where the tottering collapse of the Soviet Union in 1989 was seen as an opportunity was among members of the white apartheid government in South Africa. F.W. de Klerk became president on August 15 and inherited a regime that looked solid enough; however, its death was fast approaching. For several decades, the white regime had been the target of international sanctions, but global abhorrence of apartheid was far from universal, and South Africa managed to evade many of the most potentially damaging embargoes. The government of de Klerk faced two calamitous domestic threats. One was that within a decade, apartheid was going to be overwhelmed by demographics. The white population was shrinking through emigration and a low birth rate, while the black population was growing quickly. The mathematics were clear; already in 1989, nearly half the adult white working population was employed imposing racial segregation, and within ten years there would not be enough white people to administer apartheid. The other factor was military. The white regime relied on its military superiority to restrict the ability of Umkhonto we Sizwe (MK), the armed wing of the main anti-apartheid party, the African National Congress (ANC), to mount attacks within South Africa. To that end, the South African army and air force needed to be able to strike at ANC bases in neighbouring countries like Mozambique, Zimbabwe, and Angola. It had been remarkably successful. But between the middle of August 1987 and the end of March 1988, South African forces were engaged in the largest and most intense battle in Africa since the Second World War at Cuito Cuanavale in Angola. The South Africans were allied with the Angolan UNITA rebel movement, and ranged against them were the Angolan national army, elements of the MK wing of Nelson Mandela's ANC, and fighters from the groups seeking to liberate Namibia from South African occupation. And there was a fourth group whose involvement in the battle was decisive. This was a force of about three thousand Cubans, including tank squadrons and, crucially, MIG fighter pilots. The Cuban pilots in their MIG-21s and MIG-23s outshone the South Africans and their out-of-date Mirage aircraft. The South Africans came away from the Battle of Cuito Cuanavale facing the stark reality that they had lost air superiority across southern Africa, and without dominant air power, the superiority of their tanks and other armour counted for little.

President de Klerk came to office primed to find a political settlement with the ANC. The collapse of the Soviet Union debased the currency of communism, which had been highly influential among ANC members, whose leadership included many members of the South African Communist Party. This moment seemed to be a gift for the white regime when it could seek a political settlement with a strong hand of cards to play. Talks began with Mandela, then in Victor Verster Prison just outside Cape Town. Mandela demanded that some of his closest fellow prisoners be released as a sign from de Klerk that he meant business. On October 15, 1989, after twenty-six years in prison, Walter Sisulu, Ahmed Kathrada, and six other anti-apartheid leaders were released. This was the prelude to de Klerk's speech on February 2, 1990, in which he lifted the ban on the ANC, and to the release of Mandela himself on February 11. This opened the door to four years of negotiations, culminating in free and fair elections in 1994, in which Mandela was elected president.

The international campaign of sanctions against the white regime in South Africa may not have been the deciding factor in bringing about the end of apartheid, but it was a profound moment in the political emancipation of African-Americans. After three decades of intense activism within the US to end segregation and embed political rights, ending South African apartheid was the first international issue on which African-Americans were able to influence Washington policy.

Meanwhile, in China, the death on April 15, 1989, of Hu Yaobang, the reform-minded former head of the Chinese Communist Party, had sparked another revolution. Six days after his death, students from universities in Beijing, as well as from Xian and Nanjing, began gathering in the capital's Tiananmen Square to mount a politically charged mourning of Hu. The mourning quickly turned into protest as the students began demanding political reform and an end to corruption among party officials. The protests became an occupation of the square and gathered steam so that by mid-May, more than a million demonstrators marched through Beijing demanding not just reform but democracy. Some CCP officials tried negotiating with the protesters, but the demonstrations and occupations spread to over a hundred other cities in China and became a national uprising. With the collapse of the Communist regime in Moscow staring them in the face, CCP hard-liners forced the declaration of martial law. On the night of June 3, the People's Liberation Army moved from the outskirts toward Tiananmen Square, killing hundreds if not thousands of people in and around the centre of Beijing. In the days that followed, the occupations in the other Chinese cities were removed with equal ferocity.

While Russia under the leadership of Mikhail Gorbachev opted for reform in the face of popular unrest, the CCP in Beijing took the opposite course. In the months that followed, while China was in international purgatory because of the Tiananmen Massacre, the CCP examined what had happened and went through a period of intense reflection. Its determination was that its survival depended on crushing at birth any movement that might turn into a national challenge to the one-party state. It has followed that course with dedication and ferocity ever since.

—

THERE WERE OTHER events in 1989 that did not appear to be pivotal moments of political or cultural change at the time, but which later became so. On February 14, the first of twenty-four Global Positioning System satellites was rocketed into orbit. On March 13, British engineer and computer scientist Sir Tim Berners-Lee set out a written proposal that would become the blueprint for the World Wide Web. And on April 25, Motorola introduced the Motorola MicroTAC personal cellular telephone, then the world's smallest mobile phone, designed to fit into a shirt pocket.

The disease that propelled the first major pandemic of the modern era, acquired immune deficiency syndrome (AIDS), caused by the human immunodeficiency virus (HIV), was identified in the United States in 1981. Nearly forty years later it has, according to the World Health Organization, killed about 34 million people, 95 percent of them in sub-Saharan Africa and Asia. In the US, however, there were concerted and well-funded efforts to explore the nature of the disease and to identify treatments. As part of that process, on June 23, 1989, Dr. Anthony Fauci, the director of the

National Institutes of Health's National Institute of Allergy and Infectious Diseases, endorsed a parallel track approach to clinical trials, which gave a larger number of HIV-positive people access to experimental treatments.

By 2020, Dr. Fauci was still director of the National Institute of Allergy and Infectious Diseases; he has battled daily and in public with US President Donald Trump to take the COVID-19 pandemic seriously, to abandon political ideology and pandering to his evangelical Christian base, and to confront the disease with science and a practical strategy.

The year 1989 also presented other ripe ironies. Among them was that the Nobel Prize for Literature was awarded to the Spanish novelist Camilo José Cela "for rich and intensive prose, which with restrained compassion forms a challenging vision of man's vulnerability." There does not, however, seem to have been much compassion, restrained or otherwise, in the life of Cela, who was also the Marquis of Iria Flavia. In 1943, Cela became a censor for the dictatorship of Francisco Franco. He lost that post when his first novel, published in Argentina, was judged immoral by his fellow Spanish censors and banned. Cela, however, remained loyal to the Franco dictatorship and worked as an informer for the secret police, betraying fellow intellectuals and passing on information about political dissidents. It is both fitting and troubling that a fascist writer would receive the last Nobel Prize for writing of the Cold War.

In the middle of 1989, American political philosopher Francis Fukuyama wrote an essay in the summer edition of a journal of international affairs, *The National Interest*, which he called "The End of History?" Fukuyama argued that the collapse of communism and the end of the Cold War was a conclusive victory for democracy and free market liberalism. There could no longer be any argument about the superiority of these approaches to organizing human society. Ahead lay sunny days as those countries recently liberated from authoritarianism and those still suffering under oppressive systems embraced the now unchallenged template for human advancement, peace, and tranquillity.

"What we may be witnessing is not just the end of the Cold War, or the passing of a particular period of postwar history, but the end of history as such: that is, the end point of mankind's ideological evolution and the universalization of Western liberal democracy as the final form of human government," he wrote.

But, like any sensible scholar, Fukuyama took the precaution of scouring the horizon for any indication of challenges to liberal democracy that might confound his theory. He saw only two, and he didn't fancy their chances of toppling victorious democratic liberalism. "Two possibilities suggest themselves," he wrote. "Those are religion and nationalism." Although he saw religious fundamentalism on the rise among the Jewish, Christian, and Muslim traditions, Fukuyama found it hard to imagine any of them providing a political antidote to what he admitted was the "spiritual vacuity of liberal consumerist societies." Only Islam, he argued, had shown it could provide a political alternative to liberalism and communism. "But the doctrine has little appeal for non-Muslims, and it is hard to believe that the movement will take on any universal significance." From one perspective, Fukuyama was right. Islam has not found willing converts much beyond its established transnational Muslim community, the *umma*. But the radicalizing of Muslim communities and countries has had a profound effect on not only those countries but also others that are judged by extremists as legitimate targets for terrorist attacks.

Fukuyama should have contemplated the possibility of Christian fundamentalism becoming a determining element in American politics. The United States, after all, is the most populous Christian country in the world. Its first settlers in New England were communities of the most radical of British Puritans, and the US has a long history of puritanical Christianity playing a significant role in political outcomes.

In a similar vein, Fukuyama also underestimated tribalism as an aspect of nationalism that could challenge triumphant liberal democracy in countries and societies beset by the inequities tied to globalization. "It is not clear," he wrote, "that nationalism represents an irreconcilable contra-diction in the heart of liberalism. The vast majority of the world's nationalist movements do not have a political program beyond the negative desire of independence from some other group or people, and do not offer anything like a comprehensive agenda for socio-economic organisation." He was right in the first clause of his sentence, but wrong in the second. Truculent nationalism forged Brexit in the United Kingdom and Trumpism in the United States. Angst about immigrants and refugees sustained Viktor Orbán in power in Hungary and has won seats in national and regional assemblies for race-based parties in Germany, France, and several countries in Scandinavia. To Fukuyama's credit, he has revisited these views, and in 2018 he published *Identity: The Demand for Dignity and the Politics of Resentment*. This deals in depth with how the erosion of peoples' feelings of self-worth and status in culturally distinct communities has fuelled fear and anger that have in turn undermined democracy.

Yet for a while in the 1990s, it looked as though Fukuyama's essay on the end of history (which he expanded to a full book published in 1992) might be right. In 1989, by most counts, there were 51 democracies in the world and 105 authoritarian states. The number of democracies around the world expanded swiftly during the following decade so that by 2001 there were 88 democracies, equalling the number of autocracies.

Since then, and especially since the cataclysmic global economic crisis of 2008–09, when hundreds of thousands of people in the US and Europe lost their jobs and their homes, the view has taken hold that democracy's momentum has sputtered and stalled. Much of the persistent anger against governing elites in the North Atlantic countries stems from the failure of governments to care for their destitute citizens or to consider the fears of their middle classes, who saw destitution closing in on them. Yet at the same time, those governments were swift to produce billions upon billions of dollars to bail out banks and financial institutions whose greed, laxity, and lack of ethics had precipitated the crisis. As a result, democratic decline is evident in many countries where such a movement was previously unthinkable. With this decline has come the view that the values of economic and political liberalism are no longer supreme and unassailable. Within many democracies, challenges are coming from segments of society that have been marginalized or totally sidelined, not only by the 2008–09 crisis but more generally by the shifting sands of economics under globalization. The end of the Cold War allowed the whole world to become a marketplace for the free movement of goods and services. But it also allowed for the easy movement of the manufacturing sector from established industrialized nations to low-cost economies. As a result, middle-class and blue-collar/working-class salaries have stagnated in countries that have seen the flight of their manufacturing industries. This has created great disparities in wealth between a tiny elite of grossly rich beneficiaries of globalization and the majority of people, who can no longer aspire to the same standard of living as their parents. This in turn has fostered serious social discord and lack of faith in the structure and fairness of several democratic societies. Disillusionment is widespread, and it appears that none of the establishment classes are able to understand or respond to the plight of the bulk of the population.

One result of this disconnect is that social discord has frequently erupted as opposition to immigration or antipathy to minorities. This is an open invitation for nationalist populists, who have found ready audiences for their pandering messages, playing to the fears of the crowd with divisive and fraudulently simplistic remedies to complex social problems. Several of these rabble-rousers have managed to be elected in established democracies, including the United States, the United Kingdom, Hungary, the Philippines, Brazil, and Turkey.

What happened? Why did the victory of democracy in 1989 tip so quickly — within thirty years — into an age where the values of representative and accountable government, the rule of law, and the spectrum of liberal civil rights in North Atlantic culture are beset on all sides? It is a world that, in some respects, is more forbidding than the preceding age of the Cold War. And in several countries, where the siege is most intense, democracy is having difficulty defending itself. The forces of authoritarianism and regressive social conservatism have found that democracy's greatest weakness is its dedication to freedom and openness. It has proved unnervingly easy for the defeated states of the Cold War, Russia and China in particular, to use democracy's freedoms against it and thereby undermine confidence in those liberties.

Some democratic governments have connived in their own decrepitude. They have promoted or allowed unregulated globalization without preparing for the consequences for their own people. Sometimes that insouciance has come from blindness or apathy. In other situations, it has flowed from an ideological fixation that the marketplace would deal with the problem. But democracy has been undermined by the failure of liberal democratic governments to support the large segments of their own populations that have been displaced economically, socially, and emotionally by advances in production technology and the wholesale movement of industries to the developing world.

This shift began in the 1980s, when Ronald Reagan in the US and Margaret Thatcher in the UK launched revolutions bent on smaller governments, tax reductions, and deregulation of industry and services with the aim of generating booming economies. The theory was that everyone would benefit from a bigger economic pie — the trickle-down vision of economics.

But that is not the way it has worked out.

CHAPTER TWO

—

Letting the Gini Coefficient Out of the Bottle

THE THREADS THAT tie together attacks on modern liberal democracy — xenophobia, nationalism, populism, anti-establishment truculence, and racism — all lead back to something that began in the early 1970s, but which did not fully register until after the end of the Cold War. That is the rising disparity between the bulk of humanity and the tiny minority of the very rich, whose fortunes have multiplied, often by the momentum of interest income alone, year after year to gargantuan levels of wealth. Meanwhile, for humdrum salary earners, and even middle-rank entrepreneurs, the last thirty years have been an age of stagnation, shrivelling hopes and expectations — standards of living that have tumbled backwards. Speaking in December 2013 at a conference on poverty, US President Barack Obama said, "[there] is a dangerous and growing inequality and lack of upward mobility ... I believe this is the defining challenge of our time." Pope Francis spoke from a slightly broader perspective against the sin of greed in May 2016 when he criticized the "economy of exclusion and inequality that has increased poverty and the number of people discarded as unproductive and useless." He told a conference of business leaders to build "the foundations for a business and economic culture that is more inclusive and respectful of human dignity." In 2014, the Pew Research Center conducted a survey that found that people in general considered the gap between rich and poor one of the most pressing problems worldwide. Significantly, the Pew survey found that while people thought a good education and hard work were important attributes for getting ahead, coming from a wealthy family and having the right connections were even more so. Patronage — who you know, not what you know — was the key to advancement, the survey found. These are clear warnings that the world is in real danger of slipping into an age of oligarchs, and liberal democracies are not immune. The numbers bear this out.

This struggle to survive and prosper in societies that have become corrupt and unfair is doubly shocking and painful because for Western Europeans and North Americans, the years after the Second World War were some of the most equitable and buoyant ever recorded. According to a 2011 report by the Organisation for Economic Co-operation and Development (OECD), that began to change in the 1970s, especially in the United States and the United Kingdom, when the accelerating success of the very rich began to be evident. In the 1980s, this trend spread to the traditionally more egalitarian countries of postwar Europe, like Sweden, Denmark, and Germany. Then disparity went global with the evolution of a worldwide integrated economy and the rapid movement of manufacturing industries to developing countries with low labour and other business costs, known collectively as globalization. Oxfam, the UK charity, has made a tradition of producing new numbers on global inequality at the start of the annual Davos World Economic Forum, which brings together leaders from the business and financial sectors early each year. It is a none-too-gentle reminder to the global elite of the roiling cauldron on whose lid they sit. The headline of the charity's report for the 2019 Davos gathering declared that in the previous year, the twenty-six richest people on Earth had the same net worth as the poorest half of the world's population (about 3.8 billion people). More than that, Oxfam reported that in 2018, the world's 2,200 billionaires saw their fortunes grow by 12 percent, while the poorest half of the world's population had their assets fall in value by 11 percent.

For the 2020 Davos meeting, Oxfam reported more stark numbers. The world's 2,153 billionaires have more wealth than the 4.6 billion people who make up 60 percent of the planet's population. The twenty-two richest men in the world have more wealth than all the women in Africa.

At the same time, it must be said, the World Bank reported that about one billion people had clambered out of extreme poverty in the previous twenty-five years. Numbers from 2015 show that only 10 percent of the world's population — about 736 million —continue to survive on US$1.90 a day or less, the bank's definition of extreme poverty. In contrast, at the time of the fall of the Berlin Wall and the end of the Cold War, about 36 percent of the world's population lived in extreme poverty. Globalization has winners among the poor as well as among the very rich.

The rage of those who felt abandoned and disenfranchised by stifling inequality became clear in the wake of the 2008–09 global recession. People took to the streets all over Western Europe and North America as governments responded to the crisis by bailing out corporations and banks. Meanwhile, in many liberal democracies, those handouts were paid for by imposing austerity measures on government spending, with cutbacks in services to the general population. Significant proportions of the people who faced cuts to the social services available to them had already lost homes or jobs, or both. In 2011, major demonstrations began in the US, where the crisis had started as a result of one of the all-too-regular bouts of "irrational exuberance" on Wall Street. That phrase was coined by Federal Reserve Chairman Alan Greenspan, in a speech given at the American Enterprise Institute during a previous bout of Wall Street idiocy, the dot-com bubble of the 1990s, in which personal savings and pension funds for hundreds of thousands of people were wiped out.

The 2011 Occupy movement, as it became known, started with the setting up of a protest camp on Wall Street in September. By the middle of the following month, the protests had spread to over 600 communities in the US and 951 cities in 82 other countries. The anti-inequality movement has continued in various forms since. It has propelled the rise of far-right political parties such as the National Front in France and Alternative for

Germany, where the perceived cultural and economic threats of refugees and immigrants fuelled the sense of victimization. The two most dramatic political outcomes of these perceptions have been the 2016 UK referendum in favour of leaving the European Union and the questionable election of Donald Trump to the US presidency later the same year.

A small band of intense English nationalists accomplished the task of forcing the UK to leave the EU after forty-seven years' membership. They persuaded a majority of voters that their livelihoods and culture had either been snatched away or were threatened by the country's continued membership in the EU and the bogeyman of dictatorship from Brussels. Most of the claims of the avid Brexiteers were nonsense, but they fed embedded feelings of economic and cultural insecurity that had been festering in post-industrial Britain for years.

The 2008–09 financial crisis, and the way the newly installed administration of US President Obama responded to it, propelled the creation of the right-wing, anti-government Tea Party, which within a remarkably short period of time gained huge influence in and then control of much of the Republican Party, including in Congress. Obama also became a target of visceral personal hatred by white American blue-collar workers in particular, hundreds of thousands of whom lost their jobs and their homes. They saw Obama, who had come to office promising to be an agent of change, take the traditional route of shoring up the banks and Wall Street investment houses, while those same banks repossessed their homes and the investment houses continued to favour companies that moved their jobs to China. That hatred has continued to fester as it has been stirred and fuelled by US President Trump and his coterie. Like a bushfire, it has spread into hatred of government in general, career politicians like Hillary Clinton, and especially the media. And, with persistent prodding by US President Trump, that hatred has become racist and misogynist.

Those two events — Brexit and the arrival of Trump — and the social upheavals they caused make it clear that income inequality and the persistent pull of more and more of the national wealth into fewer and fewer hands is the most pressing core threat to the survival of liberal democracy.

IN 1912, ITALIAN statistician and sociologist Corrado Gini developed equations for measuring wealth and income distribution within countries. What has become known as the Gini Coefficient is now widely used by organizations like the World Bank, the Organisation for Economic Co-operation and Development, the World Economic Forum, and the United States' Central Intelligence Agency as a reliable indicator of the levels of inequality within countries. High Gini numbers are also used as indicators of the potential for social instability and upheaval as the citizenry rebels against disparity. Even though there is significant faith in the reliability of Gini's original equation, scholars have devised over a dozen variants of the methods of calculating the coefficient in order to take into account differences between nations and communities, such as an aging population or a baby boom. These added elements have only become of pressing significance since Gini's original work.

The value range created by Gini started with zero, representing perfect equity, and rose by fractions to one, at which point, theoretically, the entire wealth of a nation would be in the hands of one person. Some reports prefer to express the coefficient as a percentage, which is more familiar to most audiences and is what will be used here. The latest CIA World Factbook ranks 157 countries and societies by the Gini Index, from the most unequal, Lesotho, with an index of 63 percent, to the most balanced, the Faroe Islands, with 23 percent. In this report, the US is among the most unequal countries at 45 percent, sandwiched between Peru and Cameroon and in the company of China, Saudi Arabia, and Zimbabwe. A 2018 report by the World Inequality Lab, an organization based at the Paris School of Economics, with one hundred researchers reporting from seventy countries, collected statistics from the year 2016 that demonstrate a wide variation in inequality in regions around the globe. The most balanced group of communities was Europe, with a score of 37 percent on the advanced Gini measure used by the lab. Indeed, Europe was the only region that was below the level — 40 percent — at which inequity can be expected to cause social upheaval. China came next at 41 percent. Then Russia at 46 percent, followed by North America at 47 percent. Sub-Saharan Africa clocked in at 54 percent, just behind Brazil and India at 55 percent. The Middle East topped the rankings as the most unequal collection of societies, with a disparity level of 61 percent. But one of the most interesting and important findings of the World Inequality Report was that while income and wealth inequality had been growing both in the US and Western Europe over previous decades, it had been growing much more in North America.

"While the top one percent [of the population's] income share was close to ten percent in both regions in 1980, it rose only slightly to twelve percent in 2016 in Western Europe while it shot up to twenty percent in the United States. Meanwhile, in the United States, the bottom fifty percent income share decreased from about twenty percent in 1980 to thirteen in 2016," the report stated.

The report attributed Western Europe's relative victory in preserving a degree of equality and social harmony to better education systems, wage policies that favoured low- and middle-income groups, and less inclination to give tax cuts to the rich. French economist and philosopher Thomas Piketty picked up on the same issue in his seven-hundred-page manifesto, "Capital in the Twenty-First Century," written in 2014. Discussing the effects of education on social mobility and the concept of a meritocracy, Piketty's data shows that upward mobility in the US falls far behind northern Europe and even France, Germany, and the UK.

"These findings stand in sharp contrast to the belief in 'American exceptionalism' that once dominated US sociology, according to which social mobility in the United States was exceptionally high compared with the class-bound societies of Europe," Piketty found.

Canada has been no more adept than the countries of Western Europe in fending off the forces of inequality. A 2019 report by the Conference Board of Canada concluded, "Canada gets a 'C' grade and ranks twelfth out of its seventeen peer countries." Ahead of Canada on this chart are, in order, Denmark, Norway, Belgium, Finland, Sweden, Austria, France, Ireland, the Netherlands, Germany, and Switzerland. Canada comes out ahead only of Japan, Australia, Italy, the United Kingdom, and the United States.

When the Cold War ended in 1989, Canada was a solidly equitable country with a Gini Coefficient of 28 percent. Inequality rose steadily in the 1990s and early 2000s before settling down in 2008 and remaining at around 32 percent. The degree to which the rich in Canada have got richer and the poor poorer is quite dramatic. The Conference Board report divides Canada's population of 37 million people into quintiles of just over 7 million people each. In 2010, Canada's richest 7 million people took home 39.1 percent of the country's national income. The poorest 7 million people, meanwhile, got only 7.3 percent of the national income. The report says that all four quintiles below the richest group have lost income share over the twenty years since the end of the Cold War. Moreover, "The richest one percent of Canadians took almost a third of all income gains from 1997 to 2007 — the decade with the fastest-growing incomes in this generation."

There is a debate over whether this is a natural phenomenon, as Piketty contends, or if inequality is essentially a result of political decisions and management. This is the position taken by Nobel Prize–winning economist and Columbia University professor Joseph Stiglitz. The two positions are not necessarily inconsistent. A natural phenomenon is only one to which political management has not been applied. Piketty brought together and analyzed a massive amount of global economic data from twenty countries going back to the eighteenth century. His conclusion is that the world wars and the associated turmoil of the twentieth century were aberrations in the story of capitalism. Those upheavals were social levellers, he argues, that imposed unnatural equality and equity among the economic classes. Left to itself, Piketty decided, capitalism produces a high degree of inequality. The key finding of Piketty's book is relatively simple. He concluded that rich people tend to reinvest the bulk of their wealth rather than using it to create new enterprises that produce jobs. These accounts therefore grow at the current rate of interest. If the rate of interest is higher than the rate of growth of the economy, which has been the norm among mature industrialized nations for many decades, then the rich get richer ad infinitum without any effort or enterprise on their part.

Embedded in the question of why the rich have in the last few decades continued to get much, much richer is the whole issue of what economists call the "rent economy." This description first crops up approvingly in the eighteenth century in the novels of Jane Austen and Honoré de Balzac as evidence of a person's financial stability based on property ownership and the income that flows from it. But it has become a pejorative term. Piketty writes, "Today, the rents produced by an asset are nothing other than the income on capital, whether in the form of rent, interest, dividends, profits, royalties, or any other legal category of revenue, provided that such income is simply remuneration for ownership of the asset, independent of any labour." He notes that in the minds of many people, the word *rent* has come to refer to an undue or unjustified income, the result of unacceptable distortions in capitalism. But, Piketty says, the dominance of *rentiers* in the rankings of the wealthy is not the result of imperfections in the market. "In fact, it is just the opposite: the growing sophistication of capital markets and financial intermediation tends to separate owners from managers more and more and thus to sharpen the distinction between pure capital income and labour income." He warns it is "a dangerous illusion" to believe that making the market ever more open and competition increasingly acute will end the dominance of inherited or unearned wealth and create a meritocracy.

"Real democracy and social justice require specific institutions of their own, not just those of the market, and not just parliaments and other formal democratic institutions," Piketty writes.

That makes perfect sense, because many of the facilities that have allowed and, indeed, purposefully encouraged the very rich to get even wealthier while making the lives of the other 99 percent stagnant are the result of political decisions and political ideology.

The Conference Board of Canada blames rising inequity on two main forces. The first it describes as "market forces" and the second as "institutional forces." This division is common to the analyses of many economists, but, as we will see, there is little agreement on how much weight should be given to each cause.

The swift collapse after 1989 of the pro-Soviet and pro-Western camps into which much of the world had been divided during the Cold War gave a massive stimulus to developing countries. The removal of the artificial barriers and of the risks that came with picking sides between Washington and Moscow created the worldwide marketplace of globalization. Very quickly, manufacturing industries began moving to developing countries with large, low-paid populations and other attractions, such as tax breaks, cheap land, minimal environmental or labour standards, few or no regulations, and the ability to solve administrative difficulties and problems with bribes rather than costly and lengthy lawsuits. China was the biggest beneficiary, but so were other countries of Southeast Asia, India, and Bangladesh, and some countries in Latin America. At the same time, in the North Atlantic democracies, the onward march of productivity, especially innovations in robotic and other automated forms of manufacturing, made obsolete many of the blue-collar jobs that had not been moved abroad. In one article on the topic, *The Economist* magazine stated that new technologies have "pushed up demand for the brainy and well-educated" while "the integration of some 1.5 billion emerging-country workers into the global market economy ... hit the rich world's less educated folk with unaccustomed competition."

Several economists, among them Nobel laureate Paul Krugman, put more emphasis on institutional forces — in essence, the political response — as the culprit in the rise of wealth disparity. Even so, there are overlaps between the two forces. The flight of manufacturing and industrial jobs from the West, for example, has delivered a major blow to the power and influence of trade unions. In 1945, 33 percent of workers in the US belonged to a trade union. Today, that number is only 10 percent. There have been similar, though not nearly as dramatic, declines in Europe. The implications of these changes will be explored in the following chapter. But the loss of union backing sometimes, though not always, means that many people whose jobs have disappeared over the horizon of globalization have no champions and no community where they can seek support. A serious failing of Western government as globalization took hold was to do nothing serious to re-equip the people who were faced with no useful skills to address an increasingly forbidding future. Indeed, for some political parties and governments in the 1980s and 1990s, the destruction of trade union influence was a central objective of their politico-economic philosophy. This, however, has tended to make these abandoned people highly susceptible to the blandishments of populists and demagogues, like Donald Trump in the US, Boris Johnson and Nigel Farage in the UK, and Jair Bolsonaro in Brazil — flim-flam artists who peddle simplistic and unattainable solutions to complex social problems.

Other institutional factors in accelerating levels of wealth disparity and inequality include stagnant wage rates for most, except top executives; deregulation, driven by extreme free market ideology; and national taxation and other financial policies, driven by the trickle-down theory of economics, that favour the wealthy and have no benefit for the majority of the population. All of which ushers on to the stage a central character in the trials and tribulations that have befallen Western democracies in the last three decades: another economics Nobel laureate, Milton Friedman.

Friedman rocketed to economist stardom in the 1950s and 1960s for his reinterpretation of the work of the twentieth century's formative economist, John Maynard Keynes. Friedman's work on how money supply can be used to control inflation was of seminal importance, but his abiding political influence is as the intellectual mainstay for libertarianism. *The Economist* called him "the most influential economist of the second half of the twentieth century ... possibly of all of it." Friedman's defining work was his book *Capitalism and Freedom*. Published in 1962, it sold over five hundred thousand copies and was translated into eighteen languages. Friedman's quest was to address what he saw as inefficiencies in the economies of the US and other major industrialized countries. He described his remedy as being "classically liberal," by which he seemed to be echoing Henry David Thoreau's comment "that government is best which governs least." Friedman was a devotee of the freest of free trade. He advocated government staying out of all social and regulatory affairs unless absolutely necessary, arguing that social security programs created dependency. On deregulation, he even suggested an end to medical licences for doctors, apparently on the theory that rational people would avoid quacks. This theory has not proven to be true: the US medical market in particular continues to be a happy hunting ground for the purveyors of unapproved patent medicines, most of which are of no utility and some of which are harmful.

Medical quacks quickly latched on to the COVID-19 outbreak as a huge opportunity. US television stations were deluged with advertisements for all kinds of patented and expensive medications, none of them with any scientific endorsement. Some of the most outlandish advertised remedies were commercial sidelines by well-known Christian evangelists, who claimed that their potions had the added power of Heavenly Blessings. But undoubtedly the most outlandish and morally questionable snake oil merchandising came from US President Trump himself. In his rambling daily briefings to the media on the state of the coronavirus pandemic, Trump repeatedly promoted the use of the anti-malaria drug hydroxy-chloroquine as a miracle cure for COVID-19. He did this in defiance of very public advice from his most senior adviser on infectious diseases, Dr. Anthony Fauci, who consistently warned that the drug's efficacy was untested and questionable, and that taking it could provoke dangerous side effects. But Trump continued, and it did not take much digging by journalists to discover that Trump himself and several people in his close coterie, including his "personal lawyer," former New York mayor Rudi Giuliani, had investments in companies manufacturing or marketing hydroxychloroquine.

Friedman's passion for an unregulated, *caveat emptor* marketplace included a proposed system of school vouchers to propel the creation of private schools, which he believed would provide creative competition for public schools. This idea continues to bubble in the US among Republican Party libertarians. Friedman more generally expressed these ideas in his book *Free to Choose*, published in 1980.

"Economic freedom is an essential requisite for political freedom," he wrote. "By enabling people to co-operate with one another without coercion or central direction, it reduces the area over which political power is exercised. In addition, by dispersing power, the free market provides an offset to whatever concentration of political power may arise. The combination of economic and political power in the same hands is a sure recipe for tyranny."

This, of course, is an expression of the American ideal. That dream imagines that all Americans are driven by staunch communal morality, dedication to honest dealing, willingness to compromise with others' opinions, and respect for the rule of law. And while that may be an ethos that fits well enough for a pioneer society of sparse communities and untamed wilderness, Friedman's idealized vision hasn't worked so well in an age of wealth disparity, competing intolerance, and rampant tribalism. Indeed, Friedman's faulty vision and political influence has played a significant role in the erosion of modern liberalism and social cohesion, and not just in the North Atlantic countries. In Latin America, his acolytes from his thirty years teaching economics at the University of Chicago, known as the Chicago Boys, had great influence on the policies and politics of several governments. In some cases, wars and revolutions were the result.

Republicans latched on to Friedman early. He was an adviser to Barry Goldwater's presidential campaign in 1964 and played a similar role on economic policy for Ronald Reagan when the B-movie actor was governor of California from 1967 to 1975. When Reagan went to Washington as president in 1981, Friedman went with him as a member of the administration's Economic Policy Advisory Board. This produced what became known mockingly as "Reaganomics." There were four strands to Reagan's economic policies. First was reducing the growth of government spending, followed by reducing federal income and capital gains taxes. Third was reducing government regulation, and fourth was cutting inflation by limiting the money supply. Looked at with the benefit of nearly forty years of hindsight, those four imperatives, pursued with blind ideological fervour — a fervour that spread throughout the democratic industrialized world — have been a pivotal cause of the challenges to democracy today.

Margaret Thatcher, who became prime minister of the United Kingdom in 1979 at the head of a Conservative Party government, soon adopted Friedman and his theories. A contributing factor to the policies of both Thatcher and Reagan was that a major stimulus to their economies was needed, irrespective of the social consequences, because of the economic rise of both Germany and Japan. These, after all, were the countries that the alliance led by the UK and the US had defeated in the Second World War only thirty-five years before, well within living memory. To see these old enemies with thriving economies demanded a response. Thatcher and her close ideological companions Norman Tebbit and Keith Joseph were already fans of Austrian-born Friedrich Hayek, economist, philosopher, and winner of the 1974 Nobel Prize for economics. Thatcher had read Hayek's 1944 anti-socialist tract *The Road to Serfdom* when she was an undergraduate at Oxford. It influenced her deeply and no doubt played to the culture of her heritage as the daughter of alderman and Methodist preacher Alfred Roberts, who owned two grocery stores in the small ancient city of Grantham in Lincolnshire.

Thatcher and her team believed that hard work was the only social salvation. They did not flow with the milk of human kindness for those who through no fault of their own had fallen on hard times. She is often quoted as having said, "A man who, beyond the age of twenty-six, finds himself on a bus can count himself a failure."

Tebbit told a Conservative Party conference in 1981, "I grew up in the thirties with our unemployed father. He did not riot, he got on his bike and he looked for work." Thereafter, "Get on your bike" became the all-purpose response to those who railed at being put out of work by advances in productivity or the ideology of small government. It was Keith Joseph, however, who was the in-house philosopher. Chris Patten, director of the Conservative Research Department in the late 1970s and later the last British governor of Hong Kong, came up with the epithet "The Mad Monk," which caught on and stayed with Joseph the rest of his life. In 1976,

Joseph wrote a paper that argued, "Making the rich poorer does not make the poor richer, but it does make the state stronger and it does increase the power of officials and politicians, power more menacing, more permanent and less useful than market power within the rule of law. Inequality of income can only be eliminated at the cost of freedom. The pursuit of income equality will turn this country into a totalitarian slum."

That kind of thinking remains prevalent among libertarians, despite all the evidence from economists and others that the reverse is true. Sustaining and investing in the less fortunate bolsters democracy, propels economic growth, and provides enhanced opportunities for the next generation.

Hayek was brought into Thatcher's team in the late 1970s as she prepared the Conservative Party to defeat the collapsing Labour Party government. She also gathered up Friedman, and, as the Margaret Thatcher Foundation puts it, "If by this stage Hayek was the benign philosopher king, Friedman was the frenetic man of business, jetting from lecture theatre to presidential suite, all but omnipresent on the op-ed pages and the TV screen."

Thatcher, like Reagan, portrayed tax cuts, austerity, privatization, and deregulation as not only economically sound but also morally superior. That aura of godliness has plagued the practice of economic policy ever since and given a gloss of virtue to the free marketeers in what amounts to class warfare. It was, of course, a sanctity that appeared to receive unquestionable blessing when Reagan and Thatcher became the political figures who personified the West's victory in the Cold War.

It was not all smooth sailing. Reagan's argument at the time that income and capital gains tax reductions for the rich would make more money available for investment and job creation was pilloried. Comedian Will Rogers had called it trickle-down economics two generations before Reagan's presidency, intending to ridicule the whole notion. But the trickle-down theory continues to have currency, especially in the US, among the wealthy and the politicians who depend on contributions to run their campaigns. It speaks volumes that the only significant bill that US President Trump was able to get through Congress in his first year in office when the legitimacy of his presidency was still very much in doubt was a massive tax cut for the rich. A 2019 Congressional Research Service report found that, "From 2017 to 2018, the estimated average corporate tax rate fell from 23.4% to 12.1% and individual income taxes as a percentage of personal income fell slightly from 9.6% to 9.2%." It continued, "The tax law's most enduring feature is a $1 trillion permanent corporate tax cut. It also slashed tax rates for people making more than $1 million and for pass-through companies disproportionately used by the wealthy, and it rolled back the estate tax on wealthy heirs and heiresses."

The effect of giving tax cuts to the already wealthy is the reverse of claims made by advocates of trickle-down economics and of the equally fatuous idea that "a rising tide floats all boats." A rising tide does nothing for boats that have holes or that have already sunk. A 2015 study by the International Monetary Fund (IMF), "Causes and Consequences of Income Inequality: A Global Perspective," is unequivocal on this point.

"We find an inverse relationship between the income share accruing to the rich (top twenty percent) and economic growth. If the income share of the top twenty percent increases by one percentage point, GDP growth is actually 0.08 percentage point *lower* in the following five years, suggesting that the benefits do not trickle down," the study reports. "Instead, a similar increase in the income share of the bottom twenty percent (the poor) is associated with 0.38 percentage point *higher* growth. This positive relationship between disposable income shares and higher growth continues to hold for the second and third quintiles (the middle class)."

In other words, the very last people who should be given tax breaks in order to promote economic growth and diversity are the rich.

The IMF report goes on to look at the social costs of fostering income disparity by pandering to the rich, as most of the governments of industrialized democracies have done since the 1980s. The report quotes the work of another US Nobel laureate in economics, Joseph Stiglitz, who has argued that higher inequality lowers economic growth by depriving lower-income households of the ability to stay healthy (especially in a country without an effective public health service) or to accumulate physical or human resources. Stiglitz produced evidence for what is obvious to reasonable people. Those with low incomes cannot afford to give their children the best educational opportunities and therefore the best prospects for economic advancement. This is especially true in societies like the US, where an education is regarded by some political factions as a commodity rather than a right. "As a result, labor productivity could be lower than it would have been in a more equitable world," said the IMF report, quoting Stiglitz.

Stiglitz's argument is supported by evidence from the COVID-19 pandemic in the US. Figures from several states showed that victims of the virus were disproportionately people from the lower economic orders, especially African-Americans. In some states, around 70 percent of those killed by COVID-19 were African-Americans; their low standing on the economic ladder meant their health and level of immunity was compromised, they had limited or no access to health insurance, and economic necessity meant they were unable to follow instructions to go into self-isolation or practise social distancing.

The IMF report goes on to speculate about other untoward effects of inequality and disparity, all of which have become more evident since the report was written. Extreme inequality may damage trust and social cohesion, and thus it is also associated with conflicts, which discourage investment, the report says. "More broadly, inequality affects the economics of conflict, as it may intensify the grievances felt by certain groups." There is plenty of evidence for that in developing countries with intense levels of disparity. As will be set out in Chapter Twelve, protests, demonstrations, and riots have become more prevalent in the democratic industrialized world as political tribalism and disparity intensify. The yellow vest movement across France in 2019, in protest at President Emmanuel Macron's attempts at economic reform, became a model for similar protests around the world and a barometer for mistrust of governments across Europe. There are already indications that environmental movements demanding action to combat global warming, some of them intentionally disruptive, have an element of class warfare in their approaches. Debating the multitude of issues around acknowledging, assessing, and combating climate change is shaping up to be a major battlefield for both North Atlantic democracies and others further afield, such as Australia and India, in the immediate future.

The rising incomes of the rich and the stagnant incomes of the poor and middle class, continues the IMF report, can produce economic crises, such as the dot-com collapse of 2000 and the global financial crisis of 2008–09, sparked by deregulation in the US financial market. Deregulation was one of the Reagan administration's watchwords. Through the 1970s — the era of inflation and stagnation, called "stagflation" by Friedman — many business groups hitched themselves to the economist's theoretical bandwagon and advocated sweeping government deregulation. In the 1980s, the Reagan administration adopted the business groups' ideas, reducing the budgets of the Environmental Protection Agency, the Department of Energy, and the Occupational Safety and Health Administration by a quarter. Only the Democratic-controlled Congress prevented the president from abolishing these departments altogether. The Trump administration has picked up this baton and is energetically pursuing not only the eradication of environmental protections but also the promotion of skepticism about human responsibility for climate change. One of Trump's first acts as president was to take the US out of the 2016 Paris Agreement, aimed at halting and reversing global warming by committing to national programs to cut air pollution. The known political positions of some of Trump's appointees to the leadership of government departments has led to speculation that the secretaries are there not to run their domains but to destroy them. Betsy DeVos, a champion of charter schools, was made secretary of education. Trump's second head of the Environmental Agency, Andrew R. Wheeler, was a lobbyist for the coal industry. Before him, Scott Pruitt had described himself as the "leading advocate against the EPA's activist agenda" when he was attorney general of Oklahoma. Another cut was the Trump administration's 2018 dismantling of the pandemic preparedness unit under the National Security Council. Trump dismissed allegations that the closing of the unit, which had prepared several studies warning about new pandemics and suggesting strategies to confront them, led to the confusion in the White House when COVID-19 struck.

Just as pernicious was Reagan's deregulation of the financial industry, an initiative taken up by Thatcher in the UK. From New York and London, it spread throughout the financial centres of Europe and the world. This movement reduced or demolished the barriers between banks, the investment industry, insurance companies, mortgage brokers, credit and loan agencies, and all other facets of the financial sector. In essence, everything became a one-stop shop for any financial service.

Deregulation of finance changed the balance of influence and interests between the four stakeholders in any corporation: management, employees, customers, and shareholders. The interests of shareholders, and thus the exchange listings, became supreme. The compulsion of managers, whose true recompense often came in stock options, was to use any means at hand to grow the stock market value of company shares. This quickly came to have only a passing relationship to the real value or productivity of the company. The interests of the employees and the customers dropped to the bottom (and sometimes below the bottom) of matters to be considered in corporate strategy.

For a time, in the run-up to the dot-com collapse of 2000, it was fashionable to pontificate that the digital age had changed the nature of economics and that the old rules about bubbles and bursting no longer applied. But nothing had changed. Ponzi schemes were and still are subject to the inevitable laws of economic gravity, of which the 2009 collapse of Canadian world leader communications technology company Nortel is one of the more dramatic examples.

As the deregulation of the financial services industry took hold, the pay of corporate chief executives took off and, in the view of many economists, became part of the "rent economy" in which remuneration is either unearned or bears no relationship to the skills or labour involved in its acquisition. Figures from the UK show that in 1998, the average chief executive received forty-eight times as much as the average worker. By 2016, CEOs in the UK were getting 129 times the pay of the average worker. Chief executives in the US did even better. Their incomes rose from 42 times that of the average worker in 1980 to 347 times in 2017.

Newsweek magazine reported in August 2018 that compensation for the US's top executives grew 17 percent in 2017 as real wages for workers declined.

> *Despite President Trump's repeated promises to raise the salaries of average Americans, chief executives earned 312 times more than the average employee during his first year in office, according to a new analysis by the Economic Policy Institute (EPI).*
>
> *The average CEO of the largest 350 companies in the U.S. received US$18.9 million in compensation last year, up from $16 million in 2016. The main difference in pay came from stock awards and cashed-in stock options, not salary growth, the analysis found. Under the Republicans' tax plan, passed in 2017, companies spent thirty-seven times more on stock buybacks than on bonuses or increased wages for workers. These buybacks bolstered share price and benefited top executives, who usually receive stock as part of their compensation package.*
>
> *"With wages for working people barely budging, it's remarkable to see top CEO pay surging again," said Lawrence Mishel, an EPI fellow and co-author of the study. "It is difficult to believe that Congress passed a tax cut weighted so heavily toward the wealthy when the nation's top CEOs are clearly doing fine."*
>
> *The study also compared CEO pay growth with the wage growth of the top 0.1 percent of wage earners. It found that in the past 40 years, CEO pay has grown by 1,070 percent, while the top wage earners have seen growth of 308 percent.*

A central evil in the deregulation of the financial industry was that it demolished barriers purposefully put in place to deter conflicts of interest and try to ensure that the companies offering financial services operated in the best interests of their customers. With the removal of those ethical deterrents, the financial marketplace became a free-for-all where probity, honesty, and reputation went out the window. A typical example of the demons loosed by financial deregulation was what happened to London-based Barings Bank, the world's second oldest merchant bank, founded in 1762. The bank collapsed in 1995 after suffering losses of £827 million — about US$1 billion — as a result of fraudulent investments, primarily in futures contracts, conducted by its employee Nick Leeson, working at its office in Singapore. Even Coutts Bank, where the British royal family and those members of the nobility who have enough money to warrant invitation had kept their money for generations, fell afoul of forgetting acceptable behaviour. In 2011, Coutts was fined the equivalent of about US$8 million and in 2012 the equivalent of over US$10 million by the UK's Financial Services Authority. In the first case, Coutts had not warned a customer about the risks of a bond they sold him, a bond which was made all but worthless in the 2008–09 financial crisis. In the second case, Coutts was fined for failing to take proper precautions against money laundering by "failing to properly deal with customers classified as politically exposed persons."

There have always been occasions when even the most conservative and best behaved banks have made mistakes, but the cases of Barings and Coutts flowed directly from the new culture of sharp practice that came with financial deregulation. In his book *The Great Divide*, about the aftermath of the 2008–09 crisis, Joseph Stiglitz wrote about these changes.

> *We knew that the banks had mismanaged risk and misallocated capital — all the time offering huge bonuses to their leaders for the wonderful job they were doing. We knew that the bonus system itself had created incentives for excessive risk-taking and short-sighted behaviour. We knew that the credit-rating agencies had failed miserably in their job of assessing risk. We knew that securitization, long vaunted for its ability to manage risk, had provided incentives for mortgage originators to weaken standards. We knew that banks had engaged in predatory lending.*
>
> *But we didn't know the full extent of the moral depravity of the*

banks, of their willingness to engage in exploitative practices, or their recklessness.

The financial sector is emblematic of what has gone wrong in our economy — a major contributor to the growth of inequality, the major source of instability in our economy, and an important cause of the economy's poor performance over the last three decades.

The financial sector does not perform well on its own; it requires strong regulations, effectively enforced, both to prevent it from imposing harm on the rest of the society and to make sure it actually performs the functions it is supposed to perform.

—

SO, WHAT NEEDS to be done?

In the opening paragraphs of its 2018 report, the World Inequality Lab stated, "Our objective is not to bring everyone into agreement regarding inequality; this will never happen, for the simple reason that no single scientific truth exists about the ideal level of inequality, let alone the most socially desirable mix of policies and institutions to achieve this level. Ultimately, it is up to public deliberation, and political institutions and their processes to make these difficult decisions."

Indeed. What needs to be done and, equally important, what can be done depends upon a host of factors particular to individual countries and societies. There may even be perfectly reasonable disagreements with my argument that disparity and inequality are the fundamental problems that have propelled the assaults on democracy in the last thirty years. It can be proposed, for example, that the core of liberal democracy's problem is badly structured political systems that effectively further disenfranchise the already disenchanted segments of the population. And there is no doubt that a campaign to rebuild and revive democracy must be fought on several fronts at once. But there can be little argument that striving against inequality and financial disparity must be among the first forays. All the evidence is that disparity and the lack of hope and expectations for something better that accompany it are at the heart of the social despair that is fracturing democracy. There cannot be any broad buy-in to a campaign of restoration and revival unless that basic cause of repugnance and rebellion is removed first. Disparity should be tackled first, because in many democracies it will be the most politically difficult challenge to overcome. Many among the "one percent" are not going to give up their privilege easily. Though, to their credit, there are one-percenters who recognize that disparity in many liberal democracies has now reached the point where it threatens social stability and who believe that it must be healed while that is still possible. Yet there remain good reasons to anticipate a political fight.

In Canada, there is a deeply embedded wealthy class that, over the generations, has naturally assumed political influence. That class has mounted and continues to mount quiet but effective campaigns against any attempts to restrain or contain its interests. For example, the fabrication of corporate headquarters in tax havens, tax requirements on overseas income, and public registration of the beneficial ownership of property, companies, and trusts have all been resisted.

In the US, the control of political life by the very rich is more blatant and effective than in any other liberal democracy. American legislative life is dominated by pandering to the special interests that finance political parties' and candidates' campaigns. Any legislation or programs enacted for the public good often seem to be afterthoughts or collateral benefits.

Modern liberal democracy is a resilient animal, but it is also a sensitive one. As the rising to dominance of inequality and disparity shows, even a relatively light tweak of the reins or nudge with the spurs can set the economy and society off in a thoroughly unhealthy direction. Thus, efforts to redress the balance must be equally light. While the idea of a revolution can sometimes seem appealing, and even warranted, revolutions are usually messy and seldom produce the desired outcome. In thinking about how to approach the rebalancing of liberal democratic economics, the first thing to recognize is that radical solutions seldom work. The experience of the last three decades shows that as a remedy for economic problems, libertarianism and its close associates in radical conservatism are a snare and a delusion. They have driven North Atlantic culture into a cul-de-sac and are chiefly responsible for the internal attacks on democracy. However, it is evident from plenty of other examples from both North Atlantic culture and elsewhere that jerking the reins to the left, to pure socialism, would be at least as damaging as the current trend, and probably more so.

As the campaign season warms up in early 2020 ahead of presidential elections in the US in November, two early but ultimately unsuccessful candidates for the Democratic candidacy, Elizabeth Warren and Bernie Sanders, advocated the introduction of wealth taxes. They argued that even relatively low increases in the taxes paid by the very rich would provide enough government revenues to pay for social programs such as universal health care and free college and university tuition. The likely revenue from a wealth tax increase was disputed by Harvard economist and professor Lawrence Summers and Wharton School professor Natasha Sarin. They noted that the very wealthy already avoided paying at least 15 percent of their taxes through clever accounting. They calculate that that would probably rise to at least 50 percent with the introduction of wealth taxes. Warren's and Sanders's proposals also met immediate pushback from American billionaires. Bill Gates, the founder of Microsoft, voiced the thoughts of many when he said, "If you tax too much you risk the capital formation, innovation, US as the desirable place to do innovation companies — I do think you risk that." Gates's own story does not substantiate that view. When he founded Microsoft in 1975, the top marginal tax rate on personal income was 70 percent, capital gains and corporate income taxes were significantly higher than in 2020, and the estate tax was formidable. That didn't stop Gates. There are studies that conclude the main forces for innovation are young, well-educated scientists buttressed by the benefit of wealthy family backgrounds. Gates started with all those advantages.

What the numbers and the political landscape do show is that we are all social democrats to one degree or another now. In 1870, according to Thomas Piketty's numbers, tax revenues for the US and the major European economies made up less than 10 percent of national incomes. Now the range is between 30 percent (for the US at the bottom) and 55 percent (for Sweden at the top). France is close behind Sweden at about 50 percent, and the UK is at 40 percent. Back in 1870, national governments had little to spend money on except national security and some infrastructure. It is still the case that what Piketty calls the state's "regalian" responsibilities — the duties of the sovereign — take up about 10 percent of national incomes. The rest, the additional 30 to 40 percent of national incomes taken in a progressive climb that started during the Great Depression, funds governments' social responsibilities. The responsibility of states to provide education, health, and a multitude of other social services is now embedded deep at the roots of liberal democracies. Funding and managing these services is often the dominant issue in democracies, and that is not going to change. So are questions of fairness of access. These are political issues rather than purely economic ones, though they must be tackled through governments' fiscal policies. The International Monetary Fund included a comprehensive to-do list in its 2015 report on inequality. Fiscal policy already plays a positive role in curbing inequality to a degree in many advanced economies, the report states.

"But the redistributive role of fiscal policy could be reinforced by greater reliance on wealth and property taxes, more progressive income taxation, removing opportunities for tax avoidance and evasion, better targeting of social benefits while also minimizing efficiency costs, in terms of incentives to work and save," it goes on to say. "In addition, reducing tax expenditures that benefit high-income groups most and removing tax relief — such as reducing taxation of capital gains, stock options, and carried interest — would increase equity and allow a growth-enhancing cut in marginal income labor tax rates in some countries."

The IMF report goes on to say that in a world of rapid technological change that is increasing productivity by mechanizing jobs, ramping up the skill levels of people who might otherwise become permanently redundant is essential: "Improving education quality, eliminating financial barriers to higher education, and providing support for apprenticeship programs are all key to boosting skill levels in both tradable and non-tradable sectors." This investment is cumulative, says the report, because improving the education and skills standards of this generation tends to give better prospects to the next.

Reintroducing appropriate regulations and clear boundaries between various financial services is essential, claims the IMF: "Governments have a central role to play in alleviating impediments to financial inclusion by creating the associated legal and regulatory framework (protecting creditor rights, regulating business conduct, and overseeing recourse mechanisms to protect consumers), supporting the information environment (setting standards for disclosure and transparency and promoting credit information-sharing systems and collateral registries), and educating and protecting consumers."

Governments also have a clear responsibility to design and regulate labour markets in ways that reduce inequality without hindering efficiency. "For instance, appropriately set minimum wages, spending on well-designed active labor market policies aimed at supporting job search and skill matching can be important. Better use of in-work benefits for social benefit recipients also help reduce income disparities," the IMF report states. "More generally, labor market policies should attempt to avoid either excessive regulations or extreme disregard for labor conditions. Labor market rules that are very weak or programs that are non-existent can leave problems of poor information, unequal power, and inadequate risk management untreated, penalizing the poor and the middle class."

That's what happened in that careless and thoughtless era thirty years ago, and that is the topic for the next chapter.

CHAPTER THREE

—

What About
the Workers?

ÉDOUARD LOUIS IS a French novelist, but in 2018 he published a slim biographical pocket book just eighty-seven pages long, with little more than a paragraph on each page. But every word counts, and there is something of George Orwell in the young writer's spare and brutally close-up picture of his crippled and terminally ill working-class father as he approaches the end of a deeply unsatisfying and cruelly brief life. Like Orwell's *Down and Out in Paris and London* and *The Road to Wigan Pier*, the story is an epic of unrelenting hopelessness. Unlike Orwell's accounts, however, Louis's story is not from the Great Depression of the last century. This is now.

Who Killed My Father is an indictment of the French establishment and what Louis portrays as its disregard for the lives and hopes of ordinary citizens. Born into a ramshackle family, Louis's father never had a proper childhood. He didn't finish school and took a mundane manufacturing job because his family needed the money. Then he married, only, it seems, because it was expected, and plummeted into a life of quiet desperation. His back was seriously injured in an accident at work. He lost his job and was in pain for the rest of his life. Sometimes he was required by the authorities to take menial jobs in order to continue to qualify for social aid. But that work only accelerated the spread of other illnesses. At one of their last meetings, Louis comments, "You're barely fifty years old. You belong to the category of humans whom politics has doomed to an early death."

The first half of the book is a description of the uneasy and difficult relationship between Louis and his father, which masks a deep and unquestioning love. But the second half is a catalogue of the iniquities and mindless indignities heaped on the father by the officialdom of successive French governments. In the course of this dialogue, Louis recounts an incident in May 2017 when President Emmanuel Macron was confronted by two men wearing T-shirts who berated him about the austerity imposed on working people by the president's efforts at structural reform of the French economy. When challenged, Macron, who is very much a product of French upper-class elitism, tends to punch back. Louis quotes Macron as saying "in a voice full of contempt: 'You're not going to scare me with your T-shirts. The best way to afford a suit is to get a job.'" Shades of Norman Tebbit and "Get on your bike." This was far from being the only confrontation between Macron and critics of his reform program. The French media came to regularly describe the president's habitual short-tempered responses as "class contempt."

At the end of his book, Louis reels off the names of recent and current French political leaders: presidents Macron, François Hollande, Nicolas Sarkozy, and Jacques Chirac; Prime Minister Manuel Valls; High Commissioner against Poverty Martin Hirsch; Minister of Health Xavier Bertrand; and Minister of Labour Myriam El Khomri. "The history of your suffering bears these names," he tells his father. "Your life story is the history of one person after another beating you down. The history of your body is the history of these names, one after another, destroying you. The history of your body stands as an accusation against political history."

On the last page of the book, Louis recounts a final conversation with his father. "Last month, when I came to see you, you asked me just before I left, 'Are you still involved in politics?' 'Yes,' I told you, 'more and more involved.' You let three or four seconds go by. Then you said, 'You're right. You're right — what we need is a revolution.'"

Louis's book was published amid the noise of the first populist grass-roots riots on the streets of Paris in late 2018, protesting against the economic changes pursued by President Macron. These swiftly gelled into the *mouvement des gilets jaunes* (the yellow vest movement). The protests were sparked by rising fuel prices, the high cost of living, and government tax reforms that the demonstrators claimed placed a disproportionate burden on the working and middle classes. Because it was rising fuel prices that propelled the movement, the protesters wore the high-visibility yellow vests that French law required all drivers to have in their vehicles to wear during emergencies. But the vests quickly became "a unifying thread and call to arms" because of their association with working-class industries. The protests continued into 2020 and became increasingly violent. Ten people were killed in the riots, and nearly two thousand protesters and over one thousand police were injured in clashes in cities all over France. The protests were said to be the most serious civil uprising since the protests that swept across Europe, North America, and the world in 1968.

But the *gilets jaunes* protests did not swell into a revolution. Not in the classic sense, at least; when viewed, however, with a longer perspective, they are part of not a revolution but a counter-revolution against the deregulation, anti-union, and anti-employee movements among North Atlantic governments that took hold in the 1970s and 1980s. It is easy to forget now that the postwar boom of the 1950s and 1960s created a demand for labour that gave enormous power and influence to the trade unions. By the 1970s in Europe (and to a lesser but still significant extent in North America), unions were undemocratic fiefdoms whose leaders were all too often petty despots or demagogues, and union power had taken a throttling grip on national economies. Innovation and increases in productivity were near impossible, and strikes were the first resort in disputes rather than the last.

The anguished relationship in the 1970s between government and business on one side and trade unions on the other was most bitter in the

UK. The country had emerged from two world wars with massive debts, an overpriced currency, and unsustainable dependence on loans from the newly formed International Monetary Fund. (There's an insider's joke that the IMF's lavish Washington headquarters was paid for with the interest on loans to the UK.) Things began to spin out of control when the Organization of Petroleum Exporting Countries dramatically increased oil prices in October 1973. Ironically, the discovery and early exploitation in the late 1960s of oil under British sections of the North Sea only made things worse. That boosted the value of the pound sterling and made exports expensive before any counterbalance from oil revenues could take effect. The UK faced "stagflation," a deadly combination of inflation and stagnant economic growth. It was these dire prospects that pushed Conservative Prime Minister Edward Heath to successfully cajole the UK public into joining what was then the European Economic Community (EEC). But that was no instant remedy. Coal remained their main source of energy, and the largely state-owned coal mines were rapidly passing their most productive years. In opposition to the closure of uneconomic pits and layoffs of miners, the National Union of Miners (NUM) called persistent strikes, which led to power blackouts, a three-day workweek, and, in 1974, the collapse of the Heath government. The election of a Labour government led by Jim Callaghan did nothing to improve the situation. Callaghan and Chancellor of the Exchequer Dennis Healey were totally beholden to the IMF, which demanded reduced government spending, tax increases, and rises in interest rates. These years struck a fissure into the Labour Party between left-of-centre pragmatists and dedicated socialists that marks the party to this day.

When the Callaghan government died of exhaustion after the 1978–79 "Winter of Discontent," during which 1.5 million public sector workers went on strike, the Tories, led by Margaret Thatcher, came to power in a landslide victory in May 1979. She inherited a country that was on the verge of collapse and wracked by an economy dominated by a host of dying and outdated industries. And stomping through the ruins was a tribe of predominantly Marxist union leaders determined to fight for the survival of the industrial status quo. One was Derek Robinson, the shop steward and convenor of the union at British Leyland, the remaining hub of the automobile manufacturing industry. But around the time Thatcher came to office, Robinson was fired by the company for being an "insidious influence" after he had organized 523 walkouts at the Birmingham manufacturing plant over the previous thirty months. He had also vehemently opposed plans for twenty-five thousand job cuts, which was about half the remaining workforce after the sacking of eighteen thousand people had already taken place. A committed communist, and therefore known as "Red Robbo" by the tabloid press, Robinson and his supporters tried to engineer a strike that would force his reinstatement. It didn't work. Other union leaders turned against him, judging that the fate of the industry outweighed Robinson's job. A motion for a strike supporting his reinstatement was defeated by fourteen thousand votes against six hundred in his favour.

Cabinet documents from the period show that Thatcher came to power already committed to crushing the power of the unions, especially the influence of demagogue union leaders. An associated purpose was to try to impose a degree of democracy on unions, ending closed shops and allowing members to opt out of financial support for the Labour Party. For Thatcher and her coterie, it was unconscionable that union members who voted Tory or Liberal were forced to pay dues that went to sustain the Labour Party. Thatcher's advisers urged her to take on the miners. The NUM was led by the charismatic and militant near-Marxist socialist Arthur Scargill. Almost as soon as she came to office, Thatcher began preparing for the fight. In 1981 and 1982, her energy minister, Nigel Lawson, oversaw the stockpiling of coal in preparation for the showdown. Thatcher's government established a committee charged with planning to bring in the army to move coal by rail and road if need be. There followed a "phony war" in which both the union and the government tried to provoke the other into showing their hand.

But there was a very real war going on in 1982 that enhanced Thatcher's reputation and stature, leading to her being dubbed the "Iron Lady" by the German media. The Falklands War was an extraordinary feat of arms by any measure. The ten-week war began on April 2, 1982, when the

Argentine army invaded and occupied the UK's South Atlantic Falkland Islands colony. And to many, including British allies such as the United States, it appeared there was little the UK could do about it. The idea of the country that for much of the 1970s had been the sick man of Europe sending an effective invasion force thirteen thousand kilometres to retake the Falklands seemed ridiculous. Yet with extraordinary determination, resolution, and ingenuity, a task force was dispatched. The Argentine navy and air force were neutralized, and troops landed at San Carlos Water on the western shore of the east island on May 21. The head-to-head infantry fighting in the gathering austral winter was short and sharp. The war ended on June 14, when the British troops captured the capital, Port Stanley, and the commander of the Argentine garrison surrendered.

Back at home, Thatcher rode the Falklands victory into a decisive win in the 1983 general election. Victorious in war and election, she returned to her confrontation with the miners covered with honours and at the height of her personal popularity and prestige. Matters came to a head in March 1984, when the government agency that owned and operated the mines, the National Coal Board, announced that twenty collieries would close, with the loss of twenty thousand jobs. Scargill raised the temperature by claiming the Coal Board intended to close another seventy pits. The government denied this, but Cabinet documents subsequently released show that the actual number of collieries destined for closure was seventy-five.

From the start, the miners' strike was a muddled and confusing affair. Some areas of the country strongly supported the strikes and opposed the closures, but in others, miners continued to go to work. Scargill and the NUM organized "flying pickets" to try to stop miners crossing the line to work. In some cases, these tactics were successful, but in others they led to clashes between miners and the police. The strikes lasted for a year, over the course of which public opinion turned against the strikers. A series of Gallup polls taken during the year showed mounting sympathy for the employers, and by the end of 1984, 88 percent of respondents disapproved of the tactics used by Scargill and the union. In the violence fostered by the strike, 5 people died and over 120 police and miners were seriously injured. Police arrested 11,291 people, and 8,392 were charged. In the end, however, it was a clear victory for Thatcher. Trade union membership had hit a historic high of over 12 million people when she came to power in 1979, but by 2018 that membership total had fallen to 6.35 million. Government statistics show that in 2018, there were 39,000 workers involved in labour disputes, the second-lowest figure since records of these numbers started to be kept in 1893. And there were eighty-one strikes, the second-lowest number since records for stoppages began in 1930. In 2018, there were 273,000 working days lost to strikes, a tiny fraction of the 29 million lost during the Winter of Discontent in 1978–79.

Her victory over Scargill gave Thatcher the impetus to introduce other changes. Legislation ended the practice of secondary picketing — Scargill's flying pickets — and said that only workers on strike could demonstrate outside their specific workplace. Legislation also ended closed shops, which had stipulated that all workers at a particular establishment must be union members. Other reforms required compulsory secret ballots of members on union elections and other significant initiatives.

The Thatcher Revolution, however, was a lot more profound than just the crushing of the trade unions. Her dominant belief was the desirability and efficacy of free markets, rather than government intervention, to address economic problems. To that end, she pursued the privatization of state-owned industries and the removal of regulations that she felt stifled enterprise. Like her friend Ronald Reagan had done, she removed the barriers between elements in the financial sector, a move that came back to haunt the United Kingdom just as surely as it did the United States. Deregulation became a non-partisan affair. In the US it was continued by Democratic President Bill Clinton and in the UK by Labour Prime Minister Tony Blair. As a result, financial deregulation played a significant role in the housing value crash of 1990, the bursting credit bubble of 2000, and the UK's part in the global recession of 2008–09.

One of Thatcher's most profound beliefs was in what she called a "home owning democracy." She was convinced that enabling people to buy their own homes would give them not only a greater interest in and commitment to the success of society but also equity with which to borrow to start new enterprises or invest in other companies. To that end, Thatcher's government required municipalities to sell their council housing to the sitting tenants. The proportion of owner-occupied housing rose significantly through the 1980s and contributed to a general economic boom. In 1991, 67 percent of twenty-five- to thirty-four-year-old UK citizens owned their own homes. It is a measure of how swiftly things unravelled within twenty-five years that by 2016, among the same age group, only 38 percent owned their homes.

Nevertheless, the early years of Thatcher's housing initiative fed a widespread sentiment that the UK had put the dreary end-of-empire years behind it and was entering a new and more vigorous age, including being a member of the European Union. This came at some cost and didn't last for long. Unemployment through most of the 1980s stuck at about three million people, much of it among those who had worked in failing industries such as the coal mines and some antiquated manufacturing sectors. Those failures tended to be in the old industrial regions of northern England and Scotland, triggering an intense north-south divide that still defines the political map of the United Kingdom. In general, inequality rose significantly from 25 percent when Thatcher came to power in 1979 to 34 percent when she was hounded from office by her own party in November 1990.

Across the Atlantic, Ronald Reagan also saw the influence and role of trade unions in the economy as a barrier to his dream of the perfect free market. This is ironic considering that his first step from B-movie actor to politician was as president of the Screen Actors Guild, the Hollywood movie industry union, from 1947 to 1952 and again from 1959 to 1960. During those tenures, Reagan led three strikes against producers by actors demanding higher wages. As president of the United States, however, Reagan is better remembered as a union buster. In 1981, he was instrumental in the firing of eleven thousand striking air traffic controllers, all federal employees. The strikers, who belonged to the Professional Air Traffic Controllers Organization (PATCO), believed that air travel in the US would come to a screeching halt without them. That didn't happen.

Some three thousand supervisors joined two thousand non-striking controllers and nine hundred military air traffic controllers in manning airport towers. Before long, about 80 percent of flights were operating normally. Air freight remained virtually unaffected. In carrying out his threat, Reagan also imposed a lifetime ban on rehiring the strikers. In October 1981, the Federal Labor Relations Authority decertified PATCO.

The story of the destruction of the influence of unions in the United States begins with the passage of the National Labor Relations Act (NLRA) in 1935. This was part of President Franklin Delano Roosevelt's New Deal to revive the country after the economic havoc wreaked by the stock market crash of 1929. The act attempted to balance the power of employees and employers by enshrining the right of workers to create or join unions and encouraging collective bargaining to arrive at employment contracts. The legislation was only passed because it excluded agricultural and domestic workers, which made it possible for conservative southern Democrats and more progressive Republicans in the Midwest to support the act. But the legislation's passage enraged even the most enlightened industrialists, many of whom had been studying and promoting the concept of employee representation on corporate boards. This, the employers believed, would facilitate harmonious labour-management relations without the confrontations and disruptions of strikes and other "industrial actions." The idea of employee representation on corporate boards later resurfaced in the 2010s as a way of promoting workplace harmony in place of trade unionism, but through the 1940s, 1950s, and 1960s, the NLRA was the *bête noire* of US industrialists and employers. Their opposition suffered a setback during the Second World War; by 1945, the percentage of unionized wage and salaried workers in the US reached 35.4, the highest ever achieved. Employers renewed their attacks on the NLRA in 1947 with the passage of the Taft-Hartley Act, which limited the ability of labour activists to establish new unions in economic sectors that had no unions. In numerous other ways, the act aimed to shift the balance of power in the employer-employee relationship in favour of employers. The political climate of the times, with the start of the Cold War and the beginnings of the anti-communist witch hunts, aided passage of the act. Unions were seen by many as agents of creeping socialism and communism. In the early 1960s, to the surprise of many, the Supreme Court, led by Chief Justice Earl Warren, which took such an activist position on civil rights issues, turned out to be markedly pro-employer on labour matters. Emboldened by an apparently sympathetic Supreme Court, even moderates among corporate leaders began joining groups aiming to change labour laws through the legislative process. The euphemistically named Labor Law Reform Group (LLRG) included companies like AT&T, B.F. Goodrich, Ford, General Dynamics, General Electric, Macy's, Sears, U.S. Steel, and many other big beasts of US industry and commerce. The LLRG mounted an effective lobby during the presidencies of John F. Kennedy, Lyndon Johnson, Richard Nixon, Gerald Ford, and even Jimmy Carter that whittled away at the authority of the unions and affirmed the supremacy of employers in labour disputes. In this, the LLRG was aided by political infighting among union leaders over both territory and the ramifications of the civil rights movement. The liberal-leaning UAW (whose full name is now the United Automobile, Aerospace and Agricultural Implement Workers of America) and its leader, Walter Reuther, favoured demolishing barriers and aiding the integration of African-Americans. But this put Reuther and the UAW on a collision course with the American Federation of Labor and Congress of Industrial Organizations (AFL-CIO), whose president, George Meany, had no interest in helping African-Americans and was also a strong supporter of the US role in the war in Vietnam.

When Reagan came to office in 1981, much of the groundwork had already been laid to cut away the roots of trade unionism in the US. Reagan's actions against the air traffic controllers and his disbanding of their union emboldened the corporate community and disheartened the unions. Employers faced with walkouts increasingly felt they had the political cover from the Reagan administration to hire permanent replacements for striking workers and to employ union-busting companies that specialized in intimidating union members. Reagan continued the pressure on unions and their members by appointing a number of ultra-conservative members to the National Labor Relations Board, who gave consistently pro-employer rulings in disputes.

As the Reagan administration led into those of George H.W. Bush, Bill Clinton, and George W. Bush, the end of the Cold War kicked globalization into life. Unemployment rose as US-based jobs disappeared when companies started moving production to low-cost centres overseas. There was some optimism that the Obama presidency would curb the overweening power of employers and create a more level playing field for employees. Both as a senator and during his presidential campaign, Obama had supported the Employee Free Choice Act, which would instruct employers to recognize a union if a majority of their employees signed cards expressing their wish to be represented this way. However, three Chicago billionaires who supported Obama, all of whom had large, non-union workforces, let it be known that they did not support the bill. Perhaps fortunately for Obama's reputation, the forty-one remaining Republicans in the Senate after the 2008 election said they would not support the bill. They were joined by three Democrats, and with the prospect of a filibuster, the bill was never put to a vote.

In the US now, the only firmly established unions are in the public sector. Since 1980, the proportion of union members in government jobs of one sort or another has bounced between 35 and 40 percent. This is in marked contrast with union membership in private business. From a high of just over 35 percent in the mid-1950s, by 2018, only 6.4 percent of employees of private companies were union members.

The picture of public service becoming the last redoubt of trade unionism is also evident in Canada and Europe. Statistics Canada figures show the proportion of workers who are union members has dropped from 38 percent in the early 1980s — 43 percent among men — to 28.8 percent in 2014. But from 1999 to 2014, union membership in the broader public sector, including administration, education, health, and social services, grew from 70.4 percent to 71.3 percent. Levels of union membership in the private sector fell from 18.1 percent to 15.2 percent over the same years. The composition of private sector union membership also changed significantly. Membership in manufacturing industries dropped as jobs were automated or moved abroad, but most of that slack was taken up by growth in other industries, especially construction and other businesses associated with the property boom in Canada's major cities.

Canada's rate of 28.8 percent of the workforce being members of unions puts this country in the middle of the rankings of industrialized democracies in Europe. Here there is a wide range from Sweden, with 78 percent of its workforce belonging to trade unions in 2014, to France, at the very bottom with only 9.7 percent. Interestingly, only 47.9 percent of Sweden's unionized workers are in public service, while in France 66.3 percent work for some element of government. In broad terms, the European trend in union membership is down, like elsewhere. In 1995, 32.6 percent of the workforce were union members, while only 23 percent were in 2012.

Over the last century, trade unions and the movements for collective action to pressure employers into improving workplace conditions, pay, and other benefits such as health insurance and pensions have been the agents of huge advances in social equity and equilibrium. The steady decline of unionization, especially among people working in private enterprises of one sort or another, raises a host of questions about why this is happening. The questions are important because one of the significant threats to democracy is the rise of extremist politics and populist leaders among people who have lost the security of work in traditional unionized industries. If unions are becoming obsolete, what should replace them to ensure some balance of power between employers and employees in the workplace, and what must be done to ensure that workers in obsolete industries can make the transition to the new economic culture?

Most of the pressures that have eroded trade unionism have come from outside. The globalization of manufacturing and trade, as well as rapidly developing automated productivity after the end of the Cold War, have contributed to or created increased unemployment in industrialized countries. Unions have not in general responded well to the changing economic and employment landscape. They have tended to rage against the dying of the light instead of responding to reality by using common resources to help members make the transition to the new economy. At the same time, large sectors of the new economy are made up of service industries where there is little history of trade unionism and where employees are not expected or required to join a union. The relationship between managers and the managed has also developed along unique lines in the now-dominant service industries. There are some service industries where workers still demonstrate the need for a union to represent them. National or transnational retail outlets such as big box stores remain targets for unionization. However, the view that successful human resources management is an essential element in the profitable running of modern companies exists among some employers now more than it did in the past. And while this does not always achieve harmonious office cultures, it is often more successful than the mood of confrontation that often dominated in the old manufacturing industries. One result of human resources culture is that employees are offered direct routes to sorting out any workplace problems they may have. They don't experience the need for the muscle of collective action that was necessary at the beginning of the twentieth century. In addition to this, new, previously unimagined forms of employment are emerging rapidly, challenging the established and recognized norms of employee-employer relationships and leading to independent contractors, to whom digital companies, such as Uber, claim to have no relationship that is subject to regulation, taxation, or the rule of law.

Digital communication has given birth to, among many other things, the gig economy. This is an as yet largely unregulated labour market offering short-term contracts or straight freelance work without any security of employment or benefits. Even though it is still in its infancy, the digital job marketplace is already proving to be both a benefit and a curse. For people in need of immediate employment, whether it's driving an unregulated taxi or providing cleaning or care services, the digital market is a godsend. The downside is that many gig economy workers do not earn the legal minimum wage. A 2017 study of women gig workers in the UK found that nearly three-quarters did not earn enough to qualify as taxable income, a grim reminder of Orwell's kitchen skivvies in Paris and London.

Meanwhile, the owners of gig economy marketplaces are resisting efforts by governments to regulate them and classify them as employers, with all the responsibilities that go with that definition. The app owners insist they are merely facilitating the activities of independent contractors, nothing more.

But this situation is very much a First World problem. There is a more seminal problem looming in the developing countries. Studies in Latin America have found that the gig economy is creating a virtual brain drain as skilled graduates work as on-call taxi drivers and other digital marketplace jobs, either because they can't get work in their fields of expensively trained expertise or because the instant cash is attractive. A study published in August 2019 by the UK-based risk analysis company Oxford Analytica concluded the gig economy offers some advantages to workers in countries with limited opportunities or where the currency is weak. Delivery platform Rappi has over thirty thousand couriers delivering goods to over a million customers in Colombia, Mexico, Argentina, Uruguay, Chile, and Brazil. Mercadoni delivers groceries to over five hundred thousand households in Bogota and eighty thousand in Mexico City. Merged taxi app companies Easy Taxi in Brazil and Tappsi in Colombia are dominating their markets in competition with Uber. Oxford Analytica reported, "The risk of virtual brain drains in particular sectors is high, and could well happen without highly skilled professionals actually leaving their home countries." The report pointed to the online teaching site italki, which allows education graduates to earn much more than they could as traditional classroom teachers in their home countries. "If teachers are induced by the potential for relatively high earnings to teach online, it could become far more difficult for domestic education systems to attract and retain highly skilled teachers," states the report. "As the spread of the gig economy increases, such risks will extend to other new sectors."

There are other profound challenges for governments as the gig economy grows and multiplies. A simple one is the difficulty of collecting taxes from the information economy. And as much as people may recoil against paying taxes, it is tax revenue that enables governments to fulfil their responsibilities and to provide the services that citizens want and need. Among those responsibilities is the duty to regulate the legitimacy of businesses being carried on within the nation, which may include verifying the credentials of those offering services through online platforms, ensuring the quality of products, and holding inspections to be sure gig economy companies are complying with legal and ethical standards of operation. Some jurisdictions, such as California, have begun to come to grips with the difficulties of overseeing online and informal businesses operating within their boundaries. But it is one of those situations that threatens to get out of hand very quickly if governments and administrations do not make every effort to keep up with the explosive forces of the gig economy.

The potency of these challenges in some aspects of the gig economy was given a massive boost in 2020 as the shuttering of commerce and requirements for self-isolation during the COVID-19 crisis pushed many more people to start using home delivery services. Faced with the disappearance of their businesses as the bulk of the population across the North Atlantic countries followed government instructions to stay at home, restaurants and food stores rapidly developed home-delivery services. The convenience of ordering cooked meals or the ingredients for preparing meals had already caught on with segments of society. The lockdowns enforced over the coronavirus pandemic gave a major boost to these industries, just as it knocked the stuffing out of the ride-sharing drivers' economy and the demand for Airbnb tourist accommodation in people's homes.

The experience of the last thirty years contains a clear warning that unless governments and politicians pay particular attention to disruptions and tectonic shifts in the workplace, anti-establishment popular movements will arise in the name of self-preservation. It is not enough to abandon responsibility for reasons of either ideology or sheer laziness and say the marketplace will sort things out. It doesn't. There is no "unseen hand" or scientific law of economics that guides markets to make adjustments most beneficial to the largest number of people. What identified the first city states in Mesopotamia and China seven thousand years ago as civilizations was literacy and numeracy. These skills evolved by necessity as the authorities sought sustainable social order by governing the market-places and imposing rules and regulations on such things as public health, weights and measures, and the value of currency. Regulation and oversight of the marketplace is as central a responsibility of government today as it was when urban life began.

The rise of populism in the North Atlantic countries is one indication of the neglect of that basic truth.

CHAPTER FOUR

—

The Clash Between Liberalism and Democracy Lets Loose the Populists

DEFINITIONS OF DEMOCRACY, such as that cited in Chapter One, usually include a reference to tolerance, acceptance of diversity, or some other liberal catchphrase. These definitions work on the assumption that true democracy and liberalism are indivisible and that tolerance for people of other economic classes, ethnic groups, religions, cultures, or sexual orientations is a natural and essential ingredient of democracy. However, the three decades since 1998 have demonstrated that this is not true. Francis Fukuyama, in his 2018 book *Identity: The Demand for Dignity and the Politics of Resentment*, explores many of the rivulets and streams feeding the river of discontent with liberal democracy. He points out that there is a fundamental conflict between the principles of freedom and equality that are inherent in the concept of liberal democracy. This fundamental conflict arises in part because the concept of freedom means different things to different people. Freedom for US conservatives and libertarians means being unfettered by government. For other people, such as those living in authoritarian societies, freedom means the ability to participate in government, to cast meaningful votes, to have a voice. Fukuyama uses the example of the Arab Spring, the street protests and revolutions across the Middle East in 2011, to illustrate his definition of people demanding freedom to participate in the administration of their own lives.

Equality is another matter again. Fukuyama says that equality is usually seen as a commitment to an economic and social balance within society. But socialist regimes that have tried to impose pure equality have quickly found themselves running up against principles of freedom, greed, and the all-too-prevalent human desire for authority over others.

"Real-world liberal democracies never fully live up to their underlying ideals of freedom and equality. Rights are often violated; the law never applies equally to the rich and powerful as it does to the poor and weak. Citizens, though given the opportunity to participate, frequently choose not to do so. Moreover, intrinsic conflicts exist between the goals of freedom and equality: greater freedom often entails increased inequality, while efforts to equalize outcomes reduce freedoms," Fukuyama wrote. "Successful democracy depends not on optimization of the ideals, but balance: a balance between individual freedom and political equality, and between a capable state exercising legitimate power and the institutions of law and accountability that seek to constrain it."

Lost among liberal democracies in the last thirty years has been a focus on the balancing act that Fukuyama describes. One effect of that loss has been the surfacing of illiberal democratic regimes as citizens reject what they see as assaults on their values or nationality. Among North Atlantic democracies, the common cause of anti-liberal reaction is either the real or perceived threat of immigration by people of markedly different ethnicity, culture, or religion. The world knew, of course, that democracy and liberalism could be separated. Adolf Hitler and the National Socialist Party of pre-war Germany were democratically elected. So were many leaders in post-colonial Africa and Latin America who, once elected, transformed themselves from the chosen of the people into self-serving despots. But there has been an assumption that the Nazi Party's democratic credentials were an aberration born of the mistakes made by the victorious allies after the First World War and the economic chaos of the Great Depression. The success of "Big Man" leadership in Africa and Latin America is sometimes judged a failure of Western political culture to fully take root during the colonial period. What we are discovering now, however, is that there was nothing unusual about the Nazis' electoral success or the easy erosion of democracy in tough times in Africa and Latin America. These days, disaffected voters in established democracies are just as likely as anyone in transitional democracies to give their support to a populist or extremist party that plays on their fears and grievances.

Almost all countries in the North Atlantic now have in their legislatures elected members of parties that espouse some form of intense nationalism or affirmation of a conservative national culture that rejects diversity. In addition, there are several examples from the past thirty years of governments in Europe and elsewhere being democratically elected with mandates to pursue illiberal policies or in fearful reaction to perceived rampant liberalism. The United States, the United Kingdom, Turkey, the Philippines, Brazil, Hungary, and Poland come to mind. So far, none of those governments or their leaders have crossed the line into conclusively demolishing democracy to perpetuate their own power, though some, like Hungary's Viktor Orbán and Turkey's Recep Tayyip Erdoğan, are showing signs of that lust. And, as described later, Orbán and others have used the declaration of states of emergency to combat COVID-19 to override democratic institutions. Elsewhere, there are several cases, including the US, where well-established first steps in debasing democracy — such as gerrymandering political constituencies, outlandishly vilifying the opposition, and undermining the rule of law and an independent judiciary — have been taken.

One outstanding fact is the failure of leftist and left-liberal political parties to respond to the anxieties of people discarded or isolated by economic and cultural change. Almost without exception, leftist politicians in Europe and North America — many of whom call themselves "progressives" these days — have shunned disaffected citizens, who are usually poor and white. Instead, leftist parties have targeted their campaigns at a coalition of minorities and one-issue voters. This, of course, has only added to the sense of isolation and dislocation felt by those who have fallen through the cracks of political and economic change. The political playing field in the US displays this picture with blunt clarity, but the situation is much the same across Europe. Even in Canada, the Liberal government and the semi-socialist New Democratic Party are preoccupied with identifiable minorities. Rejection of that preoccupation by many voters led to the Liberals becoming a minority government in the October 2019 election. Little direct attention is paid to the trials and tribulations of the white working class facing economic and cultural upheavals. As a result, a populist conservative government, though of a cartoonish variety, was elected in 2018 in Ontario, Canada's manufacturing centre. Aggressive Conservative governments have also been elected in Alberta and Saskatchewan, both of which have economies still tied to the production of carbon fuels. Both provinces face serious economic problems because of the shrinking appetite for their products and a lack of pipelines to get them to market. Instead of recognizing that the world is changing and that they need to develop some long-term programs for economic restructuring, the political leaders in both provinces have indulged in rants that exacerbate feelings of alienation.

While growing economic disparity and employment insecurity born of globalization and technological innovation have provided the seedbed for dissatisfaction with liberal democracy, there are many other factors involved. Overall, citizens believe they have less influence on or connection with the powers that rule their lives than they had in the past. There has, of course, always been a good deal of mythology around the democratic transaction between the people and their rulers. There was never a golden age when democracy functioned perfectly, and there never will be. Even so, the contemporary dislocation between the establishment and the citizenry among the countries of the North Atlantic is very real.

The Internet has undoubtedly sharpened the focus on that dislocation. In the pre-Internet days, electoral democracy was a process of picking a representative and dispatching him or her to the legislature to exercise judgment on behalf of the voters on whatever issues arose during the term of the administration. Few voters paid more than perfunctory attention to the nuts and bolts of legislation unless they had a specific interest. Few expected to influence the outcome of legislative debates. They elected a representative whose judgment, they believed, reflected the values of the community and who, they imagined, would act accordingly. Election campaigns were referenda on past performance as much as on hopes and expectations for the future.

The Internet and social media have created a far more direct and immediate relationship between citizens and the issues of the day. Even people not in the habit of taking a regular diet of news find current events crowding in on them through the posts of their friends. Those posts usually come with strong, prepackaged opinions about whatever issues are involved. The culture of social media in particular encourages instant and ill-considered reactions to events. In the same vein, it values volume and reach over content. It is highly emotional, in part because it is impersonal.

The immediacy of social media has also thrown into sharp relief the number and opacity of the filters that now exist between citizens and the decision-making processes that affect their lives. In all the countries of the North Atlantic these days, there is a significant democratic deficit in many of the institutions with which citizens have to deal in their daily lives. US President Trump built a personal political movement by circumventing those filters and talking directly to his supporters and followers via Twitter. He has thus avoided the mediation of government officials, who tradition-ally arbitrate policy to ensure moderation and consistency, and of the media, who condense and interpret the administration's actions. Trump's tweets have revolutionized contact between leaders and their citizenry. Many other heads of government around the world have realized the political benefits of unfiltered communications with voters and have followed Trump's example. However, the sense of immediacy in the relationship between the leader and the citizens has its downsides. The public ranting and raving of a narcissistic and ignorant leader is a danger to not only national social stability but also global peace and stability. The other side of the coin is that it tends to reinforce in the minds of susceptible people the ponderous, unresponsive, and often blatantly undemocratic nature of the administration of a modern nation.

In all countries of the North Atlantic, the legislature, whether it be a parliament or a national assembly, has grown more feeble over the last thirty years. Much real power over the everyday lives of citizens has devolved to unelected institutions such as supreme courts that interpret constitutional rights and freedoms, hosts of appointed bodies that regulate multitudes of social functions, and central banks that determine interest rates and money supply without reference to the policies of governments. There is also significant impact on daily life from adherence to treaties (such as free trade agreements) and to rules set out by international organizations such as the United Nations. As Harvard University professor Yascha Mounk put it in his 2018 book *The People Vs. Democracy*, "This loss of power for the people's representatives is not a result of elite conspiracy. On the contrary, it has occurred gradually, and often imperceptibly, in response to real policy challenges. But the cumulative result has been a creeping erosion of democracy: as more and more areas of public policy have been taken out of popular contestation, the people's ability to influence politics has been drastically curtailed."

The farming out of government to single-issue bodies is an understandable response to the plethora of demands and expectations placed on a modern state by the electorate. But the price is a significant democratic deficit as these bodies, usually run by appointees, make rules and regulations affecting numerous aspects of people's lives. At the federal level in Canada, for example, there are currently 35 government departments overseen by elected ministers, but there are another 169 federal government agencies overseeing various parts of daily life. These range from the Administrative Tribunals Support Service of Canada at the head of the list down to the Windsor-Detroit Bridge Authority and Women and Gender Equality Canada at the bottom. All these appointed agencies have varying degrees of power to establish the rules for what goes on in their bailiwicks. As well, Canada is a confederation with thirteen provincial and territorial governments in addition to the central government in Ottawa. Each of these regional administrations has its own departments led by an elected government minister, and, like Ottawa, swarms of appointed agencies responsible for setting the rules and running specific functions of government. Ontario, for example, has 191 provincial agencies and over 360 community organizations and boards. In general, Canada has a better record of maintaining democratic oversight and accountability over these agencies through responsible ministries and ministers than do other countries. But, as will be discussed in Chapter Thirteen, that has to be judged in the context of a serious slide into democratic deficit in Canada.

The picture of the supremacy of appointed government agencies is similar elsewhere. Mounk reports that in 2007, the US Congress enacted 138 laws. Yet in the same year, US federal agencies issued 2,926 rules for activities under their control.

In the UK, meanwhile, there were nine hundred government agencies, known as QUANGOS (Quasi-Autonomous Non-Governmental Organizations). These are taxpayer funded but have no meaningful democratic oversight. In 2010, the Conservative–Liberal Democrat coalition government led by David Cameron and Nick Clegg responded to public concern about the number and powers of the QUANGOS by promising to cut a third of them. What happened in reality was more of a shuffle than a cull. Few QUANGOS were eliminated, and the functions of the few that were axed were passed to agencies that survived. Ironically, while Cameron was engaged in this exercise, a head of steam was building in his Conservative Party and among increasingly large elements of the public to extricate the UK from the most potent undemocratic liberal activist organization of them all, the European Union.

In some areas, however, there is strong public support for the outsourcing of political power. The Supreme Court of Canada, for example, was given significant powers of interpretation when the new Charter of Rights and Freedoms was incorporated into the Canadian Constitution in 1982. The Charter replaced the old Canadian Bill of Rights of 1960, which was only a federal statute and had no application for provincial laws. The Charter not only applied to all levels of government, it also expanded the capacity for judicial review by courts. The result has been that several federal and provincial laws have been struck down by the courts as unconstitutional. In general, the courts (the Supreme Court in particular) have made expansive interpretations of human rights. They have worked on the assumption that the purpose of the Charter is to increase the rights and freedoms of people in a variety of circumstances, at the expense of government powers. A majority of Canadians show strong support for the liberal activism of the Supreme Court, but there is significant opposition among people who contend that the court is usurping the authority of Parliament. The most contentious issues have been social mores and the rights of people accused of crimes, especially those involving drugs or firearms. Canada's Civil Marriage Act of 2005, for example, flowed from a decision by the Ontario Court of Appeal in 2003 legalizing same-sex marriage in that province. There are also more general criticisms that the existence of the Charter is a break with the tradition of British common law, where rights and freedoms are not codified in a single document. The Charter, and its interpretation by the courts, goes the argument, has tended to Americanize Canadian politics. Opinion polls, however, show that around 80 percent of Canadians approve of the Charter and the roles the courts have played in its interpretation. That support must be seen, though, as a result of the failure of the established political system to respond to the needs and aspirations of citizens.

To a degree, Canadians have adopted Americans' attitudes and see the Supreme Court as an essential element in the safeguards of minority rights against impositions by the political strength of the majority. The difference is that in the US, the role of the Supreme Court is written in to the network of checks and balances the constitutional framers constructed to ensure that the country could not become a despotism. Ironically, this has had the reverse effect and made the composition of the Supreme Court a political issue for the running of the country. The appointing of judges of Republican or Democratic leanings has become one of the first orders of business for either party winning control of the White House and the Senate. On

November 7, 2019, the Republican leader of the Senate tweeted gleefully: "As of this afternoon, one in every four judges of the federal courts of appeals will have been nominated by @POTUS Trump and confirmed by us here in the Senate. That's 45 new lifetime appellate judges committed to the key principles that judges should apply our laws and the Constitution as they are actually written, not as the judges might personally wish they'd been written."

Nothing sums up and justifies more neatly the judgment of the Economist Intelligence Unit that the US is a "flawed democracy." If an independent judiciary is one of the essential pillars of democracy, the US clearly does not have it.

Both Canada and the United Kingdom, the birthplace of many of Canada's governing institutions, resisted giving authority for political interpretations to supreme courts. Both have found it impossible to stave off that pressure when they adopted written constitutions. The situation in the UK is much more fraught than is Canada's and, as will be described later, is one of the elements that has propelled support for the country to leave the European Union, which it joined in 1973. For all its history as a parliamentary democracy, the UK has resisted giving judges the power of judicial review of political decisions. It's a simple equation: laws should be enacted and interpreted by the people's elected representatives, not appointed judges who may or may not have any idea of how ordinary people live their lives. That began to change after the UK joined the EU, whose laws gave the courts in the UK the power to review Acts of Parliament. This movement reached a seminal conclusion in 2005, when the UK's most senior judges (who had previously sat as members of the upper house, the House of Lords) were reconstituted as a new Supreme Court. There was a glaring example of just the sort of clash generations of British politicians had sought to avoid in September 2019 when the Supreme Court ruled that the new prime minister, Boris Johnson, had acted unlawfully. In the run-up to the then deadline for the UK to leave the EU on October 31, Johnson had requested Queen Elizabeth to agree to the prorogation of Parliament for five weeks. Johnson's purpose was to prevent Parliament, in which he had only minority support, from passing legislation that would tie his hands in the final negotiations with Brussels on the terms of the UK's departure or, perhaps, frustrate that intention entirely. But the Supreme Court ruled, "The decision to advise Her Majesty to prorogue Parliament was unlawful because it had the effect of frustrating or preventing the ability of Parliament to carry out its constitutional functions without reasonable justification."

For the Brexiteers, of course, this judgment only reinforced their argument that membership in the EU had eroded UK sovereignty by enabling Brussels to impose alien political and judicial concepts on the UK.

While Canadians don't have the same antipathetic attitude toward the Supreme Court and its relationship with Parliament as do many in the UK, a large majority of Canadians show little trust in the other prominent national institutions of government, business, and the media. A poll published in February 2019 by Edelman Trust Barometer found 80 percent of Canadians feel that the country's elites are out of touch with ordinary people. Half of Canadians feel "the system" is not working for them. But there is an interesting dichotomy between what Edelman calls the "informed public" — college-educated people aged twenty-five to sixty-four — and the "mass population." Among Edelman's sample of "informed" people, 74 percent trusted the key institutions of the country, while only 54 percent of the "mass" had the same confidence. Bridgitte Anderson, then general manager of Edelman Vancouver, commented that the twenty-point difference in attitude between the two social classes is a record high.

"That twenty-point gap is second only to the United Kingdom, so there is a huge differentiator for us with other global countries," she said. "It is clear that there is a real pessimism about institutions going forward."

Anderson said the poll found a deep sense of injustice and pessimism about the future. Even among the generally more optimistic "informed" public, only 53 percent thought they and their families would be better off in five years. Among the less engaged "mass" public, only 34 percent viewed the future with optimism. This was matched by just over 50 percent of respondents saying they felt they didn't have the right skills for a good job, they feared automation and innovations, and they were apprehensive their employment could be harmed by international trade policies and conflicts.

"When you dig into it and you find out more about this polarisation, and the impact it's having," said Anderson, "the data shows us that leaders — both in business and in government — need to do a better job talking to Canadians about the things that matter to them."

The Edelman poll and Anderson's comments were published a few months before Canada's October 2019 election, in which there was precious little indication that the three major political parties had any real grasp of the state of mind of Canadian voters. Indeed, just three months before the election, the Angus Reid Institute published a study showing that nearly two-thirds of Canadians — 64 percent — felt politicians cannot be trusted. Lack of trust of politicians is most prevalent among Conservative Party supporters: 71 percent. Even among committed Liberal Party supporters, the group showing the most belief in the trustworthiness of politicians, only 41 percent had confidence in their elected representatives. The cynicism about politicians is such that 32 percent told researchers they believe the primary motivation for anyone to get into politics is personal gain rather than a genuine desire to serve their communities. The object of this particular public disquiet is the professional politician, who has had no life experience outside politics and who has become increasingly common in many democracies.

Canada does not appear to have been affected as completely by this trend as other democracies. A July 2018 study for the Hansard Society's journal, *Parliamentary Affairs*, by doctoral candidate James Pow says the Canadian system produces relatively few professional politicians, unlike, for example, the United Kingdom. In the UK, a well-worn path to a political career is to join the staff of a political party research office after leaving university. Having established a reputation as a reliable, loyal, and perhaps talented party foot soldier, the objective is to get handed the nomination for a safe party seat and thus enter into the House of Commons. That is the career path taken by Chris Patten. After leaving Oxford, he joined the staff of the Conservative Party research office and parleyed that into a seat in the House of Commons. He was a minister in the governments of Margaret Thatcher and John Major before being appointed the last British governor of Hong Kong in 1992. After overseeing the handover of the territory to China in 1997, Patten went on to be appointed a member of the House of Lords and chancellor of Oxford University.

Pow points out that there is not such a dependable ladder into a political career in Canada. While in theory it is possible to enter politics by working for a political party or as a policy adviser to a minister, there is no Canadian equivalent of the Patten freeway to high office.

"In the Canadian system there are obstacles to making such plans. On the one hand, there is widespread disapproval of parties 'parachuting' candidates into winnable ridings — which is how special advisers might enjoy an electoral advantage elsewhere. On the other hand, the organisation of Canadian political parties traditionally lacks much integration between different levels of government, making it difficult to discern any real career ladder from municipal to provincial to federal office," Pow wrote.

"Indeed, based on the comparison between the winners and the runners-up in the 2011 Canadian federal election, there is no evidence that individuals with a professional background in politics enjoyed any automatic advantage in getting elected. A candidate with no experience working in politics was just as likely to win as someone with prior experience."

Pow's study found that "professional" political experience didn't even help in getting promoted to Cabinet positions. The prime minister's need to put together a Cabinet that represents the country's provinces and regions determines who gets offered ministerial posts. Abilities and political experience are useful but secondary to the need for a government seen to be representative of the whole country.

This sense among the citizenry that the pressures on political decisions have little to do with the aspirations and needs of ordinary people is reinforced by the big business of lobbying politicians on behalf of corporations and other institutions. Canada is a relative newcomer to the business of institutionalized lobbying of politicians, under an act that came into force in the bellwether year of 1989 with the intention of making transparent and subject to regulation an industry that had always existed in the shadows. As Democracy Watch recently rather overexcitedly reported, "lobbying has become an incredible growth industry in Ottawa. At a conservatively estimated $300 million in annual revenues, the industry has increased in size 10 times in the past decade. When you take into consideration the revolving door between government and lobby firms, public service is now seen by many as a mere stepping stone to more lucrative private-sector postings. It is only a slight understatement to say that lobbyists run our government."

Democracy Watch is not alone in deploring the increasing influence of lobbying operations in Canada, which has grown in parallel with the declining importance of members of Parliament as influencers on public policy. There is an increasing apprehension among the Canadian public that lobbyists hijack government policy making on behalf of their corporate employers and that government for the common good gets abandoned in the process. Canadian Commissioner of Lobbying Nancy Bélanger wrote in her 2018–19 annual report that there were 6,819 lobbyists registered with her office. Government departments are required to file monthly reports of meetings or other communications with lobbyists, and in 2018–19 there were 27,500. The top five institutions targeted by the lobbyists were, in order, members of the House of Commons; the Prime Minister's Office; the Department of Innovation, Science and Economic Development; Finance Canada; and members of the Senate. The five top issues on which lobbyists wanted to get a word in for their clients were international trade, the environment, health, industry, and economic development.

As for facing other forces eroding democracy, Canada has the perfect example to the south of what not to do. In the US, the judgment by Democracy Watch that lobbyists largely determine government and legislative activity is accurate. But in the US, money — who gives it and who gets it — is a decisive factor in politics in general and yet another example of why that country is assessed as a flawed democracy. Lobbying is only one factor in the political dominance of money in Washington. Even so, money spent on lobbying in the US has risen from about US$1.6 billion at the turn of the century to US$3.2 billion in 2016. A breakdown of who spends what on lobbying shows that for every dollar spent by non-governmental organizations and those promoting themselves as public interest groups, corporations spend $34.

Lobbying is also a boom industry in the European Union. In the 1970s there were fewer than one thousand registered lobbyists in Brussels. Today there are at least 25,000. Conservative estimates suggest that over €1.5 billion (C$2.2 billion) is spent every year on lobbying targets like the European Commission, the European Parliament, the Council of Europe, and the offices in Brussels of national governments.

SINCE 1990, THE Stockholm-based International Institute for Democracy and Electoral Assistance (International IDEA) has been keeping tabs on the levels of participation in elections by voters in democracies. A pattern has emerged. From the end of the Second World War until the end of the Cold War (1945–1989), voter turnout in democratic elections was stable at about 80 percent. It then fell sharply in the 1990s to 70 percent and continued its decline to reach 66 percent from 2011 to 2015. In a 2016 report, International IDEA commented, "Declining voter turnout signals the deep problems democracies are facing today. Lower turnout suggests that fewer citizens consider elections the main instrument for legitimizing political parties' control over political decision making. It may even show that citizens are less interested in political parties as the main bodies of democratic representation as such."

The breakdown of figures produced by International IDEA is fascinating and alarming. The highest level of decline in voter turnout has been in Europe, with the highest level of disdain for elections among voters in the new democracies of Eastern Europe that emerged from the Cold War. Average turnout across the post-communist countries has declined by around 20 percent since the first free elections held at the end of the 1980s.

This must be viewed, however, next to a consistent decline in turnout of about 10 percent in the established European democracies during the same period, albeit from a higher base. Some of the declines in voter confidence in elections are extraordinary. Most disillusioned is Albania, where voter turnout plummeted by 46 percent from the first post-communist elections held in 1991 to the elections in 2013. Slovakia is next worst, with a declining participation of 37 percent in the same period. Montenegro and Hungary are maintaining a grudging respect for democracy at the top of the list, with declining voter turnout of only 2 and 3 percent respectively.

Those are the trends. The current state of voter turnout in democracies is set out in a 2019 report by World Population Review. This is an interesting report because it shows the relationship between the percentage of voters who have turned out in recent elections and the equally important proportion of the voting-age population that is actually registered to vote. Obviously, if a democracy has a relatively low proportion of registered voters, something is wrong. That could suggest lack of voter confidence in the democratic process, lack of effort by the political parties and government to encourage participation, or efforts by political parties to ensure their opponents don't get the opportunity to vote. This last problem is, of course, a well-documented issue in the US, where the gerrymandering of constituency boundaries, barriers to voter registration, rules designed to make voting difficult, and strategic placement of inaccessible polling stations are established tricks by political parties to subvert democracy. No wonder, then, that the US comes near the bottom of the list compiled by World Population Review of voter participation in developed countries. In the US, only 55.7 percent of voting-age adults are registered to vote. This puts in context the figure of the 86.8 percent turnout in the 2016 elections. In terms of those eligible to vote, the turnout was only 86.8 percent of 55.7 percent of voting-age adults. That's 48.3 percent of eligible voters, which in turn means that Donald Trump won the presidency with the support of only 22.4 percent of those eligible to vote.

Canada does not have much to cheer about in this regard, though it has a more inclusive system than the US. In theory, Canadians are automatically put on voting lists based on their official residence. But Canadians are a mobile people who move six times during their lifetimes on average. A Statistics Canada survey done in May 2011 found four million Canadians had moved in the previous twelve months. Voter registration lists are usually months or years behind reality. It is, therefore, not a surprise that the World Population Review found that only 62.12 percent of voting-age adults are registered. Turnout was 68.3 percent in the 2015 elections. That slipped to 65.95 percent in 2019.

As in other aspects of democratic performance, the top of the list is dominated by Northern European countries, but not exclusively so. Belgium tops voter performance, with 87.21 percent of adults registered to vote and 89.37 percent of them exercising their franchise. Next comes Sweden, followed by Denmark, Australia, South Korea, the Netherlands, Israel, New Zealand, Finland, and Hungary capping off the top ten. Even some of the old Eastern Bloc countries that have seen some of the largest declines in voter participation, such as Estonia and Slovakia, still manage to make it into the top twenty of overall voter turnout.

Leading on from the nuts and bolts of participation in elections, an April 2019 paper by the Pew Research Center looked at global attitudes toward politicians and how well people believe their democracies are functioning. As in many other areas of life, Canada's feelings about these questions are very similar to those of the Nordic countries. "Assessments of how well democracy is working vary considerably across nations," found the report. "In Europe, for example, more than six in ten Swedes and Dutch are satisfied with the current state of democracy, while large majorities in Italy, Spain and Greece are dissatisfied." The Pew paper found among "key areas of public frustration: Most believe elections bring little change, that politicians are corrupt and out of touch and that the courts do not treat people fairly." In Europe, the research results suggest that dissatisfaction with the way democracy is working is tied to views about the European Union, opinions about whether immigrants and refugees are adopting the customs of their new homes, and attitudes toward populist parties. Intertwined with these disenchantments are concerns about economic security and fears that personal identity and stature within the community are under threat. One outcome of these frustrations is that support for the ideals of liberal democracy has weakened perceptibly and fuelled populist parties on both the right and left political fringes. Support for populist nationalism has become politically entrenched in the United States, the United Kingdom, Hungary, and Poland. In all those cases, the reasons for the moves away from liberal democracy and toward more intolerant versions flow from the rifts between the social and political establishment classes and voters who feel the most alienated. But all four examples are different in their details, and each has lessons to impart.

CHAPTER FIVE

—

God, Race, and Country

POPULIST LEADERS COME in all shapes and sizes, and the motives that propel them onto the podium are equally diverse. The classic image of the populist is that of Professor Harold Hill in the Broadway musical *The Music Man*, the glib-tongued orator skilled at conjuring people's hopes and fears into a few well-spun words and phrases. It is always too late when the crowds discover they have been marshalled into a movement not to overcome their own troubles but for the aggrandizement of Il Duce, whoever he, or occasionally she, may be. Hungarian Prime Minister Viktor Orbán and Poland's highly influential leader of the ruling Law and Justice Party, Jarosław Kaczyński, are different. They can be called organic populists. Their pushback against the liberal democratic and political unification agenda of the European Union and the Brussels establishment flows from a visceral understanding of the survival instincts of their people. That also makes them fundamentally different from Donald Trump and from the two prime movers of the campaign to get popular support for the UK to leave the European Union, Nigel Farage and Boris Johnson. The US and UK voters who were seduced by their populists were driven in large part by the reality or fears of economic marginalization and the belief that they no longer counted as significant members of society. In Poland and Hungary, there is no real economic component in the drive toward illiberal nationalism. Both economies have done very well out of EU membership. Poland in particular has been clocking up growth rates of about 4 percent a year for over a decade.

The populism of Orbán and Kaczyński is steeped in the culture and ethnicity of Hungary and Poland at a time when significant elements of both populations feel their heritages are threatened by the liberal democratic dictates of the European Union. Equally important is that neither country has much experience living the culture of democracy, certainly not recently. They are in transition from rule by authoritarian masters in the Soviet Union to a different kind of oversight by another empire: the EU. These transitions are never easy, and relatively few countries that have travelled this path in the last few decades have got it right on the first go. It is like trying to get a car moving uphill on icy roads. It takes a few attempts to get the balance right between playing the accelerator, the gearbox, and the brakes before finding the sweet spot where the tires bite and the car crests the rise.

The men who marketed Brexit are another matter entirely. There is nothing organic about Nigel Farage, whose founding of the United Kingdom Independence Party (UKIP) eventually forced then Tory Prime Minister David Cameron to hold the ill-conceived referendum on the issue in 2016. And Boris Johnson, who in 2019 strode out of the carnage of the pro-Brexit vote to become prime minister, cannot be called a son of the soil. Both men are limelight lovers, social eccentrics and misfits with histories of duplicity and crude ambition. Whether they believe in what they have done or have merely seen an opportunity for personal advancement in the undoubted anxiety among some UK voters about their cultural and economic survival in the EU is a question that hangs unanswered. It may be unanswerable.

At the ultra-narcissist end of the scale is US President Trump. From the way he achieved power and the way he has administered it, there is no reason to think he is driven by anything other than personal aggrandizement.

For that reason alone, he is the most dangerous of the current crop of populists leading countries of the North Atlantic because, like Louis XIV in eighteenth-century France, he regards himself as the personification of the United States. This is a continuation of his corporate life, where Trump is a marketable brand spun out of flim-flammery and theatrical obedience to his pronouncements rather than a sound corporate enterprise. To understand Trump, it is necessary to watch the so-called reality TV series *The Apprentice*, in which he played a dictatorial corporate boss, a modern-day Caesar, turning thumbs up or down, determining the fate of benighted applicants (or supplicants) who came before him. This is the Trump brand, and it is a pure fabrication, but one that won the United States presidency with the assistance of a dysfunctional electoral system and the Russian government under Vladimir Putin. Trump occupies the White House as his TV persona. He denounces the constitutional checks and balances on his power as treason and those managing the levers of law and order as traitors. Trump would be dangerous even as the popinjay demagogue of a banana republic. As the occupant of the Oval Office, he is a global threat.

As the world travels deeper into an age of anxiety — where citizens overwhelmed by the ever-increasing complexity of life, especially during the first WHO-declared pandemic, seek easy or quickly comforting answers to profound problems — it is important to understand the nuances of populism. The nature of the different populists reveals the core elements of the public disquiet and sense of alienation that has led to the demagogues' rise to power in their individual countries. This in turn shows what needs to be addressed if the trends away from democracy and toward authoritarianism are to be reversed.

———

LOOKING AT THE sweep of European history, it is extraordinary that Hungary and Poland have survived as distinct nations and cultures. Throughout recorded time, both countries have been in the collision zone between Eastern and Western powers. Both have for extended periods been part of multinational and multi-ethnic empires and managed to emerge with their sense of cultural nationhood, if not always their national borders, intact. Insecurity has bred not only profound ethnic loyalty and ingenuity but also an instinctive rebelliousness. Most recently, it was these qualities that sustained both Poles and Hungarians through the long night of the Cold War and Soviet occupation, but they also put both peoples at the forefront of the uprisings in 1989. Working in rather different ways, it was the Poles and the Hungarians as much as anyone who revealed the fundamental hollowness of Moscow's empire and who gave it the push that brought down the facade.

After the end of the Cold War, Poland and Hungary, along with most of the other Eastern Bloc countries, faced irresistible pressures to join the two main Western clubs, the European Union and the North Atlantic Treaty Organization. For the most part, the former Soviet satellites welcomed these opportunities. Reservations about the social, political, and economic upheavals involved were set aside or regarded as a price worth paying for the eventual outcome. NATO membership offered security in the event that Russia managed to achieve political stability and renew its poking and jabbing at the West, as has happened. The blandishments from the EU were even more enticing. Brussels offered many economic opportunities and promises: investment to replace grossly dilapidated infrastructure; the prospects of radical improvements in people's lives; and all of Europe as a marketplace. Those opportunities came with the requirement that the Eastern Bloc candidates buckle down to create the political, administrative, and legal framework that would allow them to function among the established European democracies. But those were attributes to which many people in Poland and Hungary had aspired for two generations.

Hungary and Poland joined NATO in 1999, eight years after the formal dissolution of the Soviet Union's Warsaw Pact in 1991, and both joined the EU in May 2004. Membership in the EU came after years of negotiations with Brussels and preparations to meet the union's standards of politics, administration, the rule of law, and judicial independence, which had started in 1997. There were referenda ahead of these accessions. In April 2003, 83.8 percent of Hungarians voted in favour of joining the EU, and the result was declared valid even though only 45 percent of registered voters had gone to the polls. The Brussels establishment preferred to ignore the fact that only a small minority of Hungary's voting-age adults had come out in favour of EU membership. In the Polish referendum in June 2003, 58.85 percent of voters turned out and 77.5 percent voted in favour of EU membership. Again, this worked out to be only a minority of registered voters. Fifteen years later, polls show majorities of citizens in both countries supporting EU membership. The economic benefits of membership continue to dominate, but close behind is seething disquiet with the social and political agendas of the bureaucrats in Brussels, which are seen as excessively liberal and destructive of EU members' nationhood. In response, both the Warsaw and Budapest governments have tacked away from the tenets of liberal democracy. Further, they have moved against some of the essential attributes of democracy, especially the rule of law and an independent judiciary. The European Commission, the EU's executive branch, has reacted by considering cutting funding to Warsaw and Budapest for failing to uphold the rule of law. There have even been calls to expel both countries because of the anti-democratic activities of their governments.

Many of the misgivings that have enabled Orbán and Kaczyński to pursue what the Hungarian leader called illiberal democracy are common throughout the EU. They stem from the perceived "democratic deficit" in the union's institutions. The European Council is widely seen as a governing body without true democratic credentials or oversight. Moreover, the council and other EU bodies are seen as creating rules and regulations with social implications that pursue a liberal agenda that is out of touch with the sensitivities of many people living within the union. The culture of legally entrenched political correctness over a spectrum of issues involving sexual orientation, the free movement of peoples from within and without the EU, and equality of respect for religions is one with which many Europeans remain uncomfortable. Brussels has stridden off along a road of liberalism without realizing or acknowledging that many citizens of the EU's members are hesitant to follow. Indeed, there are substantial minorities (and probably majorities) in Hungary, Poland, and some of the other more culturally conservative former Soviet satellites who find Brussels's liberalism abhorrent. The push for ever more political integration within the EU only exacerbates anxieties about being governed by a detached and unresponsive elite. Political integration and the creation of some kind of federation of European states will, many fear, erode and overrun the distinctive nationalities and cultures to which people cling.

On July 26, 2014, Orbán gave what had become an annual speech to a student audience at Băile Tuşnad in the ethnic Hungarian region of neighbouring Romania. It was a speech that questioned the political direction toward liberal democracy that the United States, Europe, and the European Union had taken since the collapse of the Berlin Wall. But that was only Orbán's jumping-off point. He went on to extol the virtues of illiberal democracy as a necessity for European countries to maintain their competitiveness in the face of challenges from emerging economic powers like Turkey, China, Russia, India, and Singapore. Orbán's argument took the conflict within liberal democracy between the rights of the individual and the freedoms of the collective society, and came down firmly on the side of the latter. "In other words," he said, "the Hungarian nation is not simply a group of individuals but a community that must be organised, reinforced and in fact constructed. And so in this sense the new state that we are constructing in Hungary is an illiberal state, a non-liberal state."

What was so perplexing about Orbán's lurch toward illiberal nationalism and the evident support he enjoyed from a large majority of the Hungarian people was that he was one of the last people expected to dabble in authoritarianism. Orbán had come of age in the time when the fissures in the Soviet Bloc began to expand from cracks to looming chasms. At the beginning of 1989, Orbán, one of the founding members of Fidesz, the Hungarian Civic Alliance, had received a scholarship from the foundation operated by George Soros, the Hungarian-born American philanthropist and pro-democracy activist. Orbán was studying political science at

Pembroke College, Oxford, but on June 18 he was in Heroes' Square in Budapest, where he gave a speech at the reburial of Imre Nagy, the former prime minister who had led the 1956 uprising against Moscow's rule and who had been executed by the Soviets. In his speech, Orbán demanded free elections and the withdrawal of Soviet troops. Many of those who heard or later read the speech assumed that Orbán's anti-communism equated with liberalism. They were wrong. As has been discovered, Orbán's anti-communism is not founded in liberalism but on staunch, conservative Catholic Christian values and intense dedication to Hungarian racial identity and nationalism. Even so, that day of remembrance for Nagy and redress for Moscow's excesses in 1956 led to the collapse of the communist regime in Hungary and brought Orbán wide national acclaim. He abandoned his studies at Oxford and returned to Hungary, where he was elected to the National Assembly in 1990 in the first free elections. He was appointed head of the Fidesz caucus.

Those early years in Hungary, of transition from the communist one-party state to multi-party democracy, were turbulent — as they were in all the former satellites of Moscow. Orbán stumbled through a number of failed political alliances before forming a successful coalition with the Hungarian Democratic Forum and the Independent Smallholders' Party in 1998. At thirty-five, Orbán became the second-youngest prime minister in Hungary's history, and from the start he showed scant interest in the niceties of democracy. He soon abandoned any pretence at consensus-seeking with his coalition partners, he cut the sittings of the unicameral parliament, the National Assembly, to every third week, and for ten months he failed to show up for question time in the house. Meanwhile, Fidesz was putting loyal party members at the head of key government institutions: the chief prosecutor's office, the central bank, and the public broadcasting corporation.

The 2002 elections were a hard-fought and bitter affair that saw the Hungarian Socialist Party eventually come out on top. Orbán spent eight years in opposition during which he only just managed to hang on to the leadership of Fidesz. His fortunes revived when Fidesz and its allies won a two-thirds majority in the 2010 election. This gave him the authority to change the constitution, and he grabbed the opportunity. He cut the number of seats in the National Assembly from 386 to 199. He packed the Constitutional Court with his own appointees and narrowed its jurisdiction. Constituency boundaries were gerrymandered in favour of Fidesz. Voting rights were given to the estimated three million ethnic Hungarians who live in neighbouring countries such as Romania, Slovakia, Serbia, Croatia, Slovenia, Montenegro, and Ukraine. An undercurrent of Orbán's nationalist appeal is that as a result of the partition of the old Kingdom of Hungary under the Treaty of Trianon in 1920, the country lost 70 percent of its pre–First World War territory and 30 percent of its Hungarian-speaking population. Most of the enfranchised dual-nationality Hungarians in neighbouring countries support Fidesz. A new authority was created with wide-ranging powers to confront and fine media outlets. The authority members were Fidesz loyalists.

Hungary operated under a temporary constitution from the return of democracy in 1989, but this was only a makeshift reworking of the constitution that had been enacted by the communist regime in 1949. Armed with a two-thirds parliamentary majority and the power to make fundamental constitutional changes, Orbán resolved to provide a new Fundamental Law of Hungary. This was adopted in April 2011 and is Orbán's manifesto for the country. What shouts from the rafters is that in defiance of the EU's insistence that it is a secular union, Orbán's constitution is a profoundly Christian document portraying Hungary as an unequivocally Christian country. He stakes out his ground from the opening words. "God bless the Hungarians," the preamble exhorts, and the document goes on to explicitly extol as Hungarian the Christian values of regard for family, nation, fidelity, religious faith, love, and work as an act of worship. "We recognize the role of Christianity in preserving nationhood," declares Orbán's constitution. "We hold that the family and the nation constitute the principal framework of our coexistence," it says, adding, "The life of the foetus shall be protected from the moment of conception" and "Hungary shall protect the institution of marriage as the union of a man and a woman."

In 2012, when the new constitution came into force, Orbán proclaimed, "Dear ladies and gentlemen, we Hungarians have provided our own answer. Now, twenty years after the toppling of communism and removal of the Soviets, we finally have a granite foundation for the future." But Orbán's manifesto for an illiberal Hungary has proved to be neither granite nor universally loved. In particular, there was a serious public backlash in 2013 when Orbán attempted for the fourth time to tighten provisions of the document. The definition of family was made even more restrictive. Students who received state aid would have been forbidden from leaving the country after graduation. Homeless people could be removed from public areas without forewarning. Hate speech was to be banned, but with the implication that government would be selective in the targets. The powers of the Constitutional Court to review constitutional changes were to be restricted. There were mass protests in Budapest, and the European Commission threatened reprisals if the document was implemented. Orbán backed down and modified the amendments. Since then, Orbán and Fidesz have lost their two-thirds majority in the National Assembly and thus the ability to amend the constitution without the support of other parties. Opposition parties made it clear they would not support further amendments that would make the constitution even more illiberal. However, opposition to Fidesz and Orbán is most evident among young urbanites, who show little interest at the moment in moving into national politics. And while opposition parties control most of Hungary's major cities, these are feeble platforms as the bulk of municipal council powers and responsibilities have been transferred to the central government.

A hallmark of Orbán's campaign against liberalism has been his persistent vilification of the Hungarian-born pro-democracy philanthropist George Soros. A particular target of Orbán's campaign has been Soros's Central European University (CEU), established in Budapest in 1991. The university's free or inexpensive English-language graduate courses and degrees are recognized in the US. The rector is Toronto-born Michael Ignatieff, who was the leader of the Liberal Party of Canada from 2008 to

2011, when it was the official opposition to Stephen Harper's Conservative government. Orbán and his followers charge that the university is a bastion of Soros's plan to destroy Europe by instilling left-liberal values and promoting immigration. Soros and Ignatieff stood their ground for years against efforts by Orbán to close the CEU, but gave up in 2019. On November 15, Soros opened the CEU's new campus in Vienna, beginning a year-long exodus of the university and its students from Budapest, for which Soros provided the equivalent of C$1 billion.

The declaration by the World Health Organization in mid-March 2020 that the spread of COVID-19 had become a pandemic presented Orbán with a huge opportunity, as it did other would-be autocrats. On March 30, the Hungarian National Assembly passed a raft of measures that essentially removed the checks and balances on the government. Under the new dispensation, Prime Minister Orbán could rule by decree, parliament was largely sidelined, the holding of elections and referenda were suspended indefinitely, and anyone circulating false information related to the pandemic could be imprisoned for up to five years. Of course, it was for Orbán and his regime to decide what constituted "fake news." The first edicts by the Orbán regime had far more to do with promoting his nationalist agenda than they did with combating the pandemic. Two dealt with the construction of museums and theatre management, which had nothing to do with social distancing or other anti–COVID-19 measures. They were simply moves by Orbán to remove independent powers of municipal governments. Another early edict prohibited transgender people from legally changing their sex. Others appeared to be aimed at ensuring that no evidence could be found to sustain mounting allegations that Orbán was running a profoundly corrupt regime. One decree classified as secret all information about a major Chinese railway investment, the largest single infrastructure project in Hungarian history. This had little to do with the campaign against the coronavirus but would ensure that the names of the Hungarian business people who benefited from the deal with Beijing would be kept secret for ten years. Orbán's internal coup brought a sharp rebuke from European

Commission President Ursula von der Leyen. She publicly warned Orbán that the anti–COVID-19 measures "have to be proportionate, within a limited time period, and democratically controlled." If Orbán did not respect those limitations, von der Leyen said, the EU would take legal action against the Hungarian government.

The base of support for Orbán and Fidesz was built on the disenchantment of rural and small-town conservative Hungarians with the cosmopolitan establishment. This is one of the few themes Orbán has in common with US President Trump, the UK's Brexiteers, and Poland's Jarosław Kaczyński and his Law and Justice Party (known by its Polish acronym, PiS).

Jarosław Kaczyński is an unlikely populist. For much of his political career, he has shunned the spotlight and preferred to run the government, when PiS has been in power, from just off stage. He can be described as the the éminence grise of demagogues. He served briefly as prime minister from July 2006 until November 2007, while his identical twin brother, Lech Kaczyński, was president, and he ran for but lost the presidential election in 2010. Since coming to power decisively in the elections of 2015 and then maintaining that grip in the latest elections in October 2019, Jarosław Kaczyński and PiS have followed a script very similar to Orbán and Fidesz in Hungary.

Kaczyński has concentrated on undermining or dismantling the checks and balances on executive power. Poland's Constitutional Tribunal, Supreme Court, regular courts, the National Council of the Judiciary, and electoral commissions have all been put under the control of the executive, which in the reality of Polish politics means PiS party leader Kaczyński. His justification for these actions lies in claims that the judicial and constitutional institutions are still riddled with appointees from the communist era who must be purged. The European Commission was alarmed and launched an investigation against the PiS government for breaching the rule of law and weakening democracy. There are several cases against Poland pending at the time of writing in early 2020. Polish voters don't appear to share these concerns with Brussels, having increased the number of seats PiS held in Parliament in 2019. PiS did not win control of the Senate; however, this house has very limited powers.

———

THE PASSION OF the PiS in Warsaw and Fidesz in Budapest is to keep their countries staunchly conservative, Catholic, and as racially homogeneous as possible. This became an international issue in 2015. In that year, there were an estimated 5.1 million Syrian refugees from the civil war in neighbouring countries, around 3 million of them in Turkey. And it was largely from Turkey that well over a million of these refugees made their way to Europe, seeking asylum. Brussels hastily put together a plan to allocate the arrivals to various EU countries to spread the responsibility for accommodating the refugees and to take the pressure off Greece and Italy, where most were arriving. The EU plan was to accept 160,000 asylum seekers and allocate them to member states based on the size and wealth of receiving countries. Hungary, Poland, Romania, the Czech Republic, and Slovakia refused to take any Muslim refugees.

In Poland, PiS leader Kaczyński warned that migrants carry "all sorts of parasites and protozoa, which … while not dangerous in the organisms of these people, could be dangerous here." The PiS also stated bluntly that it believed Muslim migrants could be a problem for Poland's homogenous society. Kaczyński set out his antipathy toward refugees in a 2017 interview with the *Gazeta Polska Codziennie* newspaper. He warned that Poland "would have to completely change our culture and radically lower the level of safety in our country." He also said that Poland "would have to use some repression" to prevent "a wave of aggression, especially toward women" on the part of asylum seekers.

There was a similar dynamic in Budapest, where Prime Minister Orbán explained his defiance of Brussels in politically popular terms of defending European and Christian civilization against an onslaught of outsiders. Orbán went one step further and ordered the building of a fence along the Hungarian-Serbian border to block the entry of illegal immigrants. Orbán opposes any compulsory EU long-term quota on redistribution of migrants. He wrote in the *Frankfurter Allgemeine Zeitung* at the height of the crisis in 2015: "Europe's response is madness. We must acknowledge that the European Union's misguided immigration policy is responsible for this situation." Orbán has also promoted the Great Replacement, a far right-wing conspiracy theory originally set out in a book by French author Renaud Camus in 1911. The idea is that because of low birth rates among white Europeans and North Americans, the ruling elite is promoting immigration and integration of people from Africa and the Middle East in order to sustain the economy. Replacementism, as it has become known, has been adopted by ultra-right-wing groups, most of them avowedly racist, across Europe and in the US and Canada. In 2017, *Le Journal du Dimanche* reported Orbán saying, "if we let tens of millions of migrants travel to Europe from Africa and the Middle East … the young people of Western Europe will know the day when they will be in a minority in their own country."

Of the several similarities between the populist appeals in Hungary, Poland, the United Kingdom, and the United States, antipathy toward immigrants and refugees is the common factor that stands out. Fear of immigrants taking jobs and changing the culture runs from Orbán's wall on the Serbian border to Trump's promise of an impenetrable barrier along the Rio Grande to keep out Latin Americans. It is also lurking on the surface or churning just beneath the flotsam and jetsam of Brexit.

As will be discussed later, Brexit and the rise of populist nationalism among European states are matters that must focus the minds of EU leaders and the Eurocrats in Brussels about the future and style of the union. There are two central problems for the EU from which the brunt of its problems flow and which must be addressed. One is the democratic deficit in the way the central institutions of the EU are brought together, and the other is to the lack of a consensus on what the EU is intended to be. Is it a free trade partnership or is it a federated political union?

CHAPTER SIX

—

The Smell of the Greasepaint, the Roar of the Crowd

ALTHOUGH THE EVENTS leading up to and flowing from the June 23, 2016, referendum in the United Kingdom in which 52 percent of voters opted to leave the EU are often presented as an upwelling of populism, they don't quite fit that template. There are, to be sure, characters in the story who qualify as demagogues. Nigel Farage, the gadfly leader of the United Kingdom Independence Party, and Boris Johnson, the studiously charming, dishevelled, and outrageous television personality who parlayed his notoriety into the Tory premiership, are both populists. But if an anti-establishment uprising is an essential element of a populist revolt, Brexit doesn't qualify. It was factions of the establishment, especially the more archaic reaches of the Conservative Party, that were the driving force behind the campaign for the UK to leave the EU, almost from the day it joined in 1973.

Similar qualifications should be made about the populism of Donald Trump, though his rise to the presidency of the US more closely fits the classic definition of a populist leader than does what happened in the UK. Yet Trump is more a product of a broken political system and a divided nation than he is a true populist. He is the accidental president. He has no convincing vision for the future, and his entire political appeal is to the worst instincts of disenchanted and fearful sections of society. "Make America Great Again" is a purposefully vague and unhelpful appeal to nostalgia. It can mean whatever the listener wants it to mean. It is not an agenda.

In the UK, the first signs of disquiet about the direction the EU was going came not from the grumpy corners of the Tory caucus but from Prime Minister Margaret Thatcher. When she came to office in 1979, the UK was settling in as a member of what was then the European Economic Community, a club devoted almost exclusively to enhancing trade, productivity, and competitiveness among its members. Her predecessor in the early 1970s as Tory leader and prime minister, Edward Heath, believed the UK relied too heavily on the US, to the detriment of its potential trade with mainland Europe. France vetoed early efforts by London to join the European club, but in 1973 the UK was allowed in. One year after the UK joined, Heath's Conservative government was replaced by a Labour one under Harold Wilson. The Labour party was divided over Europe and wanted the terms of membership renegotiated, so on June 5, 1975, the UK held a referendum, the country's first such ballot. It was a decisive victory, with 67.2 percent of votes cast in favour of continued membership in the EEC.

There were no immediate payoffs from EEC membership, however. The new links to Europe did nothing to sustain the UK during the economic collapse of the mid to late 1970s, although the potential of EEC membership was clear for everyone to see. But optimism about Europe among some citizens of the UK began to change in the 1980s. Margaret Thatcher became increasingly concerned that Jacques Delors, the French president of the European Commission, was intent on turning the organization into a political union with socialist instincts and with the Brussels establishment having the power to override the powers of the member states. Adding to her apprehension was the re-election to the French presidency in May 1988 of François Mitterrand on a strongly pro-Europe platform. Thatcher was also alarmed by signs that Mitterrand was trying to persuade German

Chancellor Helmut Kohl, whom she didn't like or trust, into the creation of a single currency, the euro, for the member countries. When, in September 1988, Delors gave a speech to the British Trades Union Congress outlining a vision of Europe that was socialist in inspiration and led by an all-powerful Brussels establishment, Thatcher thought it was time to fight back. "The summer of 1988 marked Thatcher's epiphany on Europe," Anthony Teasdale, an adviser to Foreign Secretary Geoffrey Howe, said later. Thatcher used as her platform a speech she gave at Bruges twelve days after Delors's presentation to the British labour movement. She affirmed that the UK's "destiny is in Europe," but went on to challenge the direction in which Delors was taking the organization. While the original Treaty of Rome framing the trade alliance had been a "charter for economic liberty," she said, the moves toward a political union represented an attempt to "introduce collectivism and corporatism" and to "concentrate power at the centre of a European conglomerate. We have not successfully rolled back the frontiers of the state in Britain, only to see them re-imposed at European level, with a European super-state exercising a new dominance from Brussels."

Thatcher's Bruges speech is now seen as the landmark moment when the Brexit campaign began. Indeed, the issues she identified dominated the argument for the following thirty years, and still do. Thatcher was reflecting mainstream UK opinion — or at least English opinion — in this speech. The English were never wholehearted Europeans, and it was always London that wanted special exclusions when Brussels came up with some new unifying initiative, whether it was the introduction of a common currency or rules for the free movement of people within the EU.

Thatcher was forced from office in November 1990 by opponents within her Tory caucus who believed she was no longer totally rational. With her went a clear vision in London of what the European community could and couldn't, or should and shouldn't, be. The fulcrum moment came in 1993 with the Maastricht Treaty, which changed the name of the European Economic Community to the European Union, and with it turned the organization from an economic union into a political one. Immediately, parties began to form in the UK that were aimed at either curtailing Brussels's power or at leaving the EU entirely. The most effective and long-lasting was the United Kingdom Independence Party (UKIP), which was formed in 1993. Among its founding members was Nigel Farage, who had quit the Tory party in 1992 over the Maastricht Treaty. Ironically, in the context of his bitter aversion to the EU and all its works, Farage was elected a member of the European Parliament in 1999. He remained there until he got the final satisfaction of delivering a bitter and contemptuous speech on the day of the UK's departure from the EU, January 31, 2020. Equally ironically, Farage has been a candidate in election for the UK Parliament seven times and has been defeated on all occasions. He was, however, leader of UKIP from 2006 to 2009 and again from 2010 to 2016. Under his leadership, UKIP became a potent electoral force both in the European Parliament and in the UK. Farage and UKIP frightened Euroskeptics in the Conservative Party that they were about to be defeated from the right. The tipping point came in 2014, when UKIP won a majority of the UK seats in the European Parliament. This was the first time in any national election in the UK since 1910 that any party other than the Conservatives or Labour had taken the largest share of the votes and seats. UKIP was never able to repeat that performance or anything close to it in elections for the UK Parliament, but anti-EU Tories saw UKIP's performance in the European elections as an opportunity to advance their own agenda. About half of Cameron's caucus was composed of Euroskeptics, convinced that the UK should leave the EU. Their rationale was substantially the same as the UKIP indictments. They believed the UK's sovereignty was being eroded with the steady drift of legislative and regulatory powers to Brussels, which operated with only marginal democratic legitimacy. The Tory backbenchers made life so difficult for Cameron that he agreed that if the Conservatives won a majority in the 2015 elections, he would hold a referendum on continued EU membership with a simple in-or-out question. Cameron had absolute confidence that voters would opt to stay in the EU, so he went further in his concessions to the Tory "awkward squad." He promised that even though the results of the referendum would only be advisory, in legal terms, he would abide by the result. Another extraordinary concession was that he allowed a simple majority for victory. A matter with such intense and long-lasting constitutional implications for the UK should have demanded a two-thirds majority of voters and a minimum turnout at the polls at the very least to effect change. And even though he himself was dedicated to the UK remaining in the EU and had confidence that the "remain" side would win, Cameron freed his ministers from party discipline and allowed them to support whichever side they chose.

It could be said that Cameron had agreed to allow the UK voting public to adjudicate on a rift within the Conservative Party by way of a referendum. Leaving aside for the moment the notion that referenda are alien and unnecessary exercises in parliamentary democracies, this was an extraordinary failure of leadership on Cameron's part, for which history will doubtless hold him accountable. The reality of Brexit as a Tory squabble gone rogue was immediately evident as the referendum campaign got going in 2016. Cameron and his chancellor, George Osborne, were the champions of the "Britain Stronger in Europe" campaign, while Conservative backbencher Boris Johnson and Secretary of State for Justice Michael Gove led the "Vote Leave" faction. And on the sidelines, but undoubtedly influential, was Farage waging his own campaign.

BY HIS OWN account, fourteen-year-old Nigel Farage's moment of political revelation came when two Conservative firebrands spoke at his school. One was Enoch Powell, whose 1968 "Rivers of Blood" speech envisaged cataclysmic consequences of unfettered immigration. The other was Thatcher's closest economic adviser, Keith Joseph. Farage became a vocal admirer of Powell. He adopted what his headmaster at the time considered fascist views, and he therefore refused to appoint Farage a prefect. Other teachers recognized that Farage thoroughly enjoyed provoking people, especially left wingers, and became very good at it. He has made that skill into a career. After leaving school in 1982, Farage became a commodities trader on the London Metal Exchange — his father had been a City stockbroker — and that was his prime employment for the next twenty years. His passion, though, was always politics, and vehement opposition to the UK's continued membership in the EU became a fixation early on. That drove him out of the Conservative Party in 1992 and into the arms of UKIP, for which he ran successfully for a seat in the European Parliament in 1999. He was re-elected throughout the 2000s and left with the completion of Brexit at the end of January 2020.

Farage's appeal as a political figure is a particularly English phenomenon. In his clothes and manner, he has cultivated an archaic image of the 1970s, a time before political correctness, the disappearance of the UK's world-famous manufacturing industry marques, and the dictatorship of health and safety edicts. Media in the UK knew in which of the several pubs he haunted they could expect to find Farage at lunchtime and that he would be propping up the bar, having a pint, dressed in his trademark tweed suit with a check shirt. It's a performance that allowed him to get away with setting out a right-wing message that might otherwise have seemed to be on the lunatic fringe. Farage's political attack is easily summed up in a couple of phrases. One was "left-behind voters" and the other was the "abandoned white working class." The first sums up anti-establishment frustration in the age of rampant liberalism and the perceived stifling of freedom of expression through the social constraints of political correctness. The second, by introducing the question of race, played into anxieties about immigration among the least skilled and adaptable industrial workers. What confounded both the Conservative and Labour parties was the way Faragism, as it is sometimes called, gathered support among working-class voters not only in what had been vibrant manufacturing and industrial towns in England and Wales but also in rural areas. Faragism seemed to steamroller over the traditional political tribalism of Labour Party support in industrial centres and loyalty to the Tories in farming country. But as events proved, Farage managed only a glancing blow to political tribalism. When push came to shove at election time, blue-collar workers set aside their agreement with Farage and voted for the Labour Party, as their parents and grandparents had done. UKIP and Farage came to dominate the United Kingdom's representation in the European Parliament, but they never had a breakthrough at Westminster. In pure domestic politics, Farage's greatest moment was the outcome of the 2016 referendum, when traditional Labour strongholds abandoned their tribal loyalties and tipped the scale for the "Leave" campaign.

BORIS JOHNSON IS also a creation of his own imagination, but a more outlandish and vivid one than Farage. Although it is not immediately evident, and can be clouded by the fog of cultural differences, Johnson's creation is very similar to the personal brand created by Donald Trump. It is founded on the belief that the normal rules of social behaviour do not apply; that the law is an irritation to be ignored; that winning is everything; and that lies become truth if repeated often and vigorously enough.

The conundrum of Johnson, that may yet prove to be his tragedy, is that he didn't have to be a liar and cheat in order to succeed in life. He was born into a well-to-do family with the gift of an exceptional intellect and imagination. As a result, he got a scholarship to Britain's most exclusive private boarding school, Eton, and went on to Balliol College at Oxford. In the UK, there is no better passport into adult life. Yet some flaw in Johnson's character has driven him to opt for lies and deception in his dealings with other people, when truth and honesty would undoubtedly have served him just as well, if not better.

Johnson's life as a political charlatan began in 1984 at Oxford when he ran for the presidency of the Oxford Union. Johnson reckoned his association with upper-class friends and his membership in the Bullingdon Club, a drinking society dominated by Old Etonians and known for trashing the rooms where it meets, would not win him votes among left-of-centre students, so he put himself forward as a supporter of the liberal Social Democratic Party during the campaign and won. Deceit came naturally to Johnson from then on. After Oxford, family connections landed him a job as a graduate trainee on the establishment newspaper *The Times*. That didn't last long. In writing an article about the discovery by archaeologists of one of the palaces of Edward II, Johnson invented a quote he attributed to his godfather, the historian Colin Lucas. Johnson's aim was to get speculation about Edward II's supposed lover Piers Gaveston into the story in order to get it on the front page of the newspaper. When the lie was discovered, Johnson was fired, but he was not deterred from twisting the truth in the cause of self-promotion. In Fleet Street in those days, the line between lying and journalistic ingenuity was often blurred or non-existent. Johnson was quickly hired by the editor of *The Daily Telegraph*, Max Hastings, to be an editorial writer. Hastings came to regret his decision and became one of Johnson's most persistent and vitriolic critics.

Johnson's path to Brexit began in 1989 when he was appointed the *Telegraph*'s correspondent in Brussels. The newspaper was and remains the most influential among Conservative Party members and supporters. For the next five years, Johnson churned out a steady stream of stories critical of the European Union and all its works. There is general agreement among political observers and commentators in the UK that Johnson's journalism from Brussels did much to create and sustain the Euroskeptic faction within the Tory party, played a part in the creation of UKIP, and generally sowed the seeds in the UK of mistrust of the EU. Journalists and officials who were there at the time say consistently that much of what Johnson wrote was either straight-out lies or gross distortions of the truth. Constant themes were claims that the European Commission, then led by Jacques Delors, was out to subjugate EU members to total rule from Brussels and mentions of the increasing economic and political influence of Germany. The latter were couched in Second World War, black-and-white movie terms that appealed to older UK citizens, Margaret Thatcher among them.

During his Brussels assignment, Johnson evolved the character he was going to present to the world from then on. He dropped his real first name, Alexander, and adopted his middle name, Boris. He also perfected the image of the likeable but powerful buffoon. One UK official told *The Guardian* newspaper in 2019, "He was great company, he was great fun, but I used to be very angry with the way he just wanted to ridicule the [EU] institution and was clearly misleading people." Among officials, "He was more seen as a colourful buffoon figure. But we didn't realise it was going to set the tone of the British debate."

Conrad Black, the Canadian proprietor of the *Telegraph* and a dedicated supporter of Thatcher and the Tory party, took a similar view. Johnson, Black said, "was such an effective correspondent for us in Brussels that he greatly influenced British opinion on the country's relations with Europe." Johnson returned to London as chief political columnist for the *Telegraph*, which inevitably led to platforms in other media, such as a new cars column in the men's lifestyle magazine *GQ* and regular appearances on a host of television programs. It was in this period that Johnson perfected his persona as a Woosterish, bumbling, but eloquently outspoken public figure. No one doubted that his career trajectory would take him into elected politics; in the 1997 general election, he made a trial run, but lost in a safe Labour Party constituency in North Wales. So when, in 1999, Black decided to offer Johnson the editorship of his influential but uneconomic weekly conservative magazine *The Spectator*, he insisted that Johnson abandon his political ambitions as a condition of taking the job. Johnson agreed, but his habits of deceiving and betraying those around him, including his wives and mistresses, were now too deeply embedded to be gainsaid. He won the safe Tory seat of Hendon in the 2001 general election. Black called Johnson "ineffably duplicitous" but decided to keep him on as editor of *The Spectator* because circulation had risen and the magazine was profitable for the first time in many years. Johnson also carried on writing columns for other publications, demanding and getting freelance fees of unheard-of amounts. His weekly column for the *Telegraph* alone brought in the equivalent of C$350,000 a year, and his other incomes made him the third-highest-earning member of Parliament. Inevitably, Johnson's attention to parliamentary business was an afterthought. In 2003, the Tories were in opposition, and new leader

Michael Howard attempted to capitalize on Johnson's public popularity by making him vice-chairman of the party and the opposition critic on the arts. That didn't last long. In 2004, a Sunday newspaper revealed that Johnson had had an affair with one of the columnists at *The Spectator*, Petronella Wyatt, and that she had had two abortions. Johnson called the story "an inverted pyramid of piffle," even though the newspaper's source was Wyatt's mother. Howard fired Johnson for lying about the affair.

It was already well established that behaviours that would destroy other political careers were merely colourful incidents along the way in the life of Johnson. In a magazine column she wrote when Johnson became leader of the Conservative Party and prime minister in 2019, Wyatt, his former mistress, explained that he "is like catnip for women." In 2007, the Conservative Party backed Johnson as its candidate for mayor of London and hired the highly regarded Australian election strategist Lynton Crosby — known in political circles as "The Wizard of Oz" and sometimes the "Master of the Dark Arts" — to run the campaign. Crosby realized that for voters the vision of Johnson as a dishevelled, funny, and unpredictable fount of political incorrectness far outweighed misgivings they might have over his propensity for lying and betrayal. Crosby was right, and Johnson rode his created image through two terms as mayor of London, which included the international exposure of hosting the 2012 Olympic Games. He followed that with his return to the House of Commons in the general election of 2015. Johnson didn't get a Cabinet post, in large part because he had again misled people about his intentions; having promised London's voters in 2012 he would see out a second term as mayor, he was still running London while also being an MP.

THE MOST PRESSING issue for Parliament in 2015 was David Cameron's promise to hold a referendum on continued membership in the EU. Despite his history as one of the founders of anti-Brussels Euroskepticism in the UK, Johnson dithered about which side of the fence on which to stand. He had two columns written: one supporting leaving the EU and another setting out the arguments for remaining in the union. What seems to have decided the matter was advice from Lynton Crosby, whose analysis had been rejected by Cameron, that the Tory leadership and the Remainers were going to lose. Johnson critics say his decision to back the Leave campaign was based entirely on his career prospects — that it might provide a pathway to the prime minister's office at 10 Downing Street — and not on any true philosophical attachment.

As prime minister, David Cameron failed to exude authority, and his leadership of the Remain campaign got off to a lame start. After winning re-election with a majority in 2015, Cameron introduced legislation to enable the referendum, while also approaching Brussels to try to change arrangements on four issues that were particular irritants for many in the UK: protection of the single market for the nine of twenty-eight EU members not using the common currency (the euro); reduction of red tape; exemption of the UK from the political agenda of an "ever closer union"; and restriction of immigration into the UK from the rest of the EU. Polls showed that a majority of voters favoured staying in the EU; however, the level of support would drop off sharply if Cameron did not secure safeguards for member states outside the euro area and guarantees for those staying away from political integration projects. A third bugbear for UK voters was that EU immigrants were immediately cashing in on the social welfare system, and a majority wanted restrictions. The first caveat was shorthand for a desire to maintain the UK's sovereignty, and the second was a clearly audible dog whistle in opposition to immigration. The results of Cameron's efforts were announced in February 2016. He had secured very few concessions. Brussels did agree to some limits on the social benefits that new EU immigrants to the UK could apply for, but then insisted on EU oversight of any measures taken by London. Cameron said later Brexit could have been avoided if the EU had given him greater control over immigration. That was never in the cards. German Chancellor Angela Merkel had repeatedly said that respecting the free movement of people was an essential requirement for EU membership, and at that time Merkel was boss.

The campaign itself was a mixture of patriotic comedy, sometimes verging on slapstick, and grim sermonizing. Boris Johnson reprised his "Captain Britannica" role from the 2012 Olympics. He toured the country in a bus decked with the false promise that leaving the EU would save the UK £350 million a week (C$600 million), which could be used to boost money for the National Health Service. The claim that this was the amount they contributed to Brussels was a gross exaggeration. But it was a simple message that suggested leaving the EU would be not only an act of liberation, but a profitable one at that. The earnest rebuttals by Remainers, bolstered by stern warnings from figures such as the governor of the Bank of England, Canadian Mark Carney, about the dire economic consequences of Brexit, largely fell on deaf ears. Johnson's amiable buffoon shtick and his clarion call that June 24, the day after the referendum, would become known as the United Kingdom's independence day caught on in the provinces. Polls showed the voters trusted Johnson's words more than those of any other political leader, including UK Prime Minister David Cameron.

Indications that a majority of UK voters had turned against the EU began to appear early as the ballots were counted on June 23. Clear majorities for Brexit began appearing in old industrial, traditionally Labour-supporting cities such as Newcastle, which had never quite recovered from the wholesale restructuring of the UK's economy in the post-Thatcher years and for which the future still looked uncertain. When all the votes were counted, 72.21 percent of registered voters had cast ballots. The option to leave the EU was supported by 51.89 percent of voters, and 48.11 percent voted to remain in the union. The real message was in the details, however. The only areas that opted to stay in the EU were Greater London, where 59.93 percent voted against Brexit, Scotland, where 62 percent voted in favour of remaining, and Northern Ireland, where 55.78 percent said they wanted stay in the EU. In most of the rest of England and much of Wales, the support for Brexit approached 60 percent.

There were clear demographic divisions among the English in particular. Among the deluge of post-mortem analysis done by a host of polling companies, many found that a significant proportion of younger voters failed to turn out, while up to 90 percent of older voters cast ballots. This was important because about 75 percent of the younger voters who did cast ballots opted to remain. That vote was overwhelmed, however, by the much higher turnout of older voters, especially those in their sixties and older, who supported Brexit.

These Brexiteers were people who remembered the UK before the economic ructions of the 1970s and 1980s and who had been unable or unwilling to adjust to the new world of EU membership. They remembered a time when the UK was still an industrial powerhouse, producing goods with time-honoured marques going back to the heydays of empire. The clarion call by Johnson and the other Brexit leaders for a new Elizabethan Age of fierce independence and buccaneering ingenuity had a visceral appeal for these voters. It may have been a nostalgic pipe dream, but it was a heady and compelling one.

Surveys of Leave voters taken immediately after the referendum found that nearly half gave reaffirming UK independence and sovereignty and removing Brussels's power and influence as the main reason for their decision. The desire for control, of course, is in order to be able to apply it. Several polls found that the major reason for regaining power from Brussels for Leave voters was to be able to control levels of immigration and rules for those who want to settle in the UK. Support for Brexit was highest in areas of England that had seen the largest influx of immigrants, especially those from Eastern Europe, since the accession to the EU of the former Soviet states in 2004. Other surveys found that economic questions weighed heavily on some minds, especially the fallout from the 2008–09 global recession and the associated crisis in the euro area. In that regard, the claims on the side of Johnson's campaign bus that the UK would save £350 million a month by quitting the EU resonated with many voters. The idea that Brussels was a financial sinkhole where the UK's contributions disappeared was factually wrong, but the picture was a compelling one for people feeling financial uncertainty.

Education levels and identity also influenced the referendum result.

Several surveys found that those with higher levels of education were likely to vote to stay in the EU, while others with less schooling or qualifications opted for Brexit. Graduates, usually insulated by stronger household finances, felt less threatened by the competition inherent in EU membership or flowing from globalization in general. Indeed, these voters saw both the EU and global economic integration as an opportunity more than a threat. The polling company YouGov found that among those who voted, 68 percent with university degrees voted to remain while 70 percent of high school graduates or those with lower scholastic attainments voted Leave. In tandem with that were findings that those with lower educational qualifications were likely to hold socially conservative views, even though they probably supported the Labour Party in parliamentary elections. Those socially conservative views opposed the liberal calls from both Brussels and the UK's political establishment, often backed with legal imperatives, for tolerance and inclusion of minorities. This cumulative sense of alienation within their own country was the deciding factor for pro-Brexit voters.

—

DAVID CAMERON RESIGNED the day after the referendum and was replaced by Theresa May. The following three years were a cavalcade of farce as the UK and its Parliament in particular demeaned themselves in the eyes of the world. There was a collective judgment that whatever the final outcome, the UK could no longer be considered a significant international player either within the EU or outside it. May and her ministers set out by trying to negotiate a deal with Brussels. Early in 2017, the Supreme Court ruled May must first pass legislation in Parliament to trigger Article 50, the EU regulation giving notice of the intention to leave the club. This Parliament did on March 16, 2017, starting a two-year negotiation process, which, in theory, would have seen the UK leaving the EU on March 29, 2019. It didn't happen like that.

On April 8, May called a general election for the end of the first week in June. It was a disastrous miscalculation. The Conservatives lost their majority, and when the smoke cleared they were dependent on the ten members of the Democratic Unionist Party, the fervent loyalists for Northern Ireland's continued union with Great Britain, for the survival of their government.

Brexit negotiations with Brussels started in June, but May and her ministers were now hamstrung by the political necessity that any agreement must meet the demands of the Democratic Unionists. That meant that May could not agree to anything that would see Northern Ireland treated differently from the rest of the UK by the EU after Brexit. But the other reality was that the only land border between the UK and the EU after Brexit would be the one between Northern Ireland and the Irish Republic. Having an open border between the two Irelands was an essential part of the Good Friday agreement of 1998 that had ended thirty years of violent civil strife in Northern Ireland. But closing that border and re-establishing checkpoints would be a necessary part of the UK leaving the EU. The governments in both Dublin and London agreed this would probably reignite the tensions between the Catholic Republicans and Protestant Unionists, and possibly restart the civil war, though no evidence for that belief has ever been produced. It was, however, a useful scare tactic for both governments.

What was called the "backstop" was devised as a way around this impasse, but it satisfied no one. It was largely responsible for May failing three times to get her deal with Brussels approved by the House of Commons. On April 5, 2019, May asked Brussels for an extension for the UK's departure to October 31. On May 24, she announced she was resigning the Tory Party leadership. This triggered a leadership contest which, on July 24, produced Boris Johnson — who had been foreign minister until he resigned in July 2018 in protest at May's deal with Brussels — as party leader and prime minister.

Johnson came to office exuding confidence that he could get a new deal from Brussels that the UK Parliament would accept and would see Brexit happen by the October 31 deadline. But his actions displayed less confidence. The first thing he did was ask the queen to prorogue Parliament from

September 9 until October 14. The result, and undoubtedly the intention of this move, was to curtail debate and create an unstoppable momentum for Brexit on October 31. It didn't work. After an emergency debate, Parliament passed a bill forcing Johnson to either get approval for a new deal with Brussels or to leave the EU without a deal, commonly known as the "hard Brexit."

Johnson by this time had not only abandoned any serious thought of bringing the Democratic Unionists on board, he had also expelled from the Tory party twenty-one MPs who had voted in favour of the emergency debate. His plan was to try to force an election and win back a majority that would allow him to command the situation. But because of the UK's fixed-term election law, Johnson needed the support of two-thirds of the members of the House of Commons. Opposition leader Jeremy Corbyn and the Labour Party were not going to give him that opportunity until they had tied his hands. In the meantime, the Supreme Court ruled that Johnson's advice to the queen to prorogue Parliament was unlawful, and they resumed sitting. On October 17, Johnson's negotiators and Brussels agreed on a new formula for the UK's departure that fudged the Northern Ireland issue and was otherwise largely the same as that previously put forward by Theresa May. On October 22, a bill to implement that agreement was passed by Parliament, but Johnson's requirement that debate be limited so Brexit could happen on October 31 was defeated. Johnson tried again to get Corbyn to agree to an election, but the Labour leader refused unless the prospect of a "no-deal Brexit" was off the table. Many hard-line Tory Brexiteers, and perhaps Johnson himself, did want to make a clean break with Brussels without any agreement on future relations and to base future trade with the EU on World Trade Organization rules alone. In the event, Brussels broke the deadlock by agreeing to yet another extension: January 31, 2020. This convinced Corbyn and the Labour leadership that Johnson could not engineer leaving the EU without a deal. It was agreed that there would be a snap election on December 12.

Johnson and the Tories won that election conclusively, winning dozens of seats in northern and central England that had never voted anything other than Labour since the party became a political force in 1922. This cleared the decks for the UK to leave the EU on January 31, 2020, beginning what was intended to be year-long negotiations toward a new trade agreement between the UK and the EU. Few observers with experience of trade negotiations of this size and weight believe the EU-UK deal can be done within such a short time frame. This says clearly that the no-deal, hard Brexit favoured by some of Johnson's most avid followers is still a possibility.

NEGOTIATIONS BETWEEN LONDON and Brussels had hardly started when COVID-19 reared its head and Europe became the centre of the pandemic. It took Johnson, much like Trump, some time to comprehend that the disease had destroyed his agenda. The Tory government dithered over options about how to respond, and for a while appeared wedded to the idea of letting the coronavirus run its course in order to create herd immunity in those who had caught the disease and survived. But they were turned from this course by predicted death tolls in the United Kingdom of many hundreds of thousands and perhaps millions. The final decision to follow the example of other countries and shut down the economy, demanding that people stay at home to stifle the spread of the disease, was made late. The UK rapidly became one of the European countries with the most infections and the highest death toll.

Among those seriously affected by COVID-19 was Johnson himself. He had carried on, meeting crowds and pointedly shaking hands with people, even when advice from epidemiologists was clear that isolation and social distancing were the only way to break the rapid pace of infection. After days in intensive care and the start of a prolonged period of convalescence, Johnson said his life had been saved by his doctors and nurses. What effect that will have on his approach to life and politics remains to be seen, but it is apparent that the pandemic has made it practically impossible for the UK to agree on a future relationship with Brussels by the January 2021 deadline. COVID-19 has made the future of Brexit just as uncertain as all the political machinations of the preceding years.

THE RESULTS OF the December election also raised questions about the survival of the United Kingdom itself. The Scottish National Party (SNP) won forty-eight of the fifty-nine seats in Scotland, and the party's leader, Nicola Sturgeon, immediately demanded that London agree to another referendum on Scottish independence. She pointed out that the situation had changed since Scots had voted narrowly to stay in the UK in the 2014 referendum. Scotland had voted by a clear majority to stay in the EU in the 2016 referendum and were now having Brexit forced upon them. Johnson refused to agree to another referendum, but if the SNP again sweeps the board in elections for the provincial parliament in May 2021, it will be difficult for London to say no again.

There was also an early warning in Northern Ireland. For the first time, Irish nationalist parties won more seats in the province than the Ulster unionists. This raised the prospect of mounting public opinion in favour of Northern Ireland leaving the UK and joining the Irish Republic, which would mean rejoining the European Union.

When all is said and done, it is hard to conclude that the Brexit experience is an example of the degradation of democracy in Europe. The principal anti-democratic mistake was Cameron's decision to allow a referendum on EU membership and then not impose sufficient safeguards to ensure an unequivocal result. The other issue is the prominence the whole affair has given to Johnson, a charlatan who flies by the seat of his pants. But on the other side, the whole Brexit episode has been pursued with sometimes painful deference to the demands of parliamentary democracy. A central reason why the UK went through the embarrassing and chaotic three years between the referendum and Brexit was a crisis of conscience for many members of Parliament. A clear majority of MPs wanted the UK to remain in the EU, and for months many struggled with the idea of finding some way to overturn or go around the referendum result. But in the end, all came to acknowledge that the sanctity and reputation of Parliament and democracy must override their own convictions. The other reason not to despair of democracy in the UK is that as the history of that country's relationship with the EU shows — more particularly England's relationship — this moment of reckoning was bound to happen at some point. In the coming months and years, when the reality of what has happened sinks in, it may prove to have been a cathartic moment. The EU is not going to agree to new terms of trade that are beneficial or attractive for the UK. Brussels cannot afford to encourage other member states to leave. If the EU manages to achieve the internal democratic and institutional reformation it needs, it is quite conceivable that, after some years out in the cold, a new generation of citizens in the UK will seek re-entry.

CHAPTER SEVEN

—

The Roar of the Greasepaint, the Smell of the Crowd

ACCORDING TO STEVE Bannon, the man regarded by many as Donald Trump's Svengali, three catchphrases made the New York reality television star president. "We got elected on Drain the Swamp, Lock Her Up, Build the Wall. This was pure anger. Anger and fear is what gets people to the polls," Bannon said in an interview with the Bloomberg news agency in February 2018. In the US in 2015 and 2016, in the run-up to the presidential elections, Bannon was undoubtedly right. There is a deep-seated and unresolved social and political conflict in the US about the essential values of the country and whose interests they should serve. In the more than 240 years since the country's founding, the early arguments about whether the US should be a classic republic, ruled by an economic and intellectual elite, or a pure democracy remain as stark and unresolved as they were in 1776.

The Civil War, from 1861 to 1865, showed what can happen in the US when the unresolved contradictions about the nature of the country are allowed to run amok. The horrors of the memory of the first war of the age of industrialized mass slaughter and the enforced discipline of the US's rise to the role of global superpower have kept those pressures under control. But since the end of the Cold War, the internal divisions among classes, races, religions, and regions in the US have welled to the surface and have again become dominant political forces. Globalization of industry and the moving of old manufacturing industries to countries with cheaper production costs have created a bitter, largely white under-class. This includes workers from the also-abandoned supporting industries, steel production and coal mining. This produced, as Bannon observed, an angry and fearful constituency of voters waiting for a Pied Piper-like Trump to appear and play a captivating tune transporting them into the world of their hopes and dreams.

The desperation of many of the people who form Trump's base can be understood by the extraordinary decline in life expectancy and rise in deaths of despair among low-income, low-education white men in the forty-five to fifty-four age group. Suicide rates among poor white baby boomers are the highest since 1941. According to the US Centers for Disease Control and Prevention (CDC), deaths of despair — attributable to drug overdoses, suicides, and alcohol abuse — accounted for 48.5 men out of every 100,000 of the population in 2002. By 2017, that figure had almost doubled to 91.6 deaths of despair for every 100,000 men. The CDC said this amounted to over a hundred thousand preventable deaths a year. There was a slight improvement in the figures in 2018, largely because of a crackdown on doctors giving prescriptions for opioids, but the CDC does not expect the overall picture to change while "their employment prospects are blighted by long-term economic restructuring and low labour mobility."

The assaults on economic security, as well as hopes and aspirations, are a common experience for Americans of all backgrounds. But instead of these commonalities drawing people closer to seek some consensus on how to respond, the old, entrenched divisions within US society are com-ing to the fore and ripping the country apart. A Pew Research Center poll in 2014 looked at the country's ideological divide over the previous twenty years and found the gap widening dramatically between those who identify as Republicans or conservatives and those who said they were Democrats or liberals.

"Partisan animosity has increased substantially over the same period (1994–2014). In each party, the share with a highly negative view of the opposing party has more than doubled since 1994. Most of these intense partisans believe the opposing party's policies 'are so misguided that they threaten the nation's well-being,'" the poll found.

The hard facts were that 36 percent of Republicans and 27 percent of Democrats believed the other party would threaten the nation's survival if it won power. This extraordinary reality — that around a third of the supporters of the two main parties believe the other party to be traitors — has been fed by events that occurred during the two presidencies prior to the 2016 election. The September 11, 2001, attacks by al Qaeda on New York and Washington stunned the American public in a way that is not readily understandable by people from countries either more used to dealing with terrorism or where the national psyche is not imbued with feelings of moral superiority and exceptionalism. The attacks loosed a welter of emotions, convictions, and responses that are now embedded in the American view of themselves and the world. The invasions of Iraq and Afghanistan launched by the administration of President George W. Bush, and the long and morally questionable wars that followed, left many Americans with ambivalent feelings or conflicting certainties, much like the previous generation's feelings about the Vietnam War.

The cataclysmic end of the Bush era with the economic crisis of 2008–09 added yet another cloud of uncertainty to a future already shrouded with threatening storms.

For many Americans, the advent of Barack Obama to the presidency in 2009 was the dawning of a new age of hope and change, the evolution of the US into a multicultural society. For others it was just the opposite. Obama's administration had many failings at home and abroad. For many white blue-collar workers, Obama was anything but a breath of fresh air after the 2008–09 economic crisis. Instead of reacting as a revolutionary, the Obama administration responded as any Washington politician might. They saved the banks and the financial houses, but did nothing for the hundreds of thousands of people who had lost their homes and their jobs.

The added insult was that not a single banker or financial wizard who had precipitated the crash faced any kind of judicial or other form of retribution. For many, this only added to the deep conviction that a black man and his family in the White House was a desecration of all they believed the United States stood for.

Conspiracy theories of all kinds were contrived to try to mark Obama as an illegitimate president. The most persistent were the "Birthers," to whom Donald Trump quickly latched on as an engine for his political ambitions. Faced with financial ruin as a failed real estate developer and casino operator, Trump had been fortunate enough to get the opportunity to rebrand himself as the star of a reality television game show, *The Apprentice*. Trump insisted that Obama, whose father was a Kenyan, had not been born in the US and was therefore not eligible to be president. Obama ignored the campaign for as long as possible, but in the end he produced his birth certificate, proving that he had been born in Hawaii.

At the same time, there was a fundamental breakdown in the US Congress's culture of respectful bipartisanship on issues of national importance. This had begun to erode during the Reagan years, but it was Republican Speaker of the House Newt Gingrich who, in the 1990s, whipped partisan animosity into a culture of "winner take all" and the rejection of all bipartisan co-operation. In 2009, on the back of the economic crisis and Obama's tepid response, the Tea Party movement was formed within the Republican Party as a libertarian faction dedicated to less government and lower taxes. As is often the case, even small groups of extremists can gain disproportionate influence over the moderate majority, and that has happened with the Tea Party.

One result of the vitriolic partisanship that has infected US politics is that the network of checks and balances put in place by the constitutional framers to prevent the emergence of some domestic version of George III have eroded and become dysfunctional. Party loyalty supersedes national interest. Personal political survival outweighs the dictates of the US Constitution. The well-being of the public comes a distant second to the requirements of lobbyists and their campaign contributions. This virus has also infected the independence of the judiciary and the rule of law. Both major parties, when they gain control of the Senate, pack the courts with judges on the basis of their liberal or conservative leanings, not their qualifications. Trump's most significant gift to his evangelical Christian and socially conservative supporters has been the opportunity to appoint two judges to the Supreme Court and a host of judges to lesser tribunals.

THE US MAY officially be a secular state, but it is the world's largest avowedly Christian country, and now and then its politics are still moved by the puritanical zeal that drove the Pilgrim Fathers from England to Massachusetts in 1620. This is one of those times. It is generally reckoned there are about 70 million evangelical Christians in the US, and they have become a potent and occasionally determining political force since the 1950s. The movement was led by evangelist pastor Billy Graham, who was a friend and spiritual adviser to presidents Dwight Eisenhower, Lyndon Johnson, and Richard Nixon, but who was called on by all presidents from Harry Truman to Barack Obama. Graham was politically restrained, unlike his son and successor Franklin Graham, who is one of the most vociferous and outspoken supporters of Trump. Other leading evangelicals with socially conservative political agendas include Jerry Falwell and Pat Robertson. There are a multitude of other, less prominent figures with large and loyal congregations, so all presidents in the last fifty years have found it politically expedient to be seen to be close to notable preachers.

Evangelical leaders began to build political influence in the 1960s. The 1963 Supreme Court ruling removing prayer and mandatory Bible reading in schools was a blow that started this purposeful politicization. That effort gained momentum with the 1965 ruling in the Griswold v. Connecticut case that it was unconstitutional to prohibit the use of birth control. A further impetus toward politicization was the 1971 ruling by the same court that stripped tax-exempt status from private institutions that discriminate on the grounds of race. Many southern Christian schools and academies discriminated against black or other non-white applicants based on their interpretation of the Bible. By and large, evangelical leaders have allied themselves with the Republican Party. They feel more comfortable with Republicans' social conservatism, however hypocritically it is expressed, than with the liberalism of the Democrats, even when in the hands of truly devout Christian presidents such as Jimmy Carter.

The pastors believe that influencing Republican presidents over appointments to the Supreme Court and other judicial appointments is the surest way to hold at bay the tides of liberalization and liberal thought. The threats they see to social values encompass issues like the extension of legal recognition and rights to the LGBTQ communities and immigration from non-Christian countries.

Increasingly, the political driving force of the evangelical movement is opposition to women's reproductive rights, specifically contraception and abortion. In Republican-controlled states, evangelicals have had success in limiting access to abortions, but their main goal is to influence the Supreme Court to overturn Roe v. Wade. This was the Supreme Court's landmark 1973 decision that concluded the US Constitution protects a pregnant woman's liberty to choose to have an abortion without excessive government restriction. However, despite these deeply held convictions, evangelicals don't always vote based on religious considerations, as public opinion samples taken after the November 2016 election showed.

No wonder *The Economist* and others judge the US to be a "flawed democracy."

—

AS 2016 DAWNED, Donald Trump appeared to be a political aberration who could not possibly win the nomination of the Republican Party, and certainly not the presidency in a contest against Democrat Hillary Clinton. In retrospect, however, he was the perfect candidate for the Republicans, though not many in the US establishment saw that at the time. That blindness, especially in the media, about what was happening in white, blue-collar America was an unforgivable failure of journalism, but also symptomatic of how dangerous the disjointed nature of US society has become.

Hillary Clinton turned out to be the perfect opponent for Trump because for almost half the voting population she epitomized the Three Hates of the Bannon strategy. Why Clinton was so despised among millions of people who had never met her remains a matter of speculation. Some theorize that she got typecast as a radical, pushy feminist willing to take ethical shortcuts when husband Bill Clinton was governor of Arkansas in the 1980s. When she arrived in Washington as First Lady in 1993, she was followed by the Whitewater scandal. She'd invested for their retirement in a real estate deal with two friends, who managed the investment illegally and lost all the money. Somehow, the smell around that deal persisted, even though there was no firm evidence the Clintons had done anything wrong. Many saw her marriage to Bill Clinton as one of convenience, conducted only to further her own ambitions for a political career. Those views were fed by his appointment of Hillary, soon after his inauguration, to prepare a report on health care reform. And when Hillary remained firmly in the shadows during the Monica Lewinsky affair in the mid-1990s, it confirmed for many the theory of a marriage of convenience. Others needed no track record of actions by Hillary Clinton to decide they didn't like her. "There's something about her manner, persona, voice, smirk that just grates on a lot of people," historian Craig Shirley said in an interview with *The Guardian* in the run-up to the election in October 2016. "People don't like to be talked down to, and she has a terrible habit of talking down to people, with that smirk."

This visceral hatred of Hillary was stoked by Trump during the campaign with references to a supposed trove of lost emails that would show how her lax sense of national security threatened the nation. He used the allegation of her security failures to accuse her of responsibility for an attack on the US consulate in Benghazi, Libya, in 2012, in which two diplomats were killed.

Some of the allegations against Clinton went beyond the bizarre. In late 2016, the far-right conspiracy theorist Alex Jones alleged on his Texas radio show that Hillary Clinton was sexually abusing children in satanic rituals in the basement of a Washington, DC, pizza restaurant. Jones's claim inspired a listener from North Carolina to grab an assault rifle, a pistol, and a hunting knife and drive to the restaurant to liberate the children. Patrons fled the restaurant as the man rushed in, but despite his frenzied search, shooting open cupboard doors, all he found was cooking equipment. The restaurant didn't even have a basement. This and other crazed stories about Clinton's demonic possession festered and multiplied, and Trump fuelled this during the campaign with his constant jabs at "Crooked Hillary," fishing for the crowd to respond, "Lock her up!" Despite all the stoked and managed hatred, on election day Clinton got more votes than any presidential candidate in American history except Barack Obama, taking 48.2 percent of the vote compared to Trump's 46.1 percent.

Donald Trump is the son of a New York real estate developer who profited greatly from the postwar boom in public housing construction. He is also the grandson of a German immigrant who founded the family fortune by running a brothel for prospectors in the Klondike gold rush in the Canadian Yukon at the turn of the twentieth century. Trump has the business acumen of his forebears, but, like them, it is the skill of a sleight-of-hand trickster. His claims to be a highly successful real estate tycoon are a good example of his duplicity. In 2018, *The New York Times* obtained printouts of Trump's official Internal Revenue Service returns, which showed that between 1985 and 1994, Trump lost money every year, with accumulated losses of more than US$1 billion. According to the article, "His core business losses in 1990 and 1991 — more than US$250 million each year — were more than double those of the nearest taxpayers in the IRS information for those years." In 1995 alone, he declared a loss of US$916 million. This, noted the *Times*, "could have allowed him to legally avoid paying any federal income tax for up to 18 years." The US tax system is indeed very generous in its treatment of real estate developers, and Trump cited tax avoidance accounting as justification for his actions in response to the articles. That would be a more convincing explanation if Trump's businesses had shown other signs of health. But they did not.

In 1991 and 1992, he declared bankruptcy for three casinos in Atlantic City and the fabled Plaza Hotel in New York.

Trump had, however, already found his true calling. In 1987, he published a ghostwritten book, *Trump: The Art of the Deal*. This became a bestseller and changed Trump from a real estate developer into a brand name that other entrepreneurs put on their products. In 2015, *Forbes* estimated Trump's net worth at US$4.1 billion, of which US$3.3 billion was the value of his brand. Trump himself claims to be worth around US$9 billion and disputes the widespread belief among business analysts that, at most, his net worth is a few hundred million. His refusal to release his recent tax returns, as has become normal for all presidential candidates, has only heightened speculation that Trump is far from being as wealthy as he claims. That said, there are many reports that the presidency is proving to be a highly profitable business for Trump and his family.

This shift is important, because once Trump became a brand rather than a true entrepreneur, maintaining the image of a tycoon was essential to generating the revenues derived from the licensing of his name.

Fortune favoured Trump in the early 2000s, when he was approached by a British-born television producer, Mark Burnett, who suggested that he appear in a new reality television show, *The Apprentice*. Trump was skeptical at first, saying this kind of television "was for the bottom-feeders of society." He changed his mind, however, when Burnett said he should appear as himself, or at least the version of himself he had created as a successful businessman with a luxurious lifestyle. The format of the program was that Trump would interview a cast of applicants for jobs running a Trump company. It was a knockout match among apprentices, with Trump periodically dismissing contestants with what became his trademark line: "You're fired!"

The show was very successful, ran for fourteen seasons, and, Trump says, made him over US$200 million. More important in relation to what followed, *The Apprentice* created an image of Trump as a decisive and demanding leader who could cut through complexities and nuance to focus on the fundamentals of any question. It was all a fantasy, of course, but in the age of movies and television, the public has come to buy into the images and personalities presented to them on the screen.

In the US in particular there is a long list of performers who have side-stepped into political careers, some with more success than others. Ronald Reagan became governor of California from 1967 to 1975 and then president of the United States. Arnold Schwarzenegger also became governor of California from 2003 to 2011. Clint Eastwood was elected mayor of Carmel-by-the-Sea, California, in 1986. Singer Sonny Bono was mayor of Palm Springs, California, from 1988 to 1992 and then the Republican congressman for California's 44th district from 1995 until his death in 1998. There are many others not only in the US but also in other countries of the North Atlantic. There is a profound difference, though, between Trump and most of the actors who made the transition to the political stage. They knew they were actors, and, while they undoubtedly capitalized on their fame to fulfil their political ambitions, they didn't see their new lives as a reprise of their most famous roles. Trump saw himself playing the role of president just as he had played the boss on *The Apprentice*, because the survival of the image was essential to his own survival. Without the image there was simply nothing there.

Through the early 2000s, Trump played with the idea of running for president, first as a Reform Party candidate, then, in 2004, as a Democrat. In 2009, he rejoined the Republican Party and began sidling up to the Tea Party right-wing fringe and developing his obsession over Barack Obama. In 2015, he did not renew his contract with *The Apprentice*. At the same time, according to an article in *The Wall Street Journal*, early in 2015 he got his fixer Michael Cohen to arrange for the manipulation of online polls for CNBC and the Drudge Report to show Trump as a popular candidate for president.

It is questionable if Donald Trump could have become the Republican Party's 2016 presidential candidate were it not for the riots and chaos around the 1968 Democratic National Convention in Chicago. The Democrats came to believe the established method of picking presidential candidates in backroom deals had gone too far when Vice President Hubert Humphrey won the nomination despite having lost all the primaries. The Democrats thereafter adopted what the party's power brokers believed would be perceived as a more open and transparent system of state primaries to test candidates' popularity and assign convention delegates.

The Republicans followed suit, with the unintended consequence that it became possible for an outsider to win the nomination.

In their 2018 book, *How Democracies Die*, Steven Levitsky and Daniel Ziblatt point out that between 1945 and 1968, under the old convention system, only one outsider, Dwight Eisenhower, the Supreme Allied Commander in the victorious closing years of the Second World War, had won the nomination for either party. Under the first two decades of the primary system, from 1972 to 1992, eight outsiders ran, five for the Democrats and three for the Republicans. In the next two decades, up to 2016, eighteen outsiders ran in the two parties' primaries, thirteen of them Republicans. Most, like televangelist Pat Robertson and mega-wealthy businessman Steve Forbes, were famous outside politics. But until Donald Trump came along, celebrity alone had not been enough for an outsider to secure the nomination.

Trump announced his candidacy on June 16, 2015, in a gaudy piece of theatre in the foyer of Trump Tower in New York that was worthy of a Russian oligarch. There was an ecstatic audience of paid performers as Trump, with his wife, Melania, on his arm, descended the escalator and proclaimed his intention to "Make America Great Again." He pointed to the four themes around which his campaign would revolve: illegal immigration, Islamic terrorism, the flight abroad of manufacturing jobs, and the national debt. Then Trump launched into a diatribe signalling his was going to be a campaign without niceties, as his acquired persona from *The Apprentice* and Steve Bannon's tasting of opinion among hardcore Republicans demanded. "When Mexico sends its people, they're not sending their best ... they're sending people that have lots of problems, and they're bringing those problems with [them]," he said. "They're bringing drugs. They're bringing crime. They're rapists. And some, I assume, are good people." Trump's answer was a promise to build "a great, great wall." His comments were a gross misrepresentation of how and why people from Central America were seeking sanctuary and better lives in the US, and his comment brought rebukes from both Republicans and Democrats. But the story led the news, which accomplished the mission.

This was the beginning of a pattern of behaviour through the primaries, the campaign, and the presidency of Trump saying something purposefully inflammatory to gain attention. Often he would retreat if the outrage was too intense. In December 2015, he issued a written statement saying, "Donald J. Trump is calling for a total and complete shutdown of Muslims entering the United States until our country's representatives can figure out what is going on." This became a mantra at Trump's rallies in the following weeks, but it sparked international condemnation, including a motion in the UK's Parliament to ban him from being allowed to enter the United Kingdom. Trump backed off, saying his proposed ban was "only a suggestion."

Polls during the last half of 2015 showed that Trump's sports bar philosophy and crude "common sense" — just like that of Nigel Farage — were resonating with Republican voters. The taproom analogy went further. At Trump's rallies, he fed on the anger of the crowds (so much so that he has made these transfusions a feature of his presidency at least once a month and often more frequently). Violence rapidly became a feature of the gatherings. Protestors were attacked by Trump loyalists, with him promising to pay legal fees if there were any repercussions. On at least one occasion, the local sheriff's office considered filing charges against Trump for inciting a riot. A series of polls over the last six months of 2015 showed Trump as the leading candidate in what was then a crowded field. And polls also showed that Trump was running head-to-head in public popularity with Democratic candidate Hillary Clinton. As the cavalcade of primaries continued, consistent messages came from delegates buttonholed by pollsters. Republican voters feared "illegal immigrants, incipient economic turmoil, and the threat of terrorist attack in the United States."

By May 2016, Trump was the presumptive nominee as other candidates dropped out. The Republican Party seemed stunned. Trump, after all, was a Republican of convenience without any historic loyalty or functional affiliation to the party. More than that, he had grabbed the candidacy by loosing something dark and malevolent in the souls of many Republican voters that the party leadership found threatening. Lindsey Graham, a senator from South Carolina, said, "I just really believe that the Republican Party has been conned here, and this guy is not a reliable conservative Republican." Trump, he continued, is a "race-baiting, xenophobic, religious bigot"; he called him the "ISIL man of the year" (referring to the Islamic State). Trump, Graham said, was a "kook," "crazy," and a man who was "unfit for office."

Senator Ted Cruz called Donald Trump a "pathological liar" who was "utterly amoral," a "serial philanderer," and a "narcissist at a level I don't think this country's ever seen."

Mick Mulvaney, a former Republican congressman, called him a "terrible human being" who had made "disgusting and indefensible" comments about women.

The ledger of invective against Trump before he won the candidacy is long and colourful. But when the outcome of the primaries became clear, one after another the Republican leaders swallowed their misgivings and, with as much good grace as they could muster while citing party loyalty and the necessity to defeat Clinton, pledged their support for Trump.

By the time Trump occupied the Oval Office in January 2017, the grip of Stockholm Syndrome on the Republican Party members in the House of Representatives and the Senate was complete. The thoroughness with which the Republicans had submitted to and even become acolytes of their captor was on display for all to see throughout the impeachment process at the beginning of 2020. The whole episode discouraged any optimism that American democracy might be dragged from the quicksand into which it was fast disappearing. Democratic House Speaker Nancy Pelosi was reluctant to start the impeachment process, and her instincts proved correct. After she succumbed to pressure from her caucus and the House Judiciary Committee heard evidence, it was clear that the Democrats did not have a cut-and-dried case. To be sure, there was clear evidence that Trump had used his position as president to halt the transfer of military aid to Ukraine in order to pressure the newly elected president, Volodymyr Zelensky, to announce an investigation into allegations, already proved unfounded, that Hunter Biden, the son of Trump's prime Democrat challenger at the time, was involved in corruption. Trump's blackmailing a foreign leader for his own political gain was an abuse of power without question. At least, it would have been a decade or two earlier. But the events around the impeachment showed how thoroughly, even within three short years, Trump had corrupted, defiled, and perverted what was considered acceptable behaviour by a president. Using the power of the presidency for personal political gain is no longer a high crime or even a misdemeanor in the age of Trump.

The White House defence was that Trump had not threatened Zelensky; and, even if he had, it didn't matter because Trump was acting for US national interest. And only Trump, as head of state, was qualified to say what that national interest was. The defence continued with the argument that the entire impeachment process was a hoax by the Democrats, who were trying to overturn the 2016 election results.

Nonetheless, Trump was impeached by the House of Representatives, largely along partisan lines. On the charge of Abuse of Power, 229 Democrats voted in favour, along with 1 Independent (a former Republican), and 195 Republicans voted against, along with 2 Democrats, with 1 abstention and 3 absences. On the charge of Obstruction of Congress, 228 Democrats voted in favour, along with the 1 Independent, and 195 Republicans voted against, along with 3 Democrats.

After impeachment by the House of Representatives came the trial in the Senate; there, Republican senators treated the matter not as a solemn duty required of them by the Constitution's checks against tyranny but as a partisan bar brawl. They fell into line with the insistence by Majority Leader Mitch McConnell that there was no need to see further evidence or to hear from any witnesses. They rushed to obey even though it was well known that Trump's former National Security Advisor John Bolton was just about to publish a book in which he confirmed the president's blackmailing of the Ukrainian leader. From then on, the outcome was inevitable. The Republican senators used their majority to vote down the articles of impeachment, with only Mitt Romney saying he found the evidence compelling and voting guilty on one count, that of Abuse of Power.

The impeachment process should have been a salutary moment when all Americans stood back to take a long, hard look at what was becoming of their country and its founding beliefs and aspirations and to develop a sense of perspective and historical context. Had they taken advantage of this moment and done so, they could only have been appalled by what they saw. But if anyone was making that judgment, it was not in public. The public discourse resembled a screaming match, with the red-hot shrapnel of partisan polarization that had become typical of American politics.

In their hearts in 2016, the Republicans had to have known what was coming. The hesitancy with which the Republican Party greeted Trump was matched by the broad political establishment, which, by and large, was not enthusiastic about Clinton either. The US Chamber of Commerce made huffy remarks about both candidates, and big business was particularly reticent about donating funds to the Trump campaign. Retirees were the most common donors to Trump's campaign funds, followed by small business owners. In surveys, both groups said they were fed up with professional politicians and trusted Trump as a Washington outsider. Both groups also pointed to their opposition to "Obamacare" — the Patient Protection and Affordable Care Act — and immigration. The belief that Trump was an outsider and would bring unbiased judgment to the presidency, a belief summed up in his pledge to "drain the swamp," was decisive for many voters. Ironically, that vision was consistently reinforced by the media every time it reported on Trump's iconoclastic or politically incorrect pronouncements. One study after the election concluded that Trump received about US$2 billion worth of free publicity during the campaign because of the media's focus on his daily outrages. The misreading by the US media of what was happening in the campaign was extraordinary. The persistent daily question in newspapers and on network and broadcast media was whether the latest affront to common decency by Trump would be the one that ensured his defeat. In fact, because of the public anger and anxiety among Rust Belt white people, every Trump affront made his victory more certain.

Probably the most potent test of Trump's invulnerability among his supporters was the release by *The Washington Post* of the *Access Hollywood* videotape on October 7, 2016, just a month before voting day. On the tape, Trump boasted about his sexual assault of women. He said that because he was a star, he could grab women "by the pussy" and get away with it. For once, Trump issued an apology of a sort. He could not resist insisting that there was a difference between words and actions and that "Bill Clinton has actually abused women and Hillary has bullied, attacked, shamed, and intimidated his victims." In the following days, several women came forward and said they had been groped or otherwise physically abused by Trump, but these revelations had no effect on his supporters, even the evangelical Christians. A book published in 2019, *All the President's Women: Donald Trump and the Making of a Predator*, by Barry Levine and Monique El-Faizy, was based on interviews with women who claimed twenty-six incidents of "unwanted sexual contact" with Trump and forty-three of inappropriate behaviour.

Even so, Trump would not have won the election that November if the US did not have such a distorted and contorted electoral system. He roared repeatedly during the campaign that the election was rigged and that he might not accept the result. It is indeed a rigged system, but, on this occasion, it benefited Trump. Americans do not vote directly for their president. They vote for party-affiliated candidates for the Electoral College in their states. It is the Electoral College that then votes for the president, and 270 votes nationally are needed to win. Trump received 304 Electoral College votes and Clinton 227. If, however, Americans had voted directly for their president, Trump would have lost and Clinton won. She received 65,853,514 votes, 48.2 percent of those cast; Trump was clearly second with 62,984,828 votes, 46.1 percent. That spread illustrates a profound weakness in the US electoral system: the opportunity to affect the result by clever gerrymandering of constituency boundaries or, in the

Internet age, by the cunning targeting of small numbers of strategically positioned voters.

Much of the post-mortem analysis of who voted for Trump and Clinton and why was predictable. People with college and university degrees voted for Clinton over Trump, 55 percent versus 38 percent. But among white voters who had not completed a college education — 44 percent of all voters — Trump won conclusively with 64 percent support to Clinton's 28 percent. It was Trump's thumping victory among lesser educated white men in five states — Florida, Pennsylvania, Wisconsin, Ohio, Michigan — that won him the election, but within that narrative are many interesting demographic details. Two stand out. One is that while an overwhelming proportion of white evangelical Christians voted for Trump — the exact percentage is disputed, but it was in the range of 75 percent — they didn't do it for the reasons that might be expected. A Pew Research Center survey found 26 percent of evangelical Trump supporters gave hopes of economic improvement as the reason for their vote, while 22 percent cited national security. That appears to refer exclusively to fears of terrorism, because only 5 percent of evangelicals said their vote was decided by immigration policy. Similarly, only 4 percent pointed to abortion policy and only 10 percent were motivated by the prospect of Trump appointing conservative Supreme Court justices. An interesting counterpoint to this is that the Pew survey then asked evangelical pastors the same questions and got very different answers. Among the pastors, what they saw as Trump's sterling character was the most important issue and swayed 27 percent of his support. This is a number that must involve a significant amount of Christian charity in the light of Trump's proven history as an adulterer, liar, fraud, bully, and confidence man.

Another interesting detail in the election results is that it was not the poor who elected Trump president. The poor and nearly poor, earning less than US$50,000 a year, voted for Clinton by a margin of more than ten percentage points. Trump was supported by well-off people who looked at the plight of the less fortunate people around them and feared for their own future. As an analysis in the *New Republic* put it, "While Trump's supporters might be comparatively well off themselves, they come from places where their neighbours endure other forms of hardship. In their communities, white residents are dying younger, and it is harder for young people who grow up poor to get ahead. Trump supporters might not be experiencing acute economic distress, but they are living in places that lack economic opportunity for the next generation."

Even as Trump was approaching his inauguration, unprecedented questions were being asked about the legitimacy of his election. In the summer and autumn of 2016, the Federal Bureau of Investigation saw evidence leading from the Trump campaign to Russia and the regime of President Vladimir Putin. There were legitimate questions about whether Putin and his agents had hacked into Democratic Party computers to steal information beneficial to Trump. There was also reason to examine whether Putin and his teams had gone further and used complex systems to identify crucial groups of American voters whose votes in marginal districts could determine the outcome of the election. Meanwhile, Trump's campaign organization had installed in senior positions people with strong financial ties to Russia, and he himself used talking points about Europe and NATO that echoed the disdain coming from the Kremlin. Even as Trump was sworn into office, there was a real possibility that Trump was a Manchurian candidate. Putin might have pulled off the ultimate coup of the age by gathering massive amounts of personal information on Americans and using unregulated social media to sway the way they voted to plant his own man in the White House.

CHAPTER EIGHT

—

Orthodoxy, Autocracy, Nationality

A CENTRAL QUESTION when looking at the assaults on European and North American democracies is why Russian President Vladimir Putin is so determined to make mischief and destroy public confidence in political institutions wherever possible. To begin to answer this question, it is necessary to go back to the speech Putin made at the Munich Security Conference on February 10, 2007. It was an outpouring of frustration and invective in which he decried what had happened since the end of the Cold War. Putin's particular target was the emergence of the US as the single superpower, dominating global affairs and bestriding the world without consideration for the interests of other countries. "One single centre of power. One single centre of force. One single centre of decision-making. It is a world in which there is one master, one sovereign," Putin railed.

Up to that moment, Putin, the former low-ranking KGB agent who had risen to command the reformed intelligence agency under President Boris Yeltsin and who then became president himself in 1999, had attracted only passing attention outside Russia. After the chaotic plunge into democracy under Yeltsin, accompanied by the corrupt sale of state assets that created the oligarch class, Putin appeared to be the uninspiring but methodical and safe pair of hands Russia needed to manage the completion of the transition to stable democracy. Washington under the leadership of President George W. Bush was focused on its war against terrorism and the quagmires churned up by its invasions of Iraq and Afghanistan. In the capitals of Western Europe and North America, the gobbling up in 2004 of most of the Eastern European satellites of the Soviet Union by both NATO and the EU was regarded almost as a matter of course, the natural result of the end of the Cold War. Putin didn't see it that way. Putin was and is a Russian patriot who has said the collapse of the Soviet Union — the end of the Russian empire — was the great disaster of the last half of the twentieth century. Having stabilized both politics and the economy with the help of rising prices for oil and gas — the core of the Russian economy — Putin looked with growing anger and anxiety at Russia's shrunken borders. He saw the US invasion of Iraq on fabricated evidence of nuclear weapons production as particularly threatening. As the growing number of US allies in Eastern Europe came ever closer to Russia's western border, Putin abandoned any thought of seeking common ground with Washington and the West. He made that clear in his 2007 Munich speech. "The process of NATO expansion has nothing to do with modernization of the alliance," he said. "We have the right to ask, 'Against whom is this expansion directed?'"

The American-led eastward expansion of the European alliance "has nothing in common with democracy, of course," Putin continued. "Today we are witnessing an almost uncontained hyper use of force in international relations — military force." Yet American military actions "have not been able to resolve any matters at all," he said, and have created only more instability and danger. The climax of Putin's outpouring was one portentous thought that may well have influenced and framed the strategy with which he fought back against US hegemony. He warned that the power churning within any nation that takes the role of supreme global leadership eventually "destroys it from within."

Putin realized he had a weak hand to play if he was to re-establish Russia as a credible power and influence in the world. The extent of

Russia's fallibility became evident the following year, 2008, when Putin ordered the invasion of Georgia, a former enclave of the Soviet empire on the Black Sea coast. Georgian independence in 1991 left only two regions, South Ossetia and Abkhazia, under the control of pro-Russian separatists. (There is a similar situation in Moldova, where the eastern territory of Transnistria has remained autonomous since 1994. There are twelve hundred Russian military "peacekeepers" stationed in the territory.) In the early 2000s, a pro-Western government in the Georgian capital, Tbilisi, began lobbying for European Union membership. The heightened tension with the separatist enclaves spilled into conflict early in August 2008, when South Ossetia began shelling Georgian villages. The Georgian army moved on South Ossetia to restore order, but Russia had already infiltrated troops into the enclave and followed up with a large-scale land and sea invasion. By mid-August, when a ceasefire was arranged, Russia had occupied much of central Georgia. Putin withdrew his troops to the two separatist enclaves, where they remain.

Putin was lucky to come out of the Georgian war the perceived winner, and he knew it. Between 60 and 70 percent of the Russian tanks and armoured vehicles had broken down during the five days of fighting. Command and control systems failed, the Russian troops were badly trained, and they were lucky to prevail against the more modern heavy armoured vehicles deployed by Tbilisi. Putin got the message, and he embarked on a massive program of military modernization in both equipment and training. Between 2007 and 2016, Russia's annual military spending doubled to US$70 billion, representing 5.3 percent of the country's gross domestic product, nearly double that of the US. Over the following years, Putin evolved a potent blend of revived military power with the more subtle weapons from his old spymaster's kit of disinformation and misinformation. The new tools of social media boosted the effectiveness of Putin's lies and helped enable a potent campaign of political influence and pressure. Above all, Putin possessed the old spymaster's skill of never presenting a clear target.

Putin's new order of battle got its first test in Ukraine, a former part of Russia with a large Russian-speaking population in the east that had been independent since 1991. In late 2013, the elected president was pro-Russian Viktor Yanukovych. Much of Ukraine favoured seeking closer ties with Western Europe, but Yanukovych was committed to economic and political links to Moscow. In November 2013, he refused to sign an association agreement with the European Union. This followed blunt warnings from Moscow that closer ties with the EU would result in sanctions from Russia, or worse. The bowing to Moscow by Yanukovych, plus the imprisonment of leading opposition figures, brought tens of thousands of people out onto the streets, especially into the central Maidan Nezalezhnosti (Independence Square) in the capital, Kyiv. Yanukovych held out until the end of February 2014, when he fled to the predominantly Russian-speaking regions of Luhansk and Donetsk in eastern Ukraine. Within days of Yanukovych's flight, armed men in green military uniforms, but without any national or other identification, began taking control of the Crimean Peninsula. At the same time, the well-armed and trained troops who became known as the Little Green Men began appearing in Luhansk and Donetsk (known collectively as the Donbass). As the war staggered on in fits and starts punctuated by ceasefires over the following years, Putin sent at least thirty thousand troops, complete with tanks and heavy artillery, to eastern Ukraine. These were all said by Moscow to be "volunteers" or "holidaying." In the meantime, Putin engineered the annexation of Crimea, giving Russia a secure port on the Black Sea.

By reinforcing the disputed territories in Georgia, Moldova, and Ukraine, Putin has stopped the eastward march of the EU and NATO. Neither organization is going to accept new members whose governments do not control large areas of their claimed territory, especially when those enclaves are occupied by Russian forces.

A central skill of the spymaster's craft is understanding and utilizing the opponent's weaknesses. Putin has shown he has lost none of his cunning since his days at the KGB outpost in Dresden. He has recognized that causing confusion is one of the most potent weapons he has, constructing doubt over whether the Donbass has actually been invaded or is simply in the grip of a civil war, or if Donald Trump is really Putin's Manchurian candidate or merely what used to be called a "useful idiot." Interfering in Western elections, even if it doesn't change the outcome, can leave voters convinced their democracy is contaminated and dysfunctional. Anything that causes citizens in democracies to doubt their institutions or that produces enough fog to frustrate decision making among Putin's adversaries is a victory.

A persistent tactic since about 2010 has been the financing, arranged either by Putin or through his allies among the oligarchs, of nationalist and right-wing groups in Europe. A common theme among the recipients of Putin's largesse is vehement opposition to the establishment classes and to the European Union. In 2014, French National Front leader Marine Le Pen borrowed the equivalent of US$14 million from a Russian-controlled bank and then a further US$3 million, both for political campaign expenses. There are also reports of Moscow making financial arrangements with far-right parties in Austria and Italy. Both stories are disputed by the purported recipients. There are also persistent reports that Russian money was funnelled into the United Kingdom Independence Party, led by Nigel Farage, and its campaign for the United Kingdom to leave the EU through Farage's main financier, businessman Aaron Banks. Farage received the equivalent of US$18 million from Banks. One of the targets of Russian infiltration in the US was the deeply pro-Republican National Rifle Association. There is clear evidence that Russian operatives close to the Kremlin developed close ties with the executive of the NRA, but no substantial evidence has surfaced that any of the US$30 million the pro-gun lobby spent boosting Trump's 2016 campaign came from Moscow.

Spreading misinformation and disinformation were staples of KGB attacks on Western democracies, and Putin has not hesitated to grasp the massive opportunities afforded by the Internet to use these tactics on a scale not possible before.

Even as the implications of Putin's March 2007 speech in Munich were being digested, he gave a taste of how he would push back against US hegemony. The following April and May, the Internet in the former

Soviet nation of Estonia was disabled by Russia. Putin was angry at plans in the Baltic state to move to a less prominent location a Second World War memorial to Russian soldiers. Estonia has one of the world's most Internet-dependent economies, and the severing of the service to government departments, financial institutions, and the national communications network brought the country to a standstill.

A similar attack was launched on Estonia's Baltic Sea neighbour, Lithuania, the following year. Again, Lithuania's crime was removing symbols of the country's Soviet past. Three months later, in August 2008, when Russian troops invaded Georgia, Moscow's hackers also attacked the Georgian Internet. This was the first known coordinated military and cyber attack, and it effectively shut down the Tbilisi government's communications network. Putin's hackers did the same thing in March 2014 when they disrupted the Internet in Ukraine as Russian troops were occupying Crimea. In May 2015, Russian hackers penetrated the computer network of the German parliament, the Bundestag, but had only limited success, according to Berlin's domestic intelligence service. In October of the same year, Russian hackers tried to get into the computers of the Dutch government in an attempt to get a report on the shooting down by Russian troops of Malaysia Airlines Flight 17 over Ukraine on July 17, 2014, killing all 298 people on board. The flight originated in Amsterdam, so the Dutch Safety Board headed the investigation and determined it was a Russian missile that had brought down the plane.

There have been several other well-documented cases of cyber attacks by Russian hackers on elections in Europe or on the communications networks of European governments. But these actions do not rise to the level of the dominant story in the catalogue of Putin's efforts to disrupt and influence Western democratic processes: the Russian government's involvement in the campaign of Donald Trump and the 2016 presidential election in the US.

THE SEVEN-HUNDRED-PAGE report submitted in March 2019 by Special Counsel Robert Mueller on foreign interference in the 2016 election is unequivocal in its verdict. Moscow used every weapon that came to hand to subvert the outcome in favour of Donald Trump. There were, however, two very significant questions left unresolved. One was whether members of the Trump campaign conspired directly with Putin's intelligence agency operatives to fix the election outcome. The other was whether the Russian campaign had achieved its purpose. The results, after all, showed that Hillary Clinton was the conclusive winner of popular support with 2.9 million more votes than Trump. It was, however, Trump's victory in several marginal states that gave him the 304 Electoral College votes necessary to grab the presidency, over Clinton's 227.

On the first question, in the introduction to his report, Mueller walks right up to the line and says, "Although the investigation established that the Russian government perceived it would benefit from a Trump presidency and worked to secure that outcome, and that the Campaign expected it would benefit electorally from information stolen and released through Russian efforts, the investigation did not establish that members of the Trump Campaign conspired or coordinated with the Russian government in the election interference activities."

A few pages later, in the executive summary, Mueller explains bluntly why he is not able to conclusively establish the link. He sets out a litany of obstructions and deceptions put in the way of his investigators by Trump campaign officials and others to block him from discovering where the leads he was following ended up. Some witnesses invoked their Fifth Amendment right not to incriminate themselves. Some lawyers used the rules of attorney-client privilege to avoid answering questions. Some witnesses just lied. Mueller and his team also found it difficult to find all the physical evidence they needed to corroborate witnesses' statements and answer the conspiracy question. Some relevant communications had been erased from the computers where they were stored. Other messages had been sent and received using encryption systems that didn't store the information. At the end, in his methodical, dogged, and unemotional way, Mueller emphasizes the possibility that the Trump campaign did conspire with Moscow to fix the 2016 election and that the evidence is still out there somewhere: "Accordingly, while this report embodies factual and legal determinations that the Office believed to be accurate and complete to the greatest extent possible, given these identified gaps, the Office cannot rule out the possibility that the unavailable information would shed additional light on (or cast in a new light) the events described in the report."

Mueller did everything he could within the restrictions under which his probe operated to point the American public and its political leaders to what he believed to be the truth. His prosecutors charged thirty-four people, including twenty-six Russian intelligence agents and other operatives. Mueller's agents got guilty pleas from seven people involved with the Trump campaign, including National Security Advisor Michael Flynn, a retired army general who served as the new president's first NSA. Another was Paul Manafort, Trump's campaign chairman in mid-2016, who was a long-time Republican political consultant with extensive business ties to Russian oligarchs and the ousted pro-Moscow president of Ukraine, Viktor Yanukovych. In 2018, Manafort was convicted by a Virginia jury of eight counts of bank and tax fraud. Four weeks later, Manafort pleaded guilty to failing to register as a foreign lobbyist while working for the Ukrainian president. Earlier in 2018, Manafort's deputy in the Trump campaign, Rick Gates, pleaded guilty to conspiring against the United States, helping to commit bank fraud, and failing to register as a lobbyist for the pro-Russian regime in Ukraine. On the fringes of the Trump campaign was Roger Stone, a friend of Trump's for over thirty years and a political hatchetman who liked to call himself the "Prince of Darkness." In public, Stone gave purposefully obtuse accounts of his role in the Trump campaign, including having advance knowledge of WikiLeaks' intention to publish emails stolen by Russian military intelligence from the Democratic National Committee (DNC) and Hillary Clinton's campaign chairman, John Podesta. In November 2019, a jury found Stone guilty of five counts of lying to Congress, one of witness tampering, and one of obstructing a congressional committee proceeding. In October 2017, National Security Advisor George Papadopoulos pleaded guilty to lying to the FBI about his Russian connections.

In May 2016, just as the presidential campaign was entering the white heat of its final months, Papadopoulos boasted to an Australian diplomat he met in London that the Trump campaign knew the Russians had dirt on Clinton in the form of thousands of emails. The diplomat passed that information along to the Australian Security Intelligence Organisation, which in turn passed it along to the FBI. After that information was assessed by the FBI, a formal counter-intelligence investigation labelled Crossfire Hurricane was launched in late July. Meanwhile, someone had slipped the FBI a copy of a report known as the Steele Dossier. This was compiled by former British intelligence officer Christopher Steele for a Washington research firm. The gestation of the Steele Dossier is a tortuous story that provides a multitude of opportunities for all political factions to point fingers at others — and those opportunities have been grasped with enthusiasm. Suffice to say, in October 2015, a conservative website, the Washington Free Beacon, hired a private investigation firm, Fusion GPS, to dig up useful dirt on Donald Trump and other Republican presidential candidates. By coincidence, in April 2016, the Hillary Clinton campaign and the Democratic National Committee approached Fusion GPS to research Trump for material that would be useful in the campaign. A few weeks later, the Free Beacon ended its arrangement with Fusion GPS, which then hired Steele to research Trump, but without initially telling him the real client was the Democrats. Steele was reportedly paid directly by Fusion GPS co-founder Glenn R. Simpson, and the investigation into Trump carried into December 2016, weeks after the election.

Steele was the head of the Russia Desk when he worked for the British Secret Intelligence Service (MI6). He brought his experience and contacts to his new work as a principal in London-based Orbis Business Intelligence. The Steele Dossier contained allegations that Trump and his campaign were conspiring with Russia to win the election. The report contained highly salacious material, including the allegation that Russian intelligence services had video of Trump cavorting with prostitutes in a hotel room while on a visit to Moscow. Trump's supporters attacked the Steele Dossier as fabrications and went on to claim that it had tainted the entire FBI investigation of the alleged Russia-Trump links. The veracity of the entire Steele Dossier remains unresolved.

By early fall 2016, polls suggested the electorate was leaning firmly in Clinton's direction. What looked at first to be the final blow for Trump came on October 7 with the publication by the *Washington Post* of a previously unseen 2005 *Access Hollywood* video in which Trump, unaware he is being recorded, talks about sexually assaulting women.

"When you're a star, they let you do it," Trump is heard saying. "You can do anything." He repeated himself. "Grab 'em by the pussy. You can do anything."

Two other things happened that day of equal importance to the way the election turned out. The first was that WikiLeaks, the international organization dedicated to publishing purloined secret or private documents, began publishing what would become a weekly diet of material from among the twenty thousand pages of emails stolen from the Democratic National Committee by Russian intelligence officers. The second was a joint warning from all the US intelligence agencies about Russian interference in the election.

"The US Intelligence Community is confident that the Russian Government directed the recent compromises of emails from US persons and institutions, including from US political organizations. The recent disclosures of alleged hacked emails on sites like DCLeaks.com and WikiLeaks and by the Guccifer 2.0 online persona are consistent with the methods and motivations of Russian-directed efforts," said the statement. "These thefts and disclosures are intended to interfere with the US election process. Such activity is not new to Moscow — the Russians have used similar tactics and techniques across Europe and Eurasia, for example, to influence public opinion there. We believe, based on the scope and sensitivity of these efforts, that only Russia's senior-most officials could have authorized these activities."

Russian cyber intelligence agents and Trump's army of digital supporters used the very skills against which the US intelligence organizations were warning to drown out both their message and the *Access Hollywood* video. On one subreddit, there was a particularly aggressive community of Trump supporters numbering around 220,000, including at least 1,000 Russian "sock puppets" operated by Russian intelligence. They deleted all references to the *Access Hollywood* tape and pushed links to the WikiLeaks pages. Something similar happened on Twitter, where about two hundred thousand pro-Trump bots, which included about fifty thousand Russian creations, drove a campaign to bury the tape and drive audiences toward WikiLeaks. A study of the campaign Twitter traffic of three hundred million tweets published in November 2016 after the election by the Bloomberg business news agency found that Trump was the subject of two-thirds of those messages versus one-third for Clinton. More than that, the messages mentioning Clinton were overwhelmingly negative, while those for Trump were positive, and this trend accelerated from the beginning of October until voting day on November 8.

Mueller and his investigative team found two principal strands to the Russian cyber attack on the US elections. The objectives of both operations were to sow discord in American society and to raise doubts among US voters about the honesty and fairness of their system. The first Russian organization to target the US election process via social media was the Internet Research Agency (IRA), an operation funded by Yevgeny Prigozhin, an associate of Putin. IRA employees began targeting the US in 2014 by opening social media accounts and group pages aimed at US audiences. Once the online presence was established, the Russian company sent groups of its employees to the US to gather intelligence, make contacts, and take photographs to be used in their social media posts.

The second line of attack was sharper edged and had a more obvious effect on the US election. In March 2016, two units of Russia's military intelligence (the Main Intelligence Directorate of the General Staff, known by the acronym GRU) began hacking into the computers and email accounts of people and organizations supporting Hillary Clinton. Over the following weeks, the two GRU units involved, Military Unit 26165 and Military Unit 74455, stole hundreds of thousands of documents from hacked email and network accounts.

Initially, when the IRA was setting up fake social media personalities and organizations, the aim of the attacks was simply to cause as much disruption and uncertainty as possible in and around the US elections. To that end, IRA agents tried to establish themselves along the obvious fracture lines in US social and political life. They created groups opposed to immigration, supported the far-right libertarian Tea Party, but also supported the Black Lives Matter campaign against the frequent killing of black people by the police. As the election primaries evolved from January to June into the campaign proper with a contest between Trump and Clinton, the IRA picked sides. Mueller's team found an IRA memo to staff from February 2016 that said, "Main idea: use any opportunity to criticize Hillary (Clinton) and the rest (except Sanders and Trump — we support them)." In the following months, the IRA created a slew of Trump-supporting social media groups, purchased over 3,500 advertisements on Facebook at a cost of over US$100,000, and even organized a number of rallies across the country in support of Trump.

"Collectively, the IRA's social media accounts reached tens of millions of US persons. Individual IRA social media accounts attracted hundreds of thousands of followers. For example, at the time they were deactivated by Facebook in mid-2017, the IRA's 'United Muslims Of America' Facebook group had over 300,000 followers, the 'Don't Shoot Us' Facebook group had over 250,000 followers, the 'Being Patriotic' Facebook group had over 200,000 followers, and 'Secured Borders' Facebook group had over 130,000 followers," the Mueller Report stated. "According to Facebook, in total the IRA-controlled accounts made over 80,000 posts before their deactivation in August 2017, and these posts reached at least 29 million US persons and 'may have reached an estimated 126 million people.'"

It was a similar story with the IRA's Twitter operation. In January 2018, Twitter said it had identified 3,814 Twitter accounts linked to the IRA. The company believed the IRA may have been in contact with 1.4 million US citizens via those accounts. Among those caught by the IRA's Twitter net and encouraged to retweet messages originating with Russian operatives were Donald Trump Jr., his brother, Eric, several other campaign officials, and, on one occasion, even Trump himself.

The aim of the Russian agents' foray into American social media was very simple: to make people angry about things they already believed to be true. This could include subliminal fears about immigration, crime, political corruption, excessive deference for minorities, or any lurking anxiety. Putin's purpose was to goad these established feelings into anger that would drive people to the polls. In the strictest sense, what he was doing was not misinformation or disinformation. It was much simpler than that.

Starting early in March 2016, the GRU sent a wave of hundreds of spear-phishing emails to people working in the Clinton campaign. Enough campaign workers responded to the messages to allow the agents to plant malicious programs that gave them access to most of the campaign's email traffic. The GRU stole tens of thousands of messages to and from campaign chairman John Podesta and from many campaign workers and advisers. With the information gained, the GRU hackers were also able to access Clinton campaign documents using a group of middle servers based in Arizona. To make public the most politically sensitive stolen documents, GRU agents created two fictitious online activists. One was a website called DCLeaks, created in April, and the other was a persona called Guccifer 2.0. In June 2016, the GRU began posting the stolen documents on DCLeaks. At the same time, the GRU started using Guccifer 2.0 to begin releasing what would eventually be thousands of documents stolen from the Democratic National Committee and the Democratic Congressional Campaign Committee.

The GRU, using its DCLeaks and Guccifer 2.0 cover identities, contacted WikiLeaks, where Julian Assange had publicly declared his organization an opponent of Hillary Clinton. Both messages said they had "sensitive information" from the Clinton campaign and were prepared to share and coordinate publishing on their sites. WikiLeaks responded swiftly, saying, "if you have anything hillary related we want it in the next two days preferably." Despite the evident enthusiasm on both sides, it took many weeks for a working relationship to be established. It blossomed fully on October 7, 2016, when less than an hour after *The Washington Post* published the *Access Hollywood* video, WikiLeaks diverted public attention by posting the first set of emails stolen by the GRU from Podesta.

WikiLeaks continued to be a channel for publishing documents stolen by the GRU until the end of the campaign.

Among the leaked Democratic National Committee emails were several that spoke derisively of candidate Bernie Sanders, who had a large band of loyal followers in the party. The messages showed that the DNC thought Sanders was too left-wing to make a credible candidate and that they were doing all it could to get him out of the race by making arrangements that favoured Clinton. The revelation of the anti-Sanders bias among the DNC angered his supporters, many of whom aimed their animosity at Clinton. The 2017 Cooperative Congressional Election Study showed that 12 percent of Sanders's supporters ended up voting for Trump. That bloc alone was not large enough to change the outcome of the election, but evidence shows that among the large percentage of registered voters who didn't cast ballots, most were Democrats. The leaked DNC emails fed into the established dislike or skepticism of Clinton, even among committed Democrat voters, and caused them to stay home on voting day.

Among cyber security experts associated with Western intelligence agencies, there is a strong belief that hacking and leaking the DNC emails was the most important boost Putin gave to the Trump campaign and that it handed the Republican candidate the presidency.

Mueller and his team went on to examine in great detail the direct contacts between Russians and members of the Trump business and campaign teams. There was a lot of information to plough through. Trump's interest in doing business in Russia started in the mid-1980s, when he met the

Soviet ambassador to Washington. He shied away, however, from putting money into Russia. It was money coming the other way, from Russia into the US, that secured the relationship. As Trump was trying to dig himself out from his bankruptcies in the early 2000s, Russian investment in properties carrying the Trump name was a significant element in his revival. A Reuters investigation in 2018 found that at least sixty-three individuals with Russian passports had bought nearly US$100 million worth of property in seven Trump-branded luxury residential towers in southern Florida. But Reuters conceded that these numbers might be conservative. About one-third — 703 — of the owners of the 2,044 units in the buildings had hidden their identities behind limited liability companies.

Appearing to be back on his financial feet in the mid-2000s, Trump took another look at trying to arrange a building bearing his name in Moscow. He used his involvement in the Miss Universe pageant in 2013 to visit Moscow and announced, "I am in talks with several Russian companies to establish this skyscraper." Trump's personal lawyer and fixer, Michael Cohen, negotiated with several Russian real estate companies over the following years, including right through the presidential campaign in 2016. Mueller sets out details of these approaches, none of which came to anything. In most cases, it was the Russian potential partner who withdrew, apparently dissatisfied with the deal being offered by the Trump organization, which by this time was interested only in selling the Trump brand to embellish the building and not becoming involved in the development nuts and bolts. Mueller makes no comment about the nature of the Trump business or why so many of the Russians backed off when they saw the deal on offer. But one footnote sets out the details of a letter of intent (LOI) between Trump and the Russian company I.C. Expert on a proposed development of 250 luxury apartments with a hotel of 150 rooms. Under the LOI, the Trump Organization would get a US$4 million "up-front fee" before construction of the hundred-storey building started. Trump would then get up to 5 percent of the value of all condominium sales, plus 3 percent of all rental revenue. On the hotel portion of the development, Trump would get a base fee of 3 percent of gross operating revenue for the first five years and 4 percent thereafter. In addition, there would be a 20 percent fee on operating profit paid to the Trump Organization. Mueller allowed himself the dry comment, "Under these terms, the Trump Organization stood to earn substantial sums over the lifetime of the project, without assuming significant liabilities or financial commitments."

Trump's personal branding is based on the belief, "When you're a star, they let you do it," but that does not seem to have extended to business deals with the Russians. Russian real estate developers seem to have been a good deal more canny than their American counterparts, but then they had not been subjected to the cultural brainwashing of *The Apprentice* television series and the mythology that the Trump brand denoted power and success.

It was not within Mueller's scope, unfortunately, to try to determine what effect the Russian interference campaign had had on the outcome of the 2016 election. The report notes that campaign manager Paul Manafort and his deputy, Rick Gates, shared with Konstantin Kilimnik, a business associate with ties to Russian intelligence, detailed information about decisive battleground states such as Michigan, Pennsylvania, and Wisconsin. But whether that information was detailed enough to enable the IRA to tailor its social media campaigns to determine the outcome in those states remains unknown.

Perhaps the most notorious of the Trump campaign meetings with Russians with close ties to the Kremlin was at Trump Tower in New York on June 9, 2016. The meeting was set up after a Moscow contact of the Trump family emailed that he had a contact who was in possession of documents that could incriminate Hillary Clinton. Donald Trump Jr. replied, "If it's what you say, I love it, especially later in the summer." He, his brother-in-law Jared Kushner, and campaign manager Paul Manafort met Russian lawyer Natalia Veselnitskaya. Donald Trump Jr. said later that Veselnitskaya used the meeting to criticize the Magnitsky Act, the bill passed in 2012 enabling the US to impose sanctions on Russian officials involved in human rights abuses. In January 2019, Veselnitskaya was indicted for obstruction of justice by the US Attorney's Office for the

Southern District of New York. The case revolves around money laundering, but Veselnitskaya has remained in Russia beyond the reach of American justice, as Russia does not have an extradition treaty with the US.

There was another meeting whose significance has not been resolved after the November election. In December 2016, Kushner and Trump's National Security Advisor Michael Flynn met Russian ambassador Sergey Kislyak at Trump Tower. According to a report in *The Washington Post*, they discussed "setting up a secret and secure communications channel" between the Trump team and the Kremlin, independent of the two countries' regular diplomatic lines of communication. Following the meeting, Kushner was put in touch with officials at a Russian bank, and Flynn had further meetings with Kislyak. When Flynn lied about these contacts to FBI investigators, he was forced to resign in December 2017. An article published by *Time* in April 2019 lists these among more than a hundred contacts between Trump associates and Russian officials during the course of the campaign.

Trump and Attorney General William Barr managed to get ahead of the story when the redacted version of the Mueller Report was published. Barr issued a brief statement saying the report had found no evidence of collusion. Trump diverted attention by threatening war with Iran. By the time anyone had read the 728-page report and assessed its damning findings, the news caravan had moved on.

The machinery of government usually churns slowly, and one gear was the Republican-led Senate Select Committee on Intelligence. It had picked up on Trump's constant refrain that the story of Russian interference in the election on his behalf was a hoax. More than that, Trump contended that the FBI, the CIA, and other elements of the US Intelligence Community were deeply corrupt and biased toward the Democratic Party. The reaction to the Mueller Report picked up on Trump's attempts to portray himself as a Washington outsider crusading against the "deep state" and intent on "draining the swamp." On April 20, 2020, the Select Committee on Intelligence presented the results of its examination of the tradecraft and analytical work behind a January 2017 Intelligence

Community Assessment (ICA) entitled "Assessing Russian Activities and Intentions in Recent US Elections," which played a part in spurring the Mueller inquiry. The committee said that it "found no reason to dispute the Intelligence Community's conclusions." The report found:

> One of the ICA's most important conclusions was that Russia's aggressive interference efforts should be considered the "new normal." That warning has been borne out by the events of the last three years, as Russia and its imitators increasingly use information warfare to sow societal chaos and discord. With the 2020 presidential election approaching, it's more important than ever that we remain vigilant against the threat of interference from hostile foreign actors.
>
> The ICA summarizing intelligence concerning the 2016 election represented the kind of unbiased and professional work we expect and require from the Intelligence Community. The ICA correctly found the Russians interfered in our 2016 election to hurt Secretary [Hillary] Clinton and help the candidacy of Donald Trump. Our review of the highly classified ICA and underlying intelligence found that this and other conclusions were well-supported. There is certainly no reason to doubt that the Russians' success in 2016 is leading them to try again in 2020, and we must not be caught unprepared.

What gave relevance to all the evidence that Vladimir Putin had taken a direct interest in the outcome of the 2016 election were the words and actions of Donald Trump both during the campaign and after he became president. During the campaign, Trump expressed his admiration for Putin and his hope that relations between the US and Russia could be improved. This raised eyebrows, coming at a time when Washington had imposed sanctions on Russia for its invasion and absorption of the Ukrainian territory of Crimea and for aiding the separatist occupation of eastern Ukraine. Well aware that anything that outraged the Washington establishment delighted his supporters, Trump went further. At a rally in Miami near the end of July 2016, Trump looked into the television cameras ranged at him. "Russia, if you're listening, I hope you're able to find the thirty thousand emails that are missing," he said, referring to Democratic nominee Hillary Clinton's deleted messages. "I think you will probably be rewarded mightily by our press." Trump raised further questions about the true relationship between himself and Putin when they met privately for over two hours in Helsinki, Finland, in July 2018. Trump insisted that no US officials be present, and he confiscated the translator's notes at the end of the meeting. Then, at the press conference following the meeting, Trump contradicted the assertion of US intelligence agencies that it was Russia that had interfered in the 2016 election. "I have great confidence in my intelligence people, but I will tell you that President Putin was extremely strong and powerful in his denial today," Trump said. "President Putin says it's not Russia. I don't see any reason why it would be."

By this time, Trump in word and deed was pursuing policies that largely favoured Moscow and not Washington's allies. Early in his presidency, Trump called the North Atlantic Treaty Organization, the hub of the Western security alliance since the Second World War, "obsolete." Trump has continued railing against the twenty-eight fellow members of NATO, accusing them of making insufficient financial or military contribution to the alliance. What he said was undoubtedly true. Few of NATO's members lived up to their financial or military commitments to the organization. Several previous US presidents had publicly admonished other members for their lack of commitment, but always with a degree of courtesy. The difference with Trump was that the level of invective reached at the summit in the UK in December 2019 meant that for the first time, the survival of the security pact became a topic of serious speculation.

Trump coupled his disdain for his NATO partners with attacks on the countries of the European Union, Washington's key allies in NATO, for what he claimed were unfair dealings in trade. More than that, his vocal support for Brexit came close to advocating the breakup of the EU. All this exacerbated the established tendency among EU members to hold different views about how friendly to get with Putin and Moscow. Russia is the source of 30 percent of the EU's petroleum imports and 39 percent of its natural gas imports. Dependence on these varies among EU members and influences how willing they are to confront Putin's perceived abuses.

A Gallup poll in late 2018 found that 40 percent of Republicans considered Russia an ally, up from 22 percent in 2014. But this was not enough to outweigh serious criticism from Republicans after Trump appeared in October 2019 to make Putin the dominant outside influence in the Middle East. In mid-October of that year, Trump made an off-the-cuff decision without consulting the Pentagon to withdraw the one thousand American troops remaining in northeastern Syria. These troops had, with those of other NATO allies, been aiding Kurdish fighters to defeat the Islamic State group that had overrun much of eastern Syria and northern Iraq in order to establish a violently puritanical Islamic caliphate. Just as Trump announced this withdrawal, Turkey's President Recep Tayyip Erdoğan, who claimed the Kurdish militia were terrorists linked to the Kurdish separatist movement in Turkey, announced his army would invade northern Syria. His aim, Erdoğan said, was to drive the Kurds thirty kilometres back from the Turkish border. It became clear that Trump had agreed to support Erdoğan's invasion. News reports late in 2019 said Trump had been blackmailed into withdrawing from Syria by Erdoğan. Turkish intelligence agencies were reported to have tapes of Trump's son-in-law Jared Kushner, adviser on the Middle East and friend of Saudi Arabia's Crown Prince Mohammed bin Salman, giving approval for Saudi agents to kidnap *Washington Post* columnist Jamal Khashoggi, a perennial critic of the Saudi royal family. The report first appeared in November in the US edition of the British conservative weekly magazine *The Spectator* and was then confirmed by Khashoggi's employer, *The Washington Post*. Khashoggi was killed and his body dismembered when he went to the Saudi Embassy in Turkey in October 2018.

Trump's abandonment of Syria and the Kurds did not sit well with some senior Republicans, who saw it as a betrayal of America's allies, who had fought shoulder to shoulder with US troops. Trump was forced to back-track on the withdrawal of US troops, though the Turkish invasion went ahead. The incident had much wider implications, however. It allowed Putin, who was already the major military support for the besieged Syrian government of Bashar al-Assad, to partner with Erdoğan in policing the Kurdish areas of northeastern Syria and to step forward as the most influential outside force in the Middle East. More broadly, it told US allies everywhere that Washington under Trump was not to be trusted.

Putin and his agents will continue to try to disrupt elections in North Atlantic democracies, both to keep his enemies off balance and to deter those among his own people who yearn for reform by saying, in effect, "See, democracy is not all it's cracked up to be." Some evidence surfaced in early 2020 that Russian hacking operations were behind the dissemination among US social media sites of conspiracy theories about the source and purported purpose of the SARS-COV-2 virus that causes COVID-19. Some of the messages promoted fake cures for the virus or equally false ways of avoiding infection. The abilities of Putin's cyber agents are formidable, but they are not insurmountable. Social media companies have begun to accept that they have a responsibility to ensure that their platforms are not used for political misinformation and disinformation. They should be held accountable, with the threat of real and painful penalties if they do not comply.

There is one essential question that is often forgotten in the rush to install digital systems to control and manage everything from election counts to national electric power networks: "What do we do if it breaks down?" There have been examples of foreign cyber attacks on electrical networks being overcome because someone on staff still knew which switch to flip to override the digital system. Digitized voting and vote counting systems have proven to be especially vulnerable to things going wrong. The chaos around the brand new but unworkable app at the hub of the voting system for the February 2020 Iowa Democratic caucuses is only one of countless similar embarrassments. In the fifty years or so of efforts to popu-larize mechanical and electronic voting systems, there have been enough breakdowns that election managers should be convinced that traditional paper ballots and manual counting should be retained. Paper ballots and manual counting are usually quicker and ensure more reliable results. The system is transparent and, therefore, the level of public confidence is high. It is also a system that is easily monitored and impossible to hack.

There is also a role for governments or other reliable institutions to demystify what many people might consider the most alarming aspects of the digital revolution. Innovations such as deepfakes, the use of sophisticated animations to create false videos of public figures doing things they never did, are more easily spotted than urban legend allows. Indeed, fostering a culture of healthy skepticism toward any information coming from the Internet is an imperative survival tool. Putin's cyber agents are moving on from Facebook and Twitter as platforms to cause uncertainty and lack of trust among Westerners in their democratic institutions. Western counter-intelligence agents see the justice system in democratic countries as a natural target for Putin and other cyber espionage actors such as China and Iran. Disrupting the justice systems, causing lack of trust in the rule of law, could be just as detrimental to democratic stability as meddling in elections.

CHAPTER NINE

—

From the *Four Basic Principles* to the *Chinese Dream* and the Covid-19 Nightmare

IN THE DAYS after the Tiananmen Square Massacre over the night of June 3–4, 1989, paramount leader Deng Xiaoping proved yet again that it takes a cool head and a firm grip to rule China. Deng and seven other veteran Chinese Communist Party leaders had come out of semi-retirement in May. They took back control after it became obvious that the new generation of frontline party leaders did not know how to respond to the hundreds of thousands of students camped out in Beijing's Tiananmen Square, demanding political reform. As the protests spread to up to one hundred other cities across China, the elders decided that any concessions to the students would plunge the country into anarchy and that it was time for a firm response. At a meeting on May 17 with the party's Standing Committee, the hub of power, Deng proposed that martial law be declared. After some strenuous debate, the committee agreed. The following day, May 18, all eight elders met with the Central Military Commission, of which Deng was still the chairman, to solidify the consensus and make sure the People's Liberation Army (PLA) would remain loyal to the CCP even when ordered to kill Chinese people. In the early hours of May 20, Premier Li Peng signed the order for martial law, which came into force that same morning. The order made the students' demonstrations illegal and gave the PLA the authority "to use all necessary means, including force, to deal with prohibited activities." Over the following weeks, the party leaders convinced themselves that the students were actually a counter-revolutionary uprising sponsored by foreign powers. The troops enforcing martial law were indoctrinated with the same message. As the leaders worked themselves into a passion, there were signs of protest fatigue and demoralization among the students in the square and a drop in the number of similar demonstrations in cities around the country. It seemed the right moment to strike. The troops moved in on the night of June 3 and the early hours of June 4.

According to the official account prepared afterwards, "Five thousand PLA soldiers and officers [were] wounded, and more than two thousand local people (counting students, city people, and rioters together) also wounded." The report declared, "The figures on the dead are these: twenty-three from the martial law troops, including ten from the PLA and thirteen from the People's Armed Police. About 200 soldiers are also missing. The dead among the city people, students, and rioters number about two hundred, of whom thirty-six are university students. No one was killed within Tiananmen Square itself."

The CCP and Chinese officials have stuck firmly to those numbers in the three decades since. Other estimates, including those from eyewitnesses, are much higher and conclude that more than one thousand people were killed in and around the square. One of the highest numbers came from the UK's ambassador to Beijing, Sir Alan Donald, who in a message to London on June 5 said he had been informed by sources in the Chinese government that at least ten thousand people had been killed.

In the following days and weeks, countries from all over Asia, Europe, and North America delivered messages of protest at the Beijing regime's action, and many imposed diplomatic and economic sanctions. While CCP leaders were congratulating themselves on putting down what they continued to see as a counter-revolutionary attempted coup, Deng was more troubled and thoughtful. At a June 6 meeting of the elders with the Politburo Standing Committee, and when he appeared three days later at the headquarters of the martial law troops, Deng made clear what he thought should happen next. He said China must continue along the road of economic reform and opening up to the outside world, especially the West. But the lesson of Tiananmen was that political reform was a different and more dangerous matter.

"For several years now, some of our comrades have buried their heads in technical things and haven't looked at big political trends. They haven't taken political thought work seriously, haven't guarded closely enough against corruption, and haven't put enough punch into their corrective measures," Deng told the June 6 meeting. "Of all China's problems, the one that trumps everything is the need for stability. We have to jump on anything that might bring instability; we can't give ground on this point, can't bend at all. And we can't care what foreigners say. Let them say what they want! All this boils down to one thing: China can't take chaos. We can't allow chaos, and we have to keep saying so bluntly and openly."

These thoughts became ever more deeply embedded in Deng's vision as he watched the Soviet Union descend into chaos and collapse over the following months. For Deng and other CCP leaders, the evisceration of the Soviet Union was the disaster scenario that awaited China if they misplayed their hand. The party must, Deng told a meeting of the Central Committee on June 23, anchor its relationship with the Chinese citizenry on the Four Basic Principles: commitment to Marxist-Leninism as modified by the thoughts of Mao Zedong, socialism, the dictatorship of the proletariat, and the leadership of the CCP. Deng was also adamant that essential to the party's survival in power was continued economic reform aimed at steadily improving the people's standard of living. When this process seemed to stall in the years after Tiananmen, Deng again came out of retirement, and in January and February 1992 he made his famous South China Tour. By visiting and publicly blessing the new and burgeoning manufacturing centres in Guangdong province, bordering

Hong Kong, Deng reinvigorated the economic reform movement. Chinese Communist Party leaders since then — Jiang Zemin, Hu Jintao, and Xi Jinping — have followed his lead. By 2019, the Chinese economy was more than eight times the size it had been in 1989 and was poised to overtake the United States as the world's largest. But Deng's successors have also followed, often brutally, his instruction to prevent political reform and to stomp on any organization or movement that threatens social stability and the CCP-led one-party state. Followers of the Falun Gong Buddhist sect, lawyers beguiled by ideas of the rule of law and an independent judiciary, the authors of Charter 08 (a manifesto for political reform), Christians, Muslims, Uyghurs, and Tibetan Buddhists have all suffered ruthless repression when their activities were judged a threat to the CCP regime.

One of the blessings for CCP leadership, however, has been that China's Western trade and diplomatic partners have not believed that it is possible to pursue economic reform without also implementing political reform. The history of North Atlantic political and economic culture is that economic advances lead naturally to the rising middle class demanding political emancipation. Western leaders expected the same thing to happen in China. In 2001, they saw accepting China into the World Trade Organization under very favourable terms as a "developing country" as an act that would precipitate political reform. The same went for the boosting of trade with China and even allowing the uninhibited movement of factories to China by North American and European companies. From the Western perspective, these acts of apparent generosity were subversive. Within China, they would promote the growth of a politically ambitious middle class, and abroad they would pressure China into becoming a "stakeholder," as one American diplomat described it, in the international order and institutions created by Washington and its allies after the Second World War. This was a profound misjudgment of the exceptionalism of Chinese social and political culture and the aspirations of the CCP. The misjudgment was doubly reprehensible because there was no secret about these things. Again, Deng had set the course in 1990 in the dark period of diplomatic and trade isolation of China after the Tiananmen Massacre. He proposed what has become known as the "Twenty-Four Character Strategy," which stated, "Observe calmly; secure our position; cope with affairs calmly; hide our capacities and bide our time; be good at maintaining a low profile; and never claim leadership."

Looking at the path of China from 1989 until the dawn of 2020, Deng's three successors have followed his script exactly. The first two decades of that period under Jiang Zemin and Hu Jintao were spent gathering and saving capabilities. The industrialization of China at breakneck speed in the 1990s and early 2000s created vast stores of wealth, both for Beijing and its state-owned enterprises and for individual CCP families (the "red nobility"). That in turn allowed for the building of infrastructure that changed the nature of the country and its society. In addition, there was the reformation of the People's Liberation Army into a modern, volunteer military, complete with the information technologies that had revolutionized Western military power. China also acquired a blue-water navy, something it had not had for over four hundred years, which has made it possible to project power throughout the western Pacific and Indian oceans.

It was Xi Jinping, who came to power in 2012, first as the general secretary of the CCP and then as president of the People's Republic of China, who decided it was time to stop hiding the country's capabilities and to end the assumption of a humble demeanour on the international stage.

Xi was born in 1953, the son of a senior CCP veteran of the revolution, Xi Zhongxun. The elder Xi had been the party's propaganda chief (a very senior post in a regime where the power of the party's message is of utmost importance) and the vice-chairman of the National People's Congress, China's highly managed version of a parliament. The elder Xi was thus a prime candidate for humiliation and re-education during the Cultural Revolution, and, like many teenagers from suspect high-ranking families, Xi Jinping was exiled to work in a rural village. After the death of Mao, Xi Jinping worked his way back into the party slowly and carefully, gaining a reputation for hard work and dependability. What set him on the path to leadership was when he was made governor of coastal Fujian province in 1999 in the wake of the exposure of the smuggling network run by Lai Changxing with the help of all the main party officials in the territory. From there, Xi went on to become CCP party boss in Shanghai, a natural stepping stone to his next appointment to the Politburo Standing Committee in 2007, where he was quickly identified as the presumed successor to President and Party Leader Hu Jintao. That expectation was reinforced when Xi was made vice-president in 2008 and vice-chairman of the Central Military Commission in 2010.

Xi's assumption of power was not a foregone conclusion. He was challenged by the charismatic, populist CCP boss of the mega-city Chongqing, Bo Xilai, a perfect example of the generation of "red nobility" who had evolved during the twenty years of unchecked economic growth. Bo was the son of Bo Yibo, a close ally of Deng Xiaoping and a man who had established strong relationships with politicians and business people in Canada and elsewhere in the 1960s. Bo Xilai followed his father's path in his relations with Westerners, many of whom saw him as a potential agent of political reform in China. Bo rocketed to political stardom, first as mayor of the northeastern port city of Dalian, then as governor of Liaoning province, and finally as minister of commerce in Beijing before his move to Chongqing. Bo, however, suffered from the common diseases of populists: narcissism and supreme confidence in his own invulnerability. His arousing of Maoist nostalgia among the thirty-five million citizens of Chongqing made him the darling of a new left movement, which regretted the passing of Marxist orthodoxy. Bo's championing of egalitarian "red culture," however, raised concerns among the party stalwarts in Beijing, many of whom, like Xi, had dark memories of the Cultural Revolution.

Bo's ambitions for leadership in Beijing collapsed on the night of February 6, 2012. His deputy mayor and long-time political ally and fixer from their days in Dalian, Wang Lijun, who was also the chief of police in Chongqing, turned up on the doorstep of the US consulate in Chengdu. Exactly what happened at the consulate during Wang's thirty hours with US diplomats remains opaque. What did become clear was that Wang, as chief of police, had fallen out with Bo over the murder of a British businessman, Neil Heywood, by Bo's wife, Gu Kailai. Heywood had been a financial adviser to Gu and had helped the couple with the education of their son, Bo Guagua, at a British private school. Later, evidence in court showed that Gu had fallen out with Heywood over money and that in November 2011 she'd arranged his poisoning while he was staying at a resort hotel outside Chongqing. Wang and his police investigators were conscripted to destroy some evidence and fabricate other evidence to make it appear Heywood died of natural causes. Wang feared the cover-up would backfire and confronted Bo, who slapped him in the face. Events cascaded quickly from there. In March, after Wang had told his story to party officials in Beijing, Gu was arrested and charged with murder. When, in mid-March, Bo failed to appear at a meeting of the twenty-five-member Politburo, rumours circulated that he had tried to launch a coup but had been foiled. Gu was convicted of poisoning Heywood and received a suspended death sentence in August 2012. In August 2013, Bo Xilai was sentenced to life in prison for bribery, abuse of power, and corruption.

As a result of Bo's fall, Xi Jinping hardly had to lift a finger to vanquish his challenger for the leadership. The racy story from Chongqing, however, gave Xi an opportunity to impress on the CCP, the Chinese people, and the world that a new day had dawned in Beijing. In his speech at the eighteenth National Congress on November 15, 2012, accepting the leadership of the CCP, Xi said he believed the high level of corruption that had grown during the boom years would "doom the party and the state." He vowed to crack down on both "tigers and flies," party officials both high and low. It had become almost obligatory for an incoming CCP leader to promise a crackdown on corruption. These campaigns usually started with a good deal of noise and activity, but they quickly petered out and life returned to normal. Xi, though, quickly showed that his campaign was going to be real and that it would be more than a drive against corrupt officials. It would be a purge aimed at eradicating contending factions that had developed in the party, especially those who had supported Bo Xilai.

Soon after Xi took over, it was announced that the first batch of inspectors from the party's much-feared Central Commission for

Discipline Inspection were being sent to half a dozen provinces. A second batch of inspectors was sent to other provinces in November 2013, and by the same month in 2015, teams had combed through the administrations of all thirty-one provinces and provincial-level municipalities such as Beijing, Shanghai, and Chongqing. When the dust settled five years later, hundreds of thousands of people in the party, the military, and state-owned companies had been indicted for corruption. Among them were hundreds of high-ranking officials, including some of the most senior serving party members ever to face formal prosecution while the CCP had been in power. The campaign continued after the first shock treatment. In 2017, party figures showed that 527,000 people were detained, investigated, and, where appropriate, punished during the course of the year. In 2018, the number was even higher: 621,000.

The anti-corruption campaign was popular among Chinese citizens, even though it was widely recognized that it was also a purge of Xi's real and potential enemies. The campaign established Xi as the most personally powerful and unassailable CCP leader since Mao. With that went the end of the collective leadership the party had adopted in reaction to Mao's predatory excesses, especially the Cultural Revolution, which ripped apart Chinese society from the mid-1960s until Mao's death in 1976. Xi capped off his anti-corruption purge with a move that tended to confirm mounting suspicions that the new leader was taking China from a merely authoritarian state into a full-blown totalitarian one. A new anti-corruption agency was created, the National Supervision Commission, whose status in the hierarchy of state institutions is higher than the Supreme Court. This, in the words of Amnesty International, "places tens of millions of people at the mercy of a secretive and virtually unaccountable system that is above the law."

In both deeds and words, Xi established from the start that he was boss and that he was going to take China on an assertive and even aggressive course. Within weeks, he had taken into his own hands the reins of control over the party, the government, the military, and a new national security apparatus. Xi also put himself at the helm of a slew of new small committees set up to examine current issues and devise new policies. These Central Leading Groups bypassed established party and government chains of responsibility and command and sent a clear message to the entire bureaucracy that on important matters, Xi was in control and watching.

Within his first six months in office, Xi oversaw the preparation of a new mandate for CCP members in their attitude toward the West. The document set out seven Western values that were dangerous and threatened the survival of China and the CCP: constitutional democracy, the concept of universal values, civil society organizations outside the party, full-blown free market capitalism, an independent media, judging the actions of past leaders through a modern lens, and questioning the socio-economic mix of what Deng had called "socialism with Chinese characteristics." Xi's condemnation of constitutional democracy included the whole three-pillar package of an accountable administration, a representative legislature, and an independent judiciary. He objected to the idea of universal rights because it implied that Western democracies could legitimately criticize the way the CCP dealt with its own citizens. Xi understood that the Western idea of civil society was based on the notion of the supremacy of individual rights, not collective rights and duties, as espoused by the CCP.

This vilification of the West added substance to the vague but alluring appeal of the "Chinese Dream" that Xi first made his mantra on a visit to Guangdong soon after he took control of the party in December 2012. It became clear that what Xi meant by the Chinese Dream was a return to the age before the Industrial Revolution in Europe and North America in the early nineteenth century, when China was the world's pre-eminent economic and political power and had been for several thousand years. Xi's message was that the humiliation of the previous two centuries, when Western industrialized nations had outstripped China's economic and political power and influence, and even established colonial enclaves on Chinese territory, was a phase that had passed. When Xi reported to the party congress after his first five years in power late in 2017, he was master of all he surveyed. That was acknowledged early in 2018 when the limit of two five-year terms for holding the highest office was removed. This limit on power had been put in place to avoid a repeat of the excesses of another unchallenged leader like Mao Zedong and to encourage a collective leadership. The 2018 amendment opened the way for Xi to remain president, head of the CCP, and chairman of the Central Military Commission until the end of 2027 at least, and perhaps much longer than that.

Internally, Xi has overseen the installation of the most sophisticated system of technological totalitarianism the world has seen. By the end of 2017, the first two hundred million of what would be over six hundred million closed-circuit television cameras were in action to reduce crime and deter social unrest. The plan is that by the end of 2020, this system will use artificial intelligence programs to keep track of citizens by facial recognition or tracking their gait, evaluate their political and economic trustworthiness by their actions, and reward or restrict them accordingly.

The uncertainties of private enterprise were being curtailed by requiring that CCP committees be established within all private companies and joint ventures with foreigners. Party members inevitably rise to policy-making management positions. The number of foreign civil society organizations operating in China had been cut from over seven thousand to around four hundred, and the room for activity by the survivors was strictly limited.

In 2018 and 2019, the hammer of Xi's passion for social control fell most heavily on the Muslim Uyghurs of northwestern Xinjiang province. In mid-2018, a United Nations human rights panel said it had credible information that about one million Uyghurs were being held by Chinese authorities in massive internment camps. The UN committee said it believed these were "political camps for indoctrination" and that the Chinese authorities were bent on brainwashing the Uyghurs out of their religious loyalty to Islam. Chinese officials insisted the camps were vocational guidance centres to which the Uyghurs had gone voluntarily, but enough first-hand accounts emerged from people who had been detained to suggest this was far from the truth. Beijing pushed back against international criticism, but late in 2019 announced that the Uyghurs had "graduated" from the centres and were now back home leading happy and productive lives.

Beyond the boundaries of China, Xi rolled out the rapid construction of his multi-trillion-dollar Belt and Road Initiative (BRI). This is a gargantuan plan to create a twenty-first-century version of the old Silk Road trading path between China and the countries of Central, South, and Southeast Asia; the Middle East; Europe; and Africa. Xi has extended the plan to include Latin America. Many of the poor countries along the route, or those with easily corrupted leaders, gobbled up the cheap money being dangled by Beijing for the construction of roads, ports, railways, and airports. But other countries, especially those in Southeast Asia with a history of being considered vassal states by imperial China, were more cautious. To some, this looked like a classic campaign for imperial expansion by Beijing, and events quickly supported this skepticism. When Sri Lanka, Kenya, and others failed to meet their debt repayments, Beijing did not, as promised, offer generous new arrangements. Chinese officials pointed to the small print and demanded long-term control of the new assets, such as the ports of Hambantota in Sri Lanka and Mombasa in Kenya. Sensing the danger, other countries like Malaysia, Bangladesh, Myanmar, Pakistan, and Sierra Leone tried to get out of their obligations to before the "debt trap" sprung on them.

China's neighbours also have before them daily reminders of China's emergence as a regional military power. Xi completed the effective occupation of the South China Sea with the construction of seven islands, which in 2017 were turned into heavily armed and fortified military outposts. About 60 percent of maritime trade and a third of global shipping uses the sea lanes of the South China Sea. This economic flow is now subject to Beijing's policing, as are the activities of the riparian states Vietnam, the Philippines, Brunei, and Malaysia, whose claimed maritime territories have been occupied by the People's Liberation Army.

Beijing's absorption of the South China Sea is a classic example of achieving a strategic objective by taking incremental steps over more than two decades. These steps were always carefully judged by Beijing so that none was assertive or aggressive enough to prompt the United States to stand up in support of Southeast Asian allies. The riparian states themselves were inconsistent in their responses to Beijing's nudging and prodding. Sometimes Vietnam or the Philippines pushed back vigorously. On other occasions, they ignored Chinese advances, which often used fishing boats conscripted as "maritime militia" as the shock troops for their creeping territorial claims. Using the fishing fleets had the advantage of deniability by Beijing of any official involvement if there was a serious confrontation.

A major benefit for Beijing in the 2000s and 2010s was Washington's focus on its problems with fundamentalist Islam and its wars in Afghanistan and Iraq. There was no appetite by either George W. Bush or Barack Obama to seek a serious showdown with China. It is with that observation that the US Department of Defense begins its annual report to Congress "Military and Security Developments Involving the People's Republic of China 2019." The executive summary starts, "China's leaders have benefited from what they view as a 'period of strategic opportunity' during the initial two decades of the 21st century to develop domestically and expand China's 'comprehensive national power.' Over the coming decades, they are focused on realizing a powerful and prosperous China that is equipped with a 'world-class' military, securing China's status as a great power with the aim of emerging as the preeminent power in the Indo-Pacific region."

The following 135 pages of the report set out these themes in simple detail. The CCP will continue to follow its long-term "Made in China 2025" plan, which aims to replace imported military and other industrial technology with domestic products by that date. As part of that objective, the civil-military integration initiative will continue to encourage civilian technology companies to cater to the defence market. China's leaders will continue to leverage the country's growing economic, military, and diplomatic influence to establish it as the pre-eminent regional power. The Belt and Road Initiative will project this power and probably drive Beijing to continue to expand its network of overseas bases to provide security for these investments. Beijing continues to see containing China's rise as the prime objective in Asia of successive US administrations. To try to prevent vigorously anti-China policies in Washington and among its Pacific Rim allies, Beijing is intensifying well-established operations to influence the media, business, and academic and political communities in the US and other target countries "to achieve outcomes favourable to its security and military strategic objectives." Strategies include persuading foreign opinion-makers to accept Beijing's benign narrative on issues such as the BRI and the South China Sea claims.

—

THE MAIN ORGANIZATION for Beijing's political warfare campaign in the US, Canada, Australia, New Zealand, Japan, Singapore, and other Pacific Rim nations is the United Front Work Department. The United Front was created in the 1940s for the purpose of convincing non-communist partners that the CCP was not really a revolutionary Marxist-Lenin organization. United Front operatives portrayed the CCP as a mild-mannered group primarily interested in reform that would improve the lives of China's rural and urban poor. Xi Jinping, however, has echoed Mao Zedong and called the United Front the CCP's "magic weapon" alongside party discipline and military preparedness. One of Xi's early drives as the new leader was to vastly expand both the responsibilities and resources of the United Front so that it has outposts in all diplomatic and other offices abroad.

In May 2019, New Zealand academic Anne-Marie Brady, perhaps the most important outside expert on the United Front, gave evidence about the organization to the Justice Select Committee of her country's parliament after a series of questions and scandals about United Front infiltration and espionage. She said that their activities fall into four categories. The first is to be active among the ethnic Chinese Diaspora, to try to make them agents of Beijing's foreign policy and to suppress as far as possible any anti-CCP activity among the emigrants. For those who co-operate, there are offers of financial opportunities or various benefits. Those who shun the advances face threats of denial of visa or passport rights and, in extreme cases, the detention or other harassment of family members still in China. These pressures are applied by United Front agents operating out of Chinese embassies and consulates and also by members of their organizations in the host countries. A strong indication of the number of Chinese diplomats in Canada who are "double hatted" is that at the end of 2018, Beijing had 162 accredited diplomats in Canada, while the US, which is by far Canada's largest and most important trade, investment, defence, and diplomatic partner, had only 142. A universal foreign United Front cover organization is the China Council for the Promotion of Peaceful National Reunification, which has branches throughout the world. In itself, this highlights the importance the CCP puts on trying to diplomatically isolate the nation of Taiwan, which Beijing continues to try to force into political union. There is also a host of country-specific United Front organizations, some of which are functioning groups and others of which are created or wheeled out for particular propaganda projects. In Canada, there are Chinese Benevolent Associations in major cities, which are used as umbrella groups when need be. These groups in Vancouver and Toronto were used as the lead organizations when a propaganda campaign was mounted against the pro-democracy protesters in Hong Kong in 2019. A key organization for watching and controlling the hundreds of thousands of young Chinese students at foreign universities is the Chinese Student and Scholars Association.

The Student and Scholars Association is linked to another academic organization that the Canadian Security Intelligence Service has identified as a United Front group and has called "espionage outposts" of the embassy and consulates. This is the network of Confucius Institutes set up in foreign universities, colleges, and schools, ostensibly managed and financed by Beijing's Ministry of Education with the aim of spreading appreciation for Chinese culture and language. As well as keeping files on the activities of Chinese students in the colleges and universities to which they are attached, agents based at the Confucius Institutes identify and coerce foreigners whose skills or positions may be useful to the CCP.

The second task of the United Front is sometimes called "foreign elite capture." The objective is to co-opt foreigners, usually non-ethnic Chinese, with money, privileges, or flattery to get them to support the CCP's foreign policy goals, including passing over technical knowledge and other useful information. United Front agents have a treasure chest of lures to capture foreign business people and politicians. The most eminent can get consultancies of up to US$150,000 a year just for being an "adviser" to a CCP-affiliated organization. Retired officials whose contacts the CCP considers useful may get invited to join the board of state-owned companies, with all the benefits that go with it. Sometimes this has had the reverse effect from what the CCP wanted. Some Canadians who have taken up these offers have been so appalled by the way the CCP companies were run and the corruption involved that they have left in disgust. Foreign politicians, business people, or officials lower down the food chain may get all-paid lavish visits to China. Companies with technologies the CCP wants may be offered a merger or preferential treatment in the Chinese market. United Front operatives also swiftly discovered that in countries like Canada, municipal governments and indigenous organizations are a lot easier to penetrate than provincial or central governments, and the rewards can be just as great. Decisions on resources and land use are often made at local levels, where politicians and officials are easily accessible and often not as wary of manipulation by foreign agents as those at more senior levels of government.

The third task of the United Front is to promote a strategic communications propaganda strategy, again with the aim of suppressing opposition and driving support for the CCP's policies on the international stage. In recent years, Chinese companies from all branches of the mass media have been active around the world, especially among the democracies of the Pacific Rim, pushing for partnerships and strategic mergers and acquisitions. This approach is known as "buying a boat to go out to sea," and it gives further conformation to the importance the CCP puts on propaganda and controlling the message. China has managed to take editorial control of most of the media companies in the independent island nation of Taiwan, either by outright purchase or by seducing local publishers with promises of access to the vastly larger market on the mainland. That lure has been used effectively on media and cultural companies from Europe and North America. Access, however, often requires some very big compromises from foreign companies. They must follow CCP policy on core national interests and not portray China in an unfavourable way, even outside of China. Those dictates extend to publishing, a global market China has come to dominate because of low production costs. Academic publishers have had to edit out material for books aimed at the Chinese market if the CCP considers it critical of China. Not only publishing companies but others doing business in China, such as airline companies, have been threatened with having their privileges withdrawn if their material does not show Taiwan as part of China.

The CCP has a very thin skin on what it considers issues of national pride. In October 2019, Chinese companies cancelled financial deals with the US National Basketball Association after Houston Rockets manager Daryl Morey tweeted support for pro-democracy protesters in Hong Kong. Two months later, in mid-December, the midfield player for London's Arsenal football club, Mesut Ozil, posted on Twitter in support of fellow Muslims, the Uyghurs of China Xinjiang province. Amid reports from the United Nations that about a million Uyghurs were in concentration camps, Ozil called them "warriors who resist persecution." The Chinese Football Association responded by calling the comment "unacceptable" and said Ozil had "hurt the feelings" of Chinese soccer fans. The Chinese state television broadcaster, CCTV, went further and removed an Arsenal–Manchester City game from its schedule, a considerable financial penalty for both clubs.

A key current element of United Front responsibility is to promote the Belt and Road Initiative, which is a central feature of Xi's economic policy, and to try to minimize criticism. This task has become more arduous for United Front groups in the target countries as worries have sunk in about the "debt traps" behind the cheap loans offered by Beijing and the economic dependence that comes with all road, rail, and seaway links leading to China. In several countries, such as Sri Lanka, Kazakhstan, and Zambia, worries about economic subservience to China have become the cause of persistent social unrest and riots.

The CCP's editorial control of Chinese-language media in Diaspora communities and its emphasis on recruiting agents of influence means Beijing has had less reason than Moscow to use social media for misinformation and disinformation campaigns. Beijing's agents do, however, emulate Moscow in their energetic efforts to hack into the computer networks of groups and individuals they consider a threat. Cyber attacks usually involve emails purporting to come from friends or contacts, but with attachments containing malicious software. The malware may contain annoying computer viruses or, more commonly, spyware that gives the agency a window into dissidents' communications networks. This enables the CCP's spies to not only follow plans and discussions within dissident groups but also know the whereabouts of individual members. It was this type of malware that was discovered in an ongoing forensic study undertaken by Citizen Lab, an interdisciplinary agency based at the Munk School of Global Affairs at the University of Toronto, regarding CCP agency cyber attacks. In 2013, Citizen Lab examined a suspicious email with an attachment that had been received by a Tibetan Canadian organization. The email purported to be from a prominent member of the Tibetan Canadian community and contained three attached documents, which, if opened, would have infected computers with the malware Citizen Lab named Surtr, after the fire giant in Norse mythology. "A computer compromised by Surtr would be susceptible to having all of its keystrokes logged, its file directories and contents listed, as well as allowing the operator to remotely execute commands," they reported. Pursuing its interest in attacks on human rights groups, in 2014, Citizen Lab published a report, "Communities @ Risk," after studying suspicious emails and attachments from ten civil society organizations that had volunteered to take part in the research project. A Tibetan Canadian group involved in this study gave a lead into which Chinese intelligence agency was behind some of the attacks. The hacker was identified as an operator known to Western agencies as APT1, which had targeted many government agencies and Fortune 500 companies. APT1 was identified by the United States Federal Bureau of Investigation and the Department of Justice as Unit 61398. This is the cover name for a cyber espionage operation in the second bureau of the third department of the Chinese People's Liberation Army. In May 2014, the US Department of Justice filed charges of economic espionage against five officers in Unit 61398, involving six American nuclear power, metals, and solar products industries.

The extent of CCP agents' infiltration into politics, academia, and businesses in the democracies of the Pacific Rim, especially Australia, New Zealand, and Canada, was largely unknown or ignored until the mid-2010s. Then, a couple of defections by CCP diplomats with information about the party's espionage activities rang alarm bells. As a result, the media and others began gathering information. At the end of 2018, Australian academic Clive Hamilton published *Silent Invasion*, which set out the pattern of CCP infiltration in his country. Soon afterwards, my book *Claws of the Panda: Beijing's Campaign of Influence and Intimidation in Canada* was published. There was also a steady stream of media reports in New Zealand on the same topic. The campaigns of espionage and attempts to gain influence were very similar in all three countries. In Australia, there were moves to prevent CCP agents from buying political influence by making donations to political parties and to tighten up restrictions and regulations governing foreign agents in Australia. There were similar moves in New Zealand.

In Canada, the publication of my book coincided with the detention of the chief financial officer of Huawei Technologies, Meng Wanzhou, in December 2018. She was arrested on an extradition warrant issued by the US Department of Justice to face charges of fraud and evading sanctions against Iran. The CCP responded by holding hostage two Canadians in China, Michael Kovrig, a Canadian diplomat on secondment to the International Crisis Group, and Michael Spavor, a businessman specializing in North Korea. The standoff created the worst crisis in Canada-China relations since mutual diplomatic recognition in 1970. More than that, it called into question the whole basis of the relationship the two countries had enjoyed since that time. The taking of the two Michaels showed very clearly to the Canadian public, business people, and political leaders that the CCP shared few if any values with Canada. The whole relationship was based on trade and trade alone. There was no meeting of minds on human rights, the rule of law, Asia-Pacific security issues, or respect for international institutions. In Canada, the crisis prompted a re-evaluation of the country's thrust into Asia, which for decades had focused on China. Canadian interest began to turn more forcefully toward Asian middle powers with which there was a broad spectrum of shared values, such as Japan, South Korea, Taiwan, Australia, New Zealand, Singapore, Indonesia, and, further afield, India and Sri Lanka.

Whatever the outcome of the case and the linked negotiations for the return of the two Michaels, Canada's relationship with China has been seriously damaged for a generation at least.

It is not just in Canada that the mania for trade and investment ties with China is being reassessed. The four Pacific Rim democracies that are members of the Five Eyes intelligence alliance — Canada, US, Australia, and New Zealand (the fifth member is the United Kingdom) — are actively exchanging information and risk analysis of the threats posed by China. The focus is beginning to tighten on the activities of the United Front and the influence it has managed to achieve in their countries among the ethnic Chinese Diaspora, all levels of government, the media, and the technical faculties of colleges and universities. These activities impose serious pressures on domestic politics and social stability that need to be addressed. All of the democracies involved, as well as other Pacific Rim nations under the same attacks from China, including Taiwan, are debating how best to confront and overcome the influence of the United Front in their countries.

―

FROM A BROADER perspective, the threat of China to global democracy is looking a lot less potent than it did a few years ago. The year 2019 exposed some serious structural weaknesses in Xi's Chinese Dream, and as China entered the Year of the Rat at the end of January 2020, the storm clouds were gathering. It is always unwise to prophesy the end of the Communist regime in China, and Xi's creation of the most technically sophisticated system of totalitarian control ever seen gives further cause for hesitation. Even so, four events in 2019 and 2020 have exposed weaknesses that the CCP cannot overcome without abandoning the psychology of the one-party state.

The first is growing skepticism among target countries about making deals with Beijing for Belt and Road Initiative projects. The message has sunk in on the back of painful experiences in countries like Sri Lanka and some of the "stans" in Central Asia that the loans for infrastructure construction extended by China come with the objective of imperial expansion. In the Central Asian state of Kazakhstan, the popular uprisings against Chinese loans and investment have another cause. The focus of outrage against the detention and brainwashing of at least one million Muslims in the Chinese territory of Xinjiang has been on the Uyghurs. But many of those detained and subjected to "re-education" are ethnic Kazakhs with relatives in neighbouring Kazakhstan. The anger and protests in Kazakhstan highlight the importance of Xinjiang as China's passageway for road and rail links through Asia and on to the Middle East and Europe. Yet the attempt to ensure security in Xinjiang by what is, according to the United Nations, cultural genocide has, ironically, aroused opposition to the BRI project in the equally crucial corridors of Central Asia.

The second exposure of fundamental weakness in the CCP's governing mentality occurred during the events in Hong Kong in 2019. An attempt by the Beijing-selected administration of the territory to introduce legislation allowing extradition from Hong Kong to mainland China prompted mass peaceful demonstrations. On at least one occasion, two million people from among the territory's population of seven million took to the streets. Their demands went well beyond objection to the extradition law. They included respect for the "high degree of autonomy" promised Hong Kong when it was returned to Chinese sovereignty by the United Kingdom in 1997, along with progress toward full democracy. But as the protests continued, violence flared, apparently provoked by the police in an attempt to turn public opinion against the demonstrators. It didn't work, and the protests continued for six months, only dying down when pro-democracy candidates conclusively won most of the seats in territory-wide district elections at the end of November 2019.

These protests, other pro-democracy campaigns over the past two decades, and the responses to them have revealed what appears to be an unbridgeable cultural divide between the CCP and the people of Hong Kong. At the heart of that gap is a fundamental conflict in their different perspectives and understanding of the relationship between the citizen and the state. For Hongkongers, the government is there to provide the services that the ordinary citizen needs in order to be able to live a secure and productive life. In mainland China, the reverse is true: the role of the citizen is to perform those duties the CCP says will enhance the state.

These conflicting views of the relationship between the citizen and the state were revealed in the third demonstration of fundamental weakness in 2019 and 2020. Since the 2016 election in Taiwan brought to power Tsai Ing-wen as president and gave her Democratic Progressive Party (DPP) control of parliament, the CCP has deployed the United Front to try to undermine the island's government. Tsai and the DPP assert that Taiwan is an independent nation, though the CCP claims, without any convincing legal or historic evidence, it is a "rebel province." For a couple of decades, the CCP has been trying without success to lure Taiwan into a political union by offering to respect the island's democracy and judicial and social institutions under the same "One Country, Two Systems" agreement offered to Hong Kong. Watching events in Hong Kong, Taiwanese voters have found nothing attractive in that offer. In anger and frustration, in the months running up to the new elections in January 2020, China mounted a massive campaign to try to get a pro-Beijing candidate elected president and to overturn the DPP majority in parliament. Both United Front operations failed. Tsai and the DPP won re-election with unprecedented majorities. The CCP has no more understanding of what makes Taiwanese different from and antagonistic to the values by which the Communist Party runs China than they do of the same feelings among the people of Hong Kong. Any notion of a negotiated political union between Taiwan and mainland China has been killed by ccp hubris and ignorance.

The fourth evidence of ccp weakness comes from the same fixation on ideological correctness. The outbreak of coronavirus in Wuhan and the ccp's response to it have, at the time of writing, not only ensured that the infection became a regional epidemic in China but also led to it becoming a pandemic. When a young Wuhan doctor, Li Wenliang, spotted the outbreak early in December 2019 and broadcast warnings, he was detained, intimidated by police, and accused of maliciously spreading rumours. The result, as with the suppression of information about the outbreak of Severe Acute Respiratory Syndrome (SARS) in southern China in 2002, was that the sickness quickly spread unchecked. The coronavirus story reinforces a perennial vulnerability. Any bad news about the state of the nation is seen as an insult to the ccp, and insulting the ccp is an offence against the nation. No one, therefore, wants to be the carrier of bad news, and responsible officials go to great lengths to avoid admitting that matters under their control are not going well.

In the ccp's China, having the courage to tell the truth can be deadly. That is what Dr. Li found. About a month after his first warning, the authorities recognized they could no longer hide what was happening in Wuhan, especially with the approach of the Lunar New Year at the end of January, when hundreds of millions of Chinese traditionally travel to their family homes for the celebrations. But it was too late for Dr Li. He had contracted coronavirus and died on February 6. In death he became a public hero, as mounting anger was aimed at the government. In the past, such incidents have led to direct challenges to the ccp's legitimacy in power.

If what became known as the COVID-19 outbreak had been confined to China, or its international spread had been limited, as happened with SARS between 2002 and 2004, the damage to the reputation of the ccp regime in Beijing would have been minimal. This has not been the case in 2020. The Wuhan coronavirus proved to be much more infectious than SARS and swiftly found human carriers among Lunar New Year holiday travellers, tourists, and cruise liner passengers to transport it around the globe. Although doctors and Chinese officials were aware early in December

2019 of the new coronavirus in Wuhan and that it was being transmit
among humans, they chose not to tell the World Health Organization until
the end of December. Even then, Beijing continued to insist there was no
evidence of human-to-human transmission, even though this was patently
untrue. The very first person identified with the new virus transmitted the
disease to his wife. The result was that the WHO, among whose officials
the CCP has courted influence for many years, took Beijing at their word.
As a result, in January and February, the WHO said there was no need to
close down international travel or for people to wear face masks in public.
It was not until March 11, by which time the disease was firmly embedded
in Europe and North America while its tentacles were getting a grip in
every other corner of the world, that the WHO could no longer avoid the
fact of the highly infectious nature of the virus. COVID-19 was declared a
pandemic on that day.

By this time, many countries, including some of China's allies, including Russia and Iran, had stopped direct flights or other transport to and
from China. The effects were dramatic. One result was the closure of a
large proportion of industry in China, which immediately showed how
dependent Western businesses and markets had become on the supply
chain of parts or products from China. European and North American
leaders were confronted with the reality of how vulnerable their globally
intertwined economies had become to a pandemic like COVID-19 or any
other major disruption to the exchange of goods and services. The realization that COVID-19 and other pandemics are a strategic security threat,
which epidemiologists and threat assessor specialists had been arguing
for years, was heightened as the countries that had become centres of
infection counted their stocks of medical supplies to fight it. They discovered that not only was China the source of the disease, it had also
become a major manufacturer of pharmaceuticals and hospital protective
equipment such as masks and gowns necessary for medical staff to be able
to care safely and effectively for infected patients. The US, for example,
did a rapid check and found that 80 percent of the active pharmaceutical
ingredients for its domestic drug manufacturing industry came from

abroad, principally China. Nearly all the ibuprofen used in the US came from China, along with 45 percent of the penicillin. This was the price to be paid for US pharmaceutical companies' persistent drive to move production to the cheapest manufacturing centres available.

Debates began immediately about the future of globalization and the networks of interdependent streams of supply and demand. At the very least, most if not all of the countries of the North Atlantic will reassess their lists of goods and services that they consider essential to national security. It seems highly likely that some states and their citizens will decide they again need to manufacture at home some of the products that are now made abroad. That will probably involve having to pay more for these products, but for a time at least, while the ravages of COVID-19 are a sharp memory, many people in Europe and North America will be willing to make this compromise. On balance, the pressures stemming from the pandemic will probably enhance democracy. At the very least, the fallout from the pandemic affirms the interests of consumers, who are also voters, and yanks the reins on the multinational corporations who have promoted and benefited from the dismantling of regulations and tariffs, resulting in the globalization of manufacture.

Very quickly, after checking what was in their hospital cupboards, the governments of Canada, the United States, and Europe were hammering on Beijing's door, bickering over who was going to get their hands on China's available stocks of equipment. The CCP immediately saw that its control of significant amounts of the world's available supply of the equipment necessary to fight COVID-19 gave it a wonderful opportunity to reverse the drubbing its reputation had taken over its response to the outbreak of the disease. In this, Xi and his officials were helped by the lack of any cohesive and coordinated reaction to the pandemic by the North Atlantic states.

IN EUROPE, THE first white-hot centres of the infection were Italy and Spain. Most members of the EU and the other European countries, as well as Canada, closed their borders, shut down their economies, and instructed people to stay home in order to stop the spread of the disease. The main outliers were the United States and the United Kingdom, where the two populist leaders, Donald Trump and Boris Johnson, were taken by surprise by COVID-19 and didn't know how to react. There were several reasons for this. Number one is that populists survive and thrive by controlling the agenda of public attention. When something untoward happens, Johnson and Trump are masters at dreaming up an even more dramatic scenario, real or imagined, to divert public attention. The coronavirus pandemic, however, doesn't lend itself to diversions or alternative facts. The disease was especially difficult because both men had risen to fame by lashing out at "experts" and persuading their followers that a major curse that blighted the lives of ordinary people was scientists and professionals who insisted that facts are facts. Johnson dithered for weeks with the reality of the UK's situation by toying with the notion of seeking herd immunity. In essence, this meant allowing people in the UK to get the disease so that those who recovered would become immune. It was only after Johnson was forced to read an Imperial College study that showed this approach would kill hundreds of thousands and perhaps over a million UK citizens that he changed his mind. Johnson and his government ordered the closure of the economy and all but essential service workers to observe self-isolation in their homes.

For Johnson himself, there was a personal penalty for downplaying the dangers of COVID-19 and trying to avoid the harsh actions needed to contain it. He contracted the disease and went into isolation in an apartment attached to his office at 10 Downing Street. After two weeks, he had failed to shake off the symptoms; indeed, they had become worse. In early April, Johnson was taken to hospital, where his condition deteriorated. He spent two days in intensive care, where he responded to treatment. He was then dispatched to the prime minister's official country residence, Chequers, to convalesce. In the meantime, he had handed over the daily running of the government to his deputy and foreign minister, Dominic Raab. Whatever other outcomes came from the COVID-19 outbreak in the UK, it was evident from the early days that shuttering the economies of both the UK and Europe, along with the inability to hold face-to-face meetings, made it impossible for London and Brussels to agree on the basis for a new relationship between the United Kingdom and the European Union by the planned date of the end of December 2021.

Ideologically, the arrival of COVID-19 was even more troubling for Donald Trump. An essential part of his political rise had been pandering to the beliefs of his evangelical and ill-educated blue-collar white base that scientists are part of a global conspiracy. One of his early moves in the White House had been to disband a section of the National Security Council that assessed pandemics and their threat. He also defunded a US official based in the embassy in Beijing whose job for several years was to liaise with the Chinese Centre for Disease Control and Prevention. The person holding that job left her post in July 2019. There was crude logic in closing down these positions because taking the advice of epidemiologists or any scientist on how to deal with epidemics would be a denial of the persona that Trump had constructed.

With COVID-19 already established in Washington State and working its way into other parts of the country, Trump tried to pass it off as no worse than a bad influenza. It would quickly disappear, he insisted. But when the WHO's declaration of a pandemic coincided with a bitter dispute between Russia and Saudi Arabia that saw oil prices tumble to single figures, the New York stock market crashed. All the gains in the market that Trump had engineered — and held up as his economic masterpiece — disappeared overnight. At first, Trump railed against the advocates of closing down the economy and requiring people to stay at home in order to stop the spread of the virus. He said he didn't believe the US should adopt a policy where "the cure is worse than the disease." But then he took the coward's way out and left the response to the pandemic almost entirely to the state governors, many of whom in the worst affected regions had already imposed economic lockdowns and self-isolation. The result was a hodgepodge of responses varying widely from state to state and even district to district. By and large, the actions taken broke down over partisan lines, with Democratic mayors and governors imposing states of emergency and

Republican local administrations trying to keep their communities open.

As the death toll in the US climbed steadily into the tens of thousands, accusations swirled around Trump that his lack of resolve and delay in acknowledging that the coronavirus was a real and present danger was responsible for America's uncoordinated response and the deaths of many, many people. As a diversionary tactic, on April 14, Trump announced that the US would stop its financial contributions to the WHO while it investigated the way the organization had reacted to the COVID-19 outbreak. As he announced the move, Trump contended the WHO had been far too willing to accept Beijing's word for what was happening and had, as a result, worked to cover up the danger of the disease. The US is the largest donor to the WHO and contributes about US$400 million of the organization's US$2.2 billion budget. The WHO claims Washington is about US$60 million in arrears in its payments. There were immediate and angry responses, including from the WHO's second-largest contributor, Bill Gates, who argued Trump's action would likely cripple the organization's work and make the extent of COVID-19 far worse and more deadly. But Trump's move was aimed at drawing support from his base and from Americans with misgivings about international organizations and the amount of money Washington contributes to them.

Xi and the Beijing regime did their best to capitalize on the situation. First, they tried to add to the confusion in the West about the source of the disease. Chinese officials pointed to deaths in California and New York months before the Wuhan outbreak that appeared to have stemmed from a coronavirus infection.

The evidence was reasonably clear, however, that coronavirus had originated among the live animals sold in a market in Wuhan. Scientists had warned as many as twelve years before the COVID-19 outbreak, in a study published by *Clinical Microbial Reviews*, that the wet markets in China were a ticking time bomb. These markets, which contain many different species of wild game, sea life, and exotic mammals, lack biosecurity. The presence of SARS- and COVID-19–like viruses in horseshoe bats made possible the genetic recombination of various viruses. The disease probably mutated among bats sold live in the Wuhan market and then infected a buyer or stall holder.

Chinese media, however, began spreading a conspiracy theory that COVID-19 was a creation of a US agency specializing in disease warfare. It had been spread purposefully by US agents to discredit China. Beijing's second offensive was to cast itself as a great humanitarian. Its supply of medical equipment allowed it to start sending doctors, masks, and ventilators to European countries, especially those that had been hard hit by the coronavirus. This effort fell flat, however, when high proportions of the equipment, such as test kits and intensive care unit masks, were found to be faulty.

Early predictions by global strategic analysts that the pandemic would be the turning point that established China as the predominant global superpower were premature. An essential element in China's rise in the past forty years was the significant degree of trust with Western political, business, and academic partners built by the CCP. There had been warnings before — at Tiananmen Square, over the SARS outbreak, and in the response to the demands for reform in Hong Kong — that the Communist Party's bottom line was to continue holding power. But on those occasions, Beijing's agents of influence in the West had always managed to reassure their audiences that the CCP really was a dependable partner. COVID-19 and the CCP's unsuccessful attempts to cover up the existence of the disease have yet again raised the question of China's dependability. In mid-2020, as the disease still rages around the world, its end, and the ultimate effects of the pandemic on the world's economies and politics, is still unfathomable; there are no evident reasons to trust what the CCP regime says or does.

It is perhaps unseemly to see in the spread of the coronavirus a reason for democracies to take comfort in the revelation that the threat posed by the CCP is not as potent as it has appeared. But while the sheer size of China's population and its economy give it influence and apparent power, the four events of 2019 and 2020 show it is a fundamentally ill-conceived structure that contains the seeds of its own destruction, among them the lack of agility to overcome the strengths of free and open societies.

CHAPTER TEN

—

Back to
the Future

THERE ARE GOOD reasons why Johannes Gutenberg has been called the most important figure of the second millennium of the Christian calendar for his invention of the printing press in around 1440. Gutenberg was a goldsmith living in the German city of Mainz. Information had already reached Europe about the Chinese method of printing books by inking hand-carved wooden type blocks and stamping them on paper in the right order one after another. By the mid-fifteenth century, books were being produced in Europe by this method, which was cheaper and quicker than employing a copyist. Gutenberg, according to what has become the established historical account, invented three major improvements on the basic Chinese model, improvements that accelerated the course of history. He developed metal type made from an alloy of lead, tin, and antimony that was both durable and capable of producing a variety of typefaces with great detail. To get the benefits of the precision of which his metal type was capable, Gutenberg created an oil-based ink that was more permanent and less inclined to smear than the water-based inks used by the Chinese. Gutenberg is also credited with inventing the flatbed printing press, which remained the industry standard until the beginning of the nineteenth century. Historians argue over whether Gutenberg deserves all the glory for these inventions, noting that there was a community of Germans working on the development of printing methods at this time; Gutenberg was only one of them. He would not be the first or last person to get exclusive credit for a communal development. The history of human technological advances is that they are based on what has gone before and that the same bright idea about how to move forward usually occurs to several people at around the same time. There's usually a lot of experimentation before a eureka moment. Gutenberg should probably be considered a collective name for the inventors of the printing press and its components, but there can be no question about the impact of the technology.

The printing and wide distribution of affordable books, starting with the Bible, enabled everything that happened in all spheres of human life up to the end of the twentieth century. Initially, books killed off the feudal Middle Ages, with its dependence on unquestioning ignorance among the bulk of the population. Getting the Bible out of the exclusive grip of the clergy and into vernacular languages enabled the Renaissance and the Reformation, with all the political and social advances that spilled out of those revolutions. Printing promoted literacy and the mass communication of knowledge and ideas, both scientific and social. Everything that has happened in the political and economic development of human society in the last nearly six hundred years owes its creation to ideas or information that were printed on paper.

It is also almost universally true that every human invention has its dark side. Whatever the benefits of a technological advance, there are ways to use it for evil or anti-social purposes. Printing and the capacity for mass communications were no exceptions. The public defamation of enemies or rivals without evidence or substance had been a crime since Roman times, and a moral sin before that, such as in the Biblical Ninth Commandment, "Thou shalt not bear false witness against thy neighbour." Unsubstantiated rumours could be devastating for people's lives, but when the audience was confined to people around a village well or in a town marketplace, the fallout was limited; the printing press opened up whole new audiences to the would-be libeller. The distribution of scandalous allegations against public figures — what the French called canards — took off in the eighteenth century. Scandal sheets revelled in tales of corruption, hypocrisy, and marital infidelities among royalty and the aristocracy. Some of these stories were even true. This period of outlandish spoofing of the powerful, rich, and famous reached its pinnacle when the scandal sheets were also able to include black and white or, for a few pence more, coloured pictures of what were often pornographic caricatures of their targets. "The period between 1760 and 1820," wrote historian Bliss Bennett, "is often referred to as the 'Golden Age of Caricature,' in part because of the prints satirising the British Royal family that proliferated during this period. But many high-ranking political and social figures besides King George and his relations found themselves the butt of a satirical print's pointed humour."

It was not only British royalty that was satirized. In revolutionary France in the 1790s, a torrent of pamphlets was published defiling Queen Marie Antoinette. She was made the target of baseless allegations of sexual depravity. Canards were published showing her with multiple male and female lovers. Others showed her as a mythical beast, the harpy, that was half woman and half bird of prey. These slurs were different from the satirical caricatures of George III and his court. Their political purpose was to embed in the minds of the public that Marie Antoinette was a pervert, a traitor, and an adulterer. It made it easier for the revolutionaries who had overthrown and imprisoned the monarchy to send her to the guillotine, something that might have engendered public disgust had she kept her regal stature.

At the same time as printing was establishing itself as a vehicle for the widespread broadcasting of rumour and salacious scandal, it was also emerging as a central aspect of nascent democracy. In 1787, there was a debate in the United Kingdom's House of Commons on a bill to allow newspapers to report on the daily business of Parliament. During the course of the debate, Irish statesman and philosopher Edmund Burke, who was a member of Parliament from 1766 to 1794, is reputed to have said there were "Three Estates in Parliament; but in the Reporters' Gallery

yonder, there sits the Fourth Estate more important far than they all."
Those are the words of Thomas Carlyle, the nineteenth-century British
polymath, writing about Burke in 1837. Even if Burke did not say those
exact words, the legally sanctioned opening to reporters of the House
of Commons debates established independent journalism as an essential
pillar of any enlightened society. Only four years later, in 1791, the United
States followed the lead of the UK and passed the First Amendment to
the Constitution, which included freedom of the press among the basic
freedoms of religion and expression. Since then, the idea has become
established throughout Europe and elsewhere that journalists are the
Fourth Estate in the quadrille of daily politics. The task of the press,
now expanded by the inclusion of broadcast and digital journalism, is to
question and inform on the actions of the three branches of government:
the executive, the legislature, and the judiciary. To that end, journalists
have always lived in a solitary and purposefully unresolved dimension
as institutionalized outsiders. The value of journalists to democracy as it
grew and became established in the nineteenth century was (and remains)
that they are marauders given licence to explore and question all the
conventions of the societies in which they work and live. This ethic is neatly
summed up in a quote usually attributed to twentieth-century polemical
writer and journalist George Orwell. "Journalism is printing what someone else does not want printed; everything else is public relations," he
is said to have remarked, though similar thoughts are attributed to several
other public figures of the era.

Journalists and their publications hold authorities to account every
day, and there are almost as many examples where the story had dramatic
consequences. The histories of Canada and all the other North Atlantic
democracies are peppered with stories of politicians who were forced to
resign, and in a few instances found themselves in prison, after exposure
of their misdeeds by journalists. Sometimes investigative journalism has
brought down governments.

In the UK in 1962, it was a gossip column in the society magazine *Queen*
that first hinted at a story which eventually revealed that Secretary of

State for War John Profumo was having an affair with a showgirl, Christine Keeler. She was also bedding Yevgeny Ivanov, a naval attaché at the Soviet Embassy. The scandal destroyed the self-confidence of Prime Minister Harold Macmillan, and he resigned in 1963.

In the US in 1971, *The New York Times* published what became known as the Pentagon Papers, which revealed that the US had secretly enlarged the scope of its actions in the Vietnam War, originally intended only to give support to the beleaguered regime in Saigon, with the bombings of nearby Cambodia and Laos and coastal raids on North Vietnam. The compilation of the papers, which ran to three thousand pages of narrative and four thousand pages of supporting documents, was ordered by Lyndon Johnson's Defence Secretary Robert McNamara in June 1967 for reasons that are still unclear. In February 1971, one of the military analysts who had worked on preparing the report, Daniel Ellsberg, met a *New York Times* reporter, Neil Sheehan, and over the following weeks gave him forty-three volumes. The paper began publishing the contents that June. Ellsberg later explained he had leaked the documents to end what he perceived to be "a wrongful war." He said the documents "demonstrated unconstitutional behavior by a succession of presidents, the violation of their oath and the violation of the oath of every one of their subordinates." Publication of the Pentagon Papers intensified the already polarized debate within the US about the justice of involvement in the Vietnam War. Even so, it was another four years before Washington finally withdrew all its troops. Facing the reality of involvement in an unwinnable war was, however, something new for Americans. That dark memory has influenced to one degree or another all US foreign policy and military adventures since, though not always as conclusively as it should have done.

In 1972, *The Washington Post*, closely followed by *The New York Times*, pursued the story of the June break-in at the Democratic National Committee offices in the Watergate Hotel in Washington. The burglary was ordered by senior officials in the campaign organization of Republican incumbent Richard Nixon with the intention of installing listening devices and copying the campaign documents of Democratic candidate

George McGovern. The dogged determination of the reporters led to congressional oversight, Senate hearings, resignations, firings, charges, and the eventual resignation of Richard Nixon.

From the start, the idea of journalists as in-house rebels raised serious practical and philosophical questions, and it continues to do so. What status within society should be given to a coterie of people whose role is to make life uncomfortable for the pillars of the community? How can they be made professional and accountable without eroding the independence that is essential to their value to society? The question of whether journalism is a profession or a trade has continued to dog the business. If it is a profession, with neatly identifiable skills and mores, then it can be regulated like the law or medicine. But as soon as a government or administration sets out lists of qualifications required to licence a journalist, the value of the journalist disappears. What has evolved instead is a nebulous ring of restraints to try to curb the excesses of which journalists might be capable. At the top are the laws of libel and below are a host of rules and regulations such as right to privacy legislation and edicts on what can and cannot be reported in courts of law, such as bans on identifying minors.

Most Western democracies have regulatory bodies, often called press councils, usually funded by publishers. In some cases, such as the UK in 1953, they grew out of threats by government to introduce legal regulation or a code of conduct for journalists. While press councils do provide the public a forum to air their grievances against the media, they cannot offer redress. That is still a matter for the courts. Some news outlets have gone a step further and appointed editors as in-house advocates for members of the public who have problems with what has been published or broadcast. The effectiveness of these editors, often called the public's ombudsperson, to impose discipline on the newsroom or get redress for aggrieved members of the public depends on the force of character of the editor and his or her status in the hierarchy of the newsroom.

There are also a multitude of conventions that spring from the individual cultures in which journalists are working. Until recently, for example, Japanese journalists were loath to publish anything negative about the royal family. They were, however, happy to report foreign media stories on sensitive matters in the royal court because that insulated them from any public backlash. That illustrates one of the inherent contradictions in the psyche of a journalist.

To fulfil their function as in-house rebels and outsiders, they must also swim in the mainstream of their societies. In far too many journalistic communities in North Atlantic democracies, that understanding of the mood of the mainstream has been lost. It is a major reason why the level of public trust in the media has fallen to dangerously low levels. The misreading by the media of the sentiments of the UK public over Brexit and of conservative white America in the 2016 US election are vivid illustrations of this failing. There are countless reasons for this decline, which in theory ought not to exist in an age when journalists have better academic training than ever before. But the essential skills of journalism are judgment born of experience and the ability to weigh the relative value of things. Those skills are not learned in the classroom, and their acquisition by a questing spirit leads to constant challenges, especially when the quintessential quality of a good journalist is a deep curiosity about what people think and how that drives their actions.

Neither journalism nor the public's right to accurate and clearly stated information have been well served by the blurring of the lines between news and entertainment. Much of what is presented as news, especially on television and digital media, is actually a form of entertainment designed to attract ratings and not, primarily, to inform.

What the world sees now in the spreading of misinformation and purposeful disinformation on digital social media also has its genesis in print. One of the first non-religious books actually predates the printing age. A direct translation from the Italian is "Book of the Marvels of the World," but it is best known in English as *The Travels of Marco Polo*, the account of the claimed journey of the Venetian merchant and some of his relatives to Cathay (now China) in 1271 and their return in 1295. The tradition is that Polo dictated the story to romance writer Rustichello da Pisa when they were in prison together in Genoa in 1298 and 1299. About 150 handwritten copies have survived in various languages. From the start, there were public questions about the authenticity of the book, and many believed Polo never went to China but cobbled together his account from stories he'd heard from merchants who travelled the Silk Road. Favourite criticisms are that he does not mention the Great Wall of China, eating with chopsticks, nor the ritual of binding women's feet. The book reached wider audiences, both critical and supportive, after the invention of printing. It has remained in print ever since, and academics continue to debate its veracity.

Disinformation is a modern word that did not appear in English diction-aries until the 1980s. It is a translation of the Russian word *dezinformatsiya*. Soviet leader Joseph Stalin promoted and authorized his secret service, the KGB, to use "black propaganda" to confuse and confound his enemies. *Dezinformatsiya* is thus defined as "distributing false information with the intention to deceive public opinion." Stalin and his successors, including Vladimir Putin, made disinformation a core element of Soviet/Russian espionage, but spreading lies for political or strategic purposes has a long history. Many literary forgeries in the centuries following the invention of printing were made for reasons of vanity, entertainment, or, like the notorious Hitler Diaries, for money. The Hitler Diaries were a series of sixty volumes of journals purportedly written by Adolf Hitler but actually forged by Konrad Kujau between 1981 and 1983. The diaries were purchased in 1983 for DM 9.3 million by the West German news magazine *Stern*, which sold serialization rights to several news organizations. One buyer, the UK's *Sunday Times*, asked historian Hugh Trevor-Roper to authen-ticate the diaries. He did, but then had second thoughts and expressed his doubts. Forensic examination of the diaries quickly proved they were fakes, but Trevor-Roper's reputation as a historian never quite recovered.

A more pernicious forgery is *The Protocols of the Elders of Zion*. This fabricated anti-Semitic text purports to describe a Jewish plan for global domination. It was first published in Russia in 1903, translated into multiple languages, and disseminated internationally in the early part of the twentieth century. According to the claims made by some of its publishers, the *Protocols* are the minutes of a late-nineteenth-century meeting where

European Jewish leaders discussed their goal of global Jewish hegemony by subverting the morals of Gentiles and by controlling the press and the world's economies. Henry Ford funded the printing of five hundred thousand copies that were distributed throughout the United States in the 1920s. The Nazis sometimes used the *Protocols* as propaganda against Jews. Some German teachers were assigned the book as required reading for German schoolchildren after the Nazis came to power in 1933, despite its having been exposed as fraudulent by *The Times* of London in 1921. It is still widely available today in numerous languages, in print and on the Internet. Some neo-Nazi and ultra-right-wing groups continue to present it as a genuine document and to use it to recruit followers.

GUTENBERG'S REVOLUTION CONCLUSIVELY changed human society and economics. But it was a slow and trundling beast when compared with the revolution that has flowed from the jottings made by computer scientist Tim Berners-Lee in March 1989. The following year, Berners-Lee created the blueprint for the World Wide Web. The explosive revolution that followed has, within a generation, overtaken and buried much of the culture of print-based communication and economics that Gutenberg engendered. There were only 2.6 million people using the Internet when Berners-Lee opened the door to the future. By the end of 2019, there were around 4 billion.

Those thirty years have been an extraordinary cascade of change. They have also been a colourful cavalcade of names and companies, some of which were household names that lasted only moments in the spotlight before being brushed aside or relegated to the back of the stage. Names like Yahoo, WebCrawler, Netscape, and Internet Explorer were for a brief moment in the 1990s the very essence of Internet use. Not anymore. Other companies conceived and founded around the same time have flourished and continue to dominate the landscape. Amazon was founded in July 1994 and by 2020 was the world's most valuable public company. The company that would become eBay was created in September 1995.

Google started as a research project in 1996 and was incorporated in September 1998. It has become the search engine that dominates the Internet.

It is a quality of revolutions that they defy control, and the digital revolution was more chaotic than most. In the 1990s, the air was heady with possibilities. Investors were quick to see that fortunes were to be made backing the next big thing. And the next big thing might be anything that could be facilitated by digital communication. The first concept of a social network, called SixDegrees.com, appeared in May 1997. WiFi was introduced in September 1998. Napster, aimed at allowing people to share their music collections, was released in June 1999. Blogger, one of the first platforms for people with opinions or expert knowledge to share their thoughts with a dedicated audience, appeared in August 1999. Investment money poured into these and a host of other ventures. It became unsustainable. A recession in Japan in March 2000 triggered the bursting of the dot-com bubble. By 2004, less than half the dot-com companies founded in the mid-1990s were still in operation. Out of the carnage of that cull came a generation of better-founded ideas backed by more astute investors; these are the names that dominate the industry as digital communications enters its fourth decade. Facebook was started in February 2004, just as the dot-com bubble was about to burst. YouTube was launched a year later. Twitter got started in March 2006, and Netflix moved from delivering DVDs into streaming video online at the beginning of 2007.

In June the same year, there was a seminal moment in the revolution when Apple began selling the first iPhone. Competition to provide rival mobile devices became very fierce very quickly. And the phone element of these hand-held machines quickly became merely an add-on to a host of other applications that were a harbinger of things to come.

The dawn of the fifth generation (5G) of mobile networks promises another leap in the revolution that was beyond imagination only a few years ago. The new capacity will expand mobile networks to support many more devices and services than has been possible to date. It will allow for the creation of new industries with improved performance, efficiency, and cost.

It will redefine a range of industries that have come to depend on digital communications, such as retail, education, transportation, entertainment, and a multitude of others. When matched with artificial intelligence, 5G and the even faster and larger mobile networks that will inevitably follow, humanity will enter an age of technological revolution that may well affect daily lives more profoundly than the arrival of household electricity.

Futurists are asking whether in this new world human beings will actually be able to determine their own futures. There is a real fear that, once started, the symbiotic relationship between artificial intelligence and its host machines for digital communications will make human intervention unnecessary. One of the most prominent thinkers on this stage is Dr. Douglas Rushkoff, professor of media theory and digital economics at the City University of New York. Rushkoff, an acolyte of Canadian media philosopher Marshall McLuhan, holds that the digital revolution has been hijacked by business interests. As a result, digital media have lost their promise of becoming an uninhibited highway for human interaction. Instead, operations like Facebook, Google, YouTube, Twitter, and other social media platforms have turned their customers into commodities. What they see on these sites, who they meet, the ideas that are placed before them — all are geared to herding them toward particular goods and services the record of their online behaviour says they are likely to purchase. Rushkoff's quest is to retrieve human control and autonomy in the digital age. The turning of human beings into commodities has profound social and political implications, and it is clear that there is already a good deal of ground to recover.

Rushkoff's *bête noire* is Facebook; Rana Foroohar, associate editor at the *Financial Times*, has similar antipathy toward Google, the biggest political lobbyist in the US. In her book *Don't Be Evil: The Case Against Big Tech*, published at the end of 2019, she argues that big Silicon Valley companies have succeeded in nullifying the effectiveness of the federal government departments that ought to be overseeing them. Foroohar shows that, far from being stimulators of innovation, Big Tech companies gobble up small start-up ventures or use lax patent protection laws to steal their ideas.

Meanwhile, their main drive is to promote the psychology of addiction among the hundreds of millions of people who use their sites. Foroohar has little faith that this or any US government will bring the Big Tech companies to heel. She has more confidence that it will be the European Union that imposes regulations on the companies, and she puts forward several suggestions, such as taxing income at its source rather than allowing accountants to construct fictions that these enterprises are managed from tax havens. Her arguments were both reinforced and eroded in 2019 when French President Emmanuel Macron proposed to tax American digital companies operating in France. US President Donald Trump rushed to protect the tech giants and threatened to impose a 100 percent tax on French wine and cheese imports. Macron backed down.

Digital technology has already had a huge impact on mass communications and, through that, on how politics and social intercourse function. The world of contemporary news gathering and dissemination is almost unrecognizable when held up next to media in 1989. There have been vast shifts in the way people acquire daily news — or don't — and the fallout from those changing habits has been the near total destruction and then the reconstruction of mass communication. Indeed, while traditional news outlets such as newspapers, magazines, radio, and television wither and die as their revenues disappear, one of the most vibrant industries to rise from the flames is the business of analyzing what is happening to the news media. The shelves of university libraries and better bookstores creak under the weight of books and treatises exploring every conceivable aspect of the rolling revolution that has overtaken news media. The upheaval generated by technological change is one thing, but more central to the issue of the importance of reliable information to the working of democracy is a rapidly declining lack of faith in the news media across Europe and North America.

The Reuters Institute for the Study of Journalism, based in Oxford, England, says in its 2019 report that trust in the media worldwide continues to slip by around 2 percent a year; it is currently 42 percent. But there are significant differences between countries, even those of the

North Atlantic. In Canada and several European countries, trust in mass media remains strong, though not overwhelmingly so. A survey in 2019 by the German data portal Statista found the highest level of trust was in Finland at 59 percent, closely followed by Portugal at 58 percent and Denmark at 57 percent. The Netherlands and Canada tied for fourth place at 52 percent. Several surveys show that events can quickly and sharply affect public trust in the media. The Reuters Institute survey says that in France over the course of 2018–2019, trust in the media as a reliable source of information fell by eleven percentage points to just 24 percent, largely because of the way the riots and other clashes associated with the yellow vest movement were reported. Americans, too, remain largely mistrustful of the mass media at 41 percent, according to a Gallup poll covering the same period as the Reuters survey. Disturbing as this number may be, it's well above the record low of 32 percent in 2016 when Republicans' trust of news media dropped precipitously and drove the overall level of confidence in the media down during the divisive presidential campaign. The gap in the view of the mainstream media between Republicans and Democrats is extraordinary, yet another example of the dangerous polarization of American society: 69 percent of Democrats say they have trust and confidence in mainstream media, while only 15 percent of Republicans say the same.

Trust in the media is also affected by level of education. A Reuters Institute poll for its 2019 report found that across the countries it surveyed, 26 percent of respondents said they had started relying on "reputable" sources of news and a further 24 percent said they had stopped using sources that had dubious reputations. Within those numbers, however, are significant differences depending on education levels. In the United States, among those with the highest levels of education, 47 percent said they had started seeking out reputable sources of news. Among the less well educated, only 18 percent said they looked for dependable information. The figures are similar in the United Kingdom, with 35 percent of the better educated wanting reliable news and only 20 percent of the lesser educated.

Conviction that the media is part of the establishment and is biased against segments of society or political parties is common throughout the North Atlantic countries. There are, however, several factors that have made people mistrustful of their news media and the information it brings. The first is the overwhelming volume of news, information, analysis, and outright propaganda that washes over even the most determined, discerning, and loyal consumer of daily news. Coupled with that has been the irresponsible, confused, and inconsistent response to the digital revolution by traditional news outlets.

The mounting difficulty the audience has had as the revolution progressed in hanging on to information sources they felt could be trusted has been compounded by media outlets mashing together news and opinion into a messy stew. That has made it easy for demagogues and despots to lash out at the media, portraying outlets as purveyors of falsehoods — "fake news" — or as the electronic equivalent of partisan piffle sheets.

Shrinking trust has led to shrinking revenues for news outlets, in particular the closure of legions of local newspapers, opening the door to corruption and political trickery at the municipal and regional level. The degradation of professional, trustworthy media has created a vicious cycle in which misinformation and purposeful disinformation flourish.

The one overriding factor in many of the countries of the North Atlantic is that the media has lost the people's trust because the outlets no longer reflect the interests and anxieties of the mainstreams of their populations. In far too many democracies, the media has become the voice of the establishment, chanting and sometimes leading the chorus of liberal shibboleths that large segments of the population have either come to fear or no longer agree with. One of the unusual creations of this age of disruption is liberal despotism. Another trend that has crept in is the belief that news will not attract an audience unless it is dramatic and entertaining. This development is most evident among the twenty-four-hour news channels such as CNN, MSNBC, and Fox News in the United States, the BBC in the United Kingdom, and even the CBC and CTV in Canada. The American channels have abandoned the pretence of carrying news and serious, competent analysis; instead, most of their programming day is taken up with what amounts to political propaganda and theatrics. The BBC World Service still manages to be a reasonably reliable global news outlet, but there is an unnecessary and often counterproductively aggressive style of questioning among its interviewers. In Canada, the CBC stands out as an agent for the promotion of social liberalism. The choices it makes about the relative newsworthiness of events and the topics it chooses for features are a performance of political correctness and are far too often detached from the concerns of many Canadians.

This detachment from the mainstream of their societies is not limited to the twenty-four-hour TV channels. In 2016, much of the media in the UK failed to understand what was driving voters in the stagnating blue-collar central and northern regions to vote for Brexit. The obvious conclusion is that too many reporters were listening to the message from bankers and politicians that it would be cataclysmic for the UK to leave the European Union. They were not listening to the voters in the regions of dying industries, who saw Brussels and the EU bureaucracy as a threat to their identity and sense of self-worth. What is astonishing is that after that experience, the bulk of the media made the same mistake again in the December 2019 general election, many of them portraying the campaigns as a tight race between the governing Conservatives, led by Boris Johnson, and the Labour Party, led by Jeremy Corbyn. Even from a distance, it was evident that Johnson's simple message of "Let's get Brexit done" and his air of energy and optimism for the UK's future prospects were far more likely to appeal to even traditional Labour voters than the dour recitation of decades-old socialist cant offered by Corbyn.

It was the same story in the United States ahead of the 2016 presidential election. By and large, the mainstream media could not imagine that conservative and religious American voters would vote for Donald Trump. There was no question, after all, that he was a persistent liar and narcissist with a very public record of adultery and betrayal of friends and relatives. He had a history of dishonesty and failure as a businessman, and his only claim to fame was starring as a sociopathic tycoon in a television show. Reporters didn't bother to go to the states where America's disenchanted voters lived to ask them how they evaluated their choices in the election. Trump's barking that the media is an enemy of the state is a dangerous idea to put in the minds of his followers. But there can be little question that the media in the United States, as in the United Kingdom, Canada, and democratic Europe, needs a period of introspection in order to redefine its role in an age of information overload.

A 2018 study done in the US for the Knight Foundation by the Gallup organization found that 58 percent of adult Americans thought the increased amount of news and information that accompanied the digital revolution made it harder for them to be well informed. On the other side, 38 percent of respondents thought more information made it easier to keep up to date with national and international events. The Reuters Institute for the Study of Journalism looked at the same issue in 2019 and found that the problem of overload is worst in the US, the market with the largest and most persistent bombardment by "news." Predictably, in countries where the number of news outlets is smaller, public anxiety is correspondingly lower. In Denmark, only 20 percent of respondents to the Reuters survey found the volume of news overwhelming, and in the Czech Republic the number was 16 percent.

Reuters found respondents had adopted a simple answer to the problem of a surfeit of news: "More people say they actually avoid news — thirty-two percent — than when we last asked this question two years ago. Avoidance is up six percentage points overall and eleven points in the UK, driven by boredom, anger, or sadness over Brexit. People say they avoid the news because it has a negative effect on their mood — fifty-eight percent — or because they feel powerless to change events."

It would have been easier for news consumers if the established media, and newspapers in particular, had in the 1990s better comprehended the enormity of the approaching revolution in mass communications and reacted appropriately. They did not. Many newspapers believed their readers would remain loyal to the culture of printed paper and the sense of command over events that goes with the physical possession of a newspaper. Some proprietors had nagging doubts that tactile nostalgia was not going to be enough. They tiptoed cautiously into the digital era, usually by posting a faithful copy of their print edition on a web page. These looked odd and didn't last long.

From the start, there was confusion about revenue and where the money was going to come from to pay for the journalism that readers were increasingly absorbing from their computer screens. Many newspapers took the plunge and gave free access to their online editions. They saw circulation revenue plummet because no one was paying for subscriptions. Some swallowed hard and charged for the web editions by putting up paywalls. They also saw circulation and revenue plummet as readers gravitated to the multitude of free news sites that were now available. As the new century gathered pace, readers became more and more used to having access to free news on the web. It got to the point where many expected news to be free, almost as a human right, and saw no justification for paying for it.

Advertising revenue for traditional media inevitably began declining in line with subscriptions, readership, and audiences. Publishers began closing newspapers that were recording astonishing losses at a dramatic rate, or cutting staff to the bare bones to get costs in line with shrinking revenues. All too often, these cuts affected the quality of the journalism and made the product vastly less attractive and useful than it had been. Those that managed to survive frequently did so by making themselves into multimedia platforms. Their reporters would use Twitter to send instant messages from a news scene while also using their phones to record videos to be posted on the newspaper's website. In theory, when the reporters finally got around to writing a story for the newspaper, it would be the complete account of the event, bolstered by context and analysis. That outcome, however, tended to be the exception.

A few metropolitan daily newspapers, like *The New York Times*, *The Guardian*, *The Sydney Morning Herald*, and Hong Kong's *South China Morning Post*, are robust enough to survive and thrive in the new age. They have done this, however, by becoming international products with global audiences as the World Wide Web has extended their reach. Meanwhile, a new generation of news sites has begun to poke its head above the chaos of the revolution. These are newspapers — for want of a better word — with all the journalistic virtues of a classic news publication but designed exclusively for digital production. Again, finding a reliable revenue stream is a common problem. Advertisers do not believe the news audience is as receptive to ads in online publications as they are in print editions and therefore pay much less for space in digital news sources. In response, many online news outlets include advertising that is far more pervasive and intrusive than in the past; others have constructed subscription paywalls or various donation and financial trust schemes.

It has taken a few years, but many people for whom a daily diet of news and current affairs is important have come to realize that the era of free information was a snare and a delusion. There has been a distinct growth in Europe and North America of people taking out subscriptions for one or more online news outlet. The most dedicated daily news subscribers are in the Nordic countries. The proportion of adults in Norway who subscribe to a daily news outlet is 34 percent, in Sweden 27 percent, and in Finland 16 percent. Canada still has only 9 percent, but there has been an interesting twist in the US. In 2016, the number of people subscribing to news there was in steady decline and had shrunk to only 8 percent. But the election of Trump that year appears to have awakened many Americans to the need for reliable information in uncertain times. The percentage of Americans subscribing to a daily news feed doubled to 16 percent in 2017 and has stayed there since.

Among the young, both in Europe and North America, the trend is to garner news online rather than from radio, television, or newspapers. A 2018 Pew Research Center report found that among young people aged eighteen to twenty-nine, the main daily news source for 73 percent was online, with television and radio coming in distant second and third, and only 12 percent using newspapers. More than that, another Pew survey in 2018 found that in the US, 64.5 percent of Internet users got their breaking news from social media. Of those, 43 percent relied on

Facebook, 21 percent on YouTube, and 12 percent on Twitter. The survey found that a strong proportion of those people — 57 percent — then went on to a news site to read more fully about the story that had caught their attention on social media. However, because social media contacts tend to be like-minded, and because Facebook and similar companies manage their sites to appeal to people's preferences, readers are unlikely to be exposed to ideas outside their preconceptions.

Social media is a threat to democracy, even without the intervention of outside players such as Russia. Governments in North America and Europe must at some point — preferably sooner rather than later — assert that operations like Facebook, Twitter, YouTube, and the myriad of other social media platforms are publishers and not just chat rooms or virtual social meeting places, as they like to insist. These companies must be told very clearly by means of legislation and regulation that they are the new Fourth Estate in the hierarchy of democratic institutions. With that status comes binding responsibilities to present citizens with truthful information, professionally sorted, and to hold those in power to account.

THE COVID-19 PANDEMIC in 2020 was an overwhelming media event both for good and for ill. On the plus side, the worldwide audience for news was out hunting for reliable sources of information about the virus, its potency, how its spread should be addressed, and the likely efficacy of the responses being put forward by political leaders and public health officials. The issue quickly dominated the twenty-four-hour news cycle to the exclusion of almost all other news stories. And even those other topics — sports, arts, everything — very quickly became news only to the degree that they could be viewed through the COVID-19 lens. Inevitably, the quality of the journalistic response to the coronavirus story has been uneven. Some of that was because journalism is, like all professions, crewed by people and institutions with a wide variety of skills and judgment. It was also because the story itself was rapidly evolving as doctors and scientists learned more about what COVID-19 is and how it behaves. Those bumps evened out rapidly, and by early April there were reasonably consistent descriptions in the news media of what the virus is, how it is transmitted, how infection runs its course through the human body, and how best to prevent the virus running rampant. The most dangerous role played by some media was to pass on to the public speculative remedies or ways of preventing infection. Some of these bits of quackery got into professional news media, but most of the stories were passed on through social media channels. Some of the misinformation included claims that drinking a lot of water or taking a potion of diluted chlorine would stop infection or cure the illness. A few people died from the effects of this advice. In the US, where quack remedies are a largely unregulated medical fringe, there was an outburst of advertising for various potions. Even evangelicals got into the act, with some ministers advertising remedies that they claimed had the additional benefit of religious blessing. Quackery even reached into the White House when US President Trump began promoting the anti-malaria drug hydroxychloroquine. Most medical experts were strongly opposed to use of the drug, which can cause strong and even lethal reactions. Several newspapers produced evidence that the Trump family business had invested in hydroxychloroquine.

In most countries of the North Atlantic, the governments and health authorities responded to the quack remedies by producing short and clear statements on how best to minimize the chances of getting infected by COVID-19 and what to do if symptoms emerged. The media reproduced these statements, and by and large reporters followed the rules themselves as they did their jobs. There were some worrying turns, however, when governments began imposing states of emergency in order to give themselves the powers they felt necessary to confront the virus. Some governments tacked on sweeping restrictions of the news media under the guise of preventing misinformation and the dissemination of fake news.

Early in April, *Columbia Journalism Review* published a compendium of information it had gathered from around the world about media crack-downs by various governments, most of them with a penchant for despotism at the best of times. Venezuela had arrested a journalist for reporting on the extent of the COVID-19 infection in that country. Iran imposed restrictions on what could be reported about the virus and its spread. Egypt pressured reporters to limit their coverage of the number of infections and reprimanded several foreign journalists for not obeying these rules. Turkey, already one of the worst countries for imprisoning journalists, detained seven for their reporting. And when, in mid-April, Turkey decided to free ninety thousand detainees so that coronavirus infections would not run riot through prisons, journalist detainees were explicitly excluded from the amnesty. South Africa has cherished its reputation as one of the few havens of press freedom in Africa, but when it adopted emergency measures in March, they included making the publishing of disinformation about COVID-19 a criminal offence. As was previously mentioned, in Hungary, emergency measures made publishing false information punishable by up to five years in prison, with the government deciding what constituted false information.

These measures against the media in the context of the imposition of emergency powers in general have raised questions among civil rights activists about when these powers will be lifted. The historical record suggests politicians and officials are slow to lift restraints once imposed, and it is common for not all the restrictions to be withdrawn even when the emergency is clearly over.

CHAPTER ELEVEN

—

Trolls, Bots, and Deepfakes

IN MARCH 2018, *The New York Times* in the United States and *The Observer* in the United Kingdom reported their investigations into the political consulting company Cambridge Analytica Ltd. These reports appeared to confirm all the prevailing fears about manipulating voters' decisions. The two newspapers said the company had acquired personal data on 270,000 Facebook users from a researcher who had gathered the material with the permission of Facebook. The profiles had been passed on with the agreement of the Facebook users for development of an app called "This Is Your Digital Life." However, Cambridge Analytica was given access to the app and the data without any of the caveats and restrictions the researcher had followed. As a result, Cambridge Analytica was able to tap into all the Facebook friends of the 270,000 users in the study, amounting in total to about 87 million people.

The newspaper articles were based on material leaked by a Cambridge Analytica employee, Canadian data consultant Christopher Wylie. "We exploited Facebook to harvest millions of people's profiles," Wylie told *The Observer*, "and built models to exploit what we knew about them and target their inner demons. That was the basis the entire company was built on."

That quote about targeting inner demons sums up a multitude of fears about the powers of geeks in basements with laptops. The film and television industry has created multiple narratives about twisted masterminds who, with a few keyboard instructions, can change the course of history. It was but a short stretch to suggest that people could be sent out to vote as instructed by their cell phones. This was the fantasy Cambridge Analytica was selling.

The story took on a more salacious aspect the day after the newspaper stories appeared, when BBC Channel 4 News aired the result of a four-month investigation of Cambridge Analytica, including undercover footage of an interview with the company's CEO, Alexander Nix. The reporter posed as someone working for a candidate in a Sri Lankan election wanting to see what services Cambridge Analytica could offer. In the video, Nix, in the full flood of salesmanship, says the company had worked on over two hundred elections around the world and was skilled in using honey traps, bribery, and prostitutes to discredit opposing candidates. After the program was broadcast, Nix swiftly backtracked, saying the editing of the video misrepresented the conversation, while admitting that as part of his sales pitch he had "entertained a series of ludicrous hypothetical scenarios." The company immediately suspended Nix, saying the allegations did not represent the ethics of the company.

Cambridge Analytica worked on the campaign of Leave.EU, one of the organizations pressing voters to support the UK leaving the European Union in the June 2016 referendum. At the same time, it also worked on Donald Trump's presidential campaign, after having been hired by Ted Cruz's team during the primaries. The inference to be drawn from the stories was that Cambridge Analytica had used its skills in the so-called dark arts of psychographics to develop profiles of and manipulate enough voters to win the referendum for Brexit and the presidency for Trump. Psychographics is the theory that populations can be classified according to attitudes or fears. At Cambridge University's Psychometrics Centre, Michal Kosinski postulated that a psychological profile of an individual can be created by analyzing even a small number of "likes" they make on Facebook. He used as his base the five personality attributes developed by psychologists: openness, conscientiousness, extroversion/introversion, agreeableness, and neuroticism. Kosinski's work was taken up by an American psychologist of Soviet heritage, Aleksandr Kogan. Kogan, who sometimes went by the name "Dr. Spectre," fashioned Kosinski's work into an app that allowed Cambridge Analytica to mine the data it had acquired from Facebook.

Cambridge Analytica had raised eyebrows from the company's birth in 2013. It was founded by Robert Mercer, a hedge fund operator and major financier of right-wing political causes in the US and Europe. Mercer's investments include Breitbart News, a libertarian online propaganda sheet then run by Steve Bannon. Mercer is widely reported to have stumped up US$15 million and Bannon to have put in US$1 million or so to start Cambridge Analytica. The company said it was involved in forty-four campaigns in the 2014 cycle of elections in the US, and soon afterwards it was taken on by the Ted Cruz presidential campaign. But the Cruz campaign fired Cambridge Analytica in February 2016 after seeing clear evidence that the psychographic technique was failing to identifying potential Cruz supporters in any number and with any consistency. One Cruz campaign aide told *The New York Times*, "more than half the Oklahoma voters whom Cambridge had identified as Cruz supporters actually favoured other candidates."

Cambridge Analytica's backers, Mercer and Bannon, were already deeply involved in the Trump campaign, and the company shifted loyalties without difficulty. Mercer was running a Super PAC called Make America Number 1, which supported Trump and campaigned on his behalf.

Super PACs grew out of a 2010 Supreme Court ruling that determined that political action committees are legally able to collect unlimited amounts of money to support candidates and parties, but they are barred from coordinating those activities with the people and parties they support. Super PACs operate, in theory, at arm's length from the campaigns. They often finance and produce the nastier aspects of the campaigns, especially attack ads aimed at opponents. Cambridge Analytica CEO Nix referred to this in the undercover video broadcast by Channel 4 News. He said Make

America Number 1 handled all the negative attacks on Democrats and presidential candidate Hillary Clinton, thus allowing the Trump campaign to "take the high road." Nix implied that there was coordination between the campaign and the Super PAC, though this has been denied by the company and has never been fully investigated. More than that, any separation from Trump would appear to have been superfluous. No one could accuse Trump of taking the high road and being gentlemanly in his dealings with Clinton during the campaign.

Under the warped political system in the US, Trump lost the popular vote in 2016, but Clinton's additional 2.86 million votes counted for nothing because Americans don't vote directly for the presidential candidate. They vote in each state for candidates for the Electoral College, who in turn vote for the president according to rules set out by the various states' legislatures. By this count, Clinton lost conclusively. Trump won 304 Electoral College votes, and she received 227. This was the fifth occasion in the history of the United States when a candidate has won the presidency while losing the popular vote. The disparity was because much of Clinton's support was in the most populous states, California and New York. Trump, how-ever, won four crucial states by less than 1.2 percent of the vote. His tight victories in Florida, Pennsylvania, Wisconsin, and Michigan handed him the presidency. This raises the question of whether Cambridge Analytica's campaign of aiming Facebook and other social media propaganda at small numbers of susceptible voters in critical districts turned the election for Trump.

There are no convincing arguments that it did.

In a *New York Times* article in February 2018, Brendan Nyhan, profes-sor of government at Dartmouth College in New Hampshire, wrote, "a growing number of studies conclude ... that most forms of political persuasion seem to have little effect at all." Nyhan went on to explain that much more needs to be learned about the effects on elections of online advertising such as that placed by Cambridge Analytica and of the mes-sages put out by Russian trolls and bots. "But people should not assume they had huge effects," he noted. Even television advertising for commercial products has a very small impact on consumers, Nyhan wrote, and "recent meta-analysis of numerous different forms of campaign persuasion, including in-person canvassing and mail, finds that their average effect in general elections is zero."

Nyhan continued, "We shouldn't be surprised — it's hard to change people's minds! Their votes are shaped by fundamental factors like which party they typically support and how they view the state of the economy. 'Fake news' and bots are likely to have vastly smaller effects, especially given how polarized our politics have become."

He also warned that while the numbers involved in the promotion of disinformation and misinformation may sound massive, they are often small when put in context. While Twitter reported that Russian bots had tweeted 2.1 million times on behalf of Trump before the election, this represented only 1 percent of all election-related tweets and only 0.5 percent of election tweets that were actually looked at by voters. Equally, studies done by Andrew Guess of Princeton in partnership with Jason Reifer at the University of Exeter in the UK found that only 40 percent of Trump supporters visited fake news websites. Among those people, however, the visits to pro-Trump fake news sites represented only 6 percent of their total news intake.

Other academics in the field agree with Nyhan that the microtargeting of voters is little understood and probably doesn't work. Eitan Hersh, a professor of political science at Tufts University and author of *Hacking the Electorate: How Campaigns Perceive Voters*, wrote that there is clearly a relationship between people's personality traits and their political values, but that relationship is weak. Therefore, it can be counterproductive for a political campaign to use consumer purchasing patterns as a basis for targeting partisan messages. Hersh said his research showed that predicting whether or not someone is Latino based on their name and where they live was right only two-thirds of the time. Further research showed that people who wrongly received campaign material intended for Latinos often didn't like it, and it soured their view of the candidate involved. This skepticism was summed up in comments made by Tom Dobber, a doctoral candidate studying political microtargeting at the University of Amsterdam, in the wake of the Cambridge Analytica revelations. "We don't really know much about the effects of microtargeting, let alone targeting on the basis of someone's psyche," he said. "I think Cambridge Analytica is a better marketing company than a targeting company."

Dobber makes a good point. Smothered under the bafflegab of the Cambridge Analytica promotional material lies the essential question about the ultimate value of microtargeting the personalities and predilections of voters. Human beings are not automatons. There is no reset button that can change or reverse their political or social preferences simply by subjecting them to a deluge of advertisements. The most Cambridge Analytica could hope to achieve was to encourage someone to vote or dissuade them from voting. The ability to direct votes one way or another appears to be negligible at best.

The fallout from the Cambridge Analytica affair was fast and furious. Bannon had parted ties with the company when he joined Trump's White House staff early in 2017. Two days after the first news reports of the scandal, on March 20, 2018, the value of the market capitalization of Facebook dropped by US$37 billion. Surveys found that as a result of Facebook having sold personal data that became political ammunition, only 41 percent of Facebook users trusted the company. Official investigations into the company's actions were launched in both the US and the UK. On May 1, 2018, Cambridge Analytica and its parent company, the SCL Group (subsequently reformed as Emerdata Ltd.), filed for bankruptcy and closed down operations.

———

AMONG WELL-QUALIFIED OBSERVERS, there is a belief that the Russian trolls and bots, with their focus on turning voters' established political convictions into anger, were more effective than Cambridge Analytica in tipping the election in Trump's favour. James Clapper, the Director of National Intelligence from mid-2010 until the inauguration of the Trump administration, said in an interview with *The New Yorker*, published in

September 2018, "it stretches credulity to think the Russians didn't turn the election." Kathleen Hall Jamieson, professor of communications at the University of Pennsylvania, bases her judgment on a combination of experience and circumstantial evidence. The title of her book, *Cyber: How Russian Hackers and Trolls Helped Elect a President — What We Don't, Can't and Do Know*, sums up her certainties and ambivalences. Her book also underlines that tracking and calculating the impact of cyber attacks on elections is still a new science with much basic work to be done.

The cyber invasion of the 2016 US presidential election by Russia and its now infamous St. Petersburg "troll farm," the Internet Research Agency, was a far more professional operation than whatever it was Cambridge Analytica did. The IRA began operations in 2013 with the objective of influencing online communications, mainly social media chatter, to promote Russian interests. For the most part, this involved trying to intensify political polarization and social confrontation in the target countries of Europe and North America. It is a distinctive human trait to respond vigorously to drama, and social media has intensified the impact of this weakness. People are more likely to trust wrong information if it makes them angry or mirrors what they already believe. If they are angry or outraged, they are more likely to share the story with their social media connections. The Russians work on the theory that over time, playing on these weaknesses can create societies that are politically and socially polarized and are misinformed about central issues. To try to create these instabilities in North Atlantic countries, IRA operatives — trolls —use artificial social media accounts to inject increasingly aggressive and divisive elements into the online conversations. The IRA also uses automated scripts — bots — designed to spread disinformation. It also sometimes uses paid advertisements, as it did on Facebook to boost Trump in the 2016 US election.

The Russian efforts to disturb the 2016 presidential election left a clear trail of the IRA's activities. In the spring of 2019, NATO published a paper that is an early step in a strategic counterattack. Two academics, John D. Gallacher, a doctoral student in cyber security at Oxford University, and

Dr. Marc Heerdink, a professor of social psychology at the University of Amsterdam, studied the IRA footprints in order to develop methods for measuring the impact of disinformation operations. Such measuring tools are necessary in order to be able to judge the risks posed by this form of cyber warfare and to calculate accurately the effects they have had on democratic elections. Heerdink and Gallacher picked one issue that emerged during the course of the campaign that had clear boundaries and distinct protagonists. The Black Lives Matter movement arose over clear evidence that US police were far more likely to shoot to kill a black person when responding to an incident than they were a white person. Opposing movements were established on social media, arguing that the lives of police officers and white people matter too. Gallacher and Heerdink further refined their model by tracking IRA activities on just two social media forums: the social networking service Twitter and Reddit, a discussion website where registered members submit material that is then voted up or down by other members.

The NATO study found that the IRA operatives intervened on all sides of the Black Lives Matter debate, inserting provocative messages aimed at fostering antagonism. "On Twitter, increases in Russian IRA activity predicted subsequent increases in the degree of polarisation of the conversation surrounding the Black Lives Matter movement," stated the report. "On Reddit, comment threads started by Russian IRA accounts contained more toxic language and identity-based attacks." The study found clear evidence that on Twitter, the IRA succeeded in heightening the polarization of the debate. But Gallacher and Heerdink found there was a time lag as the tweets posted by the IRA worked their way around the audience. The polarized effect usually peaked between the seventh and ninth day after the intervention. The level of invective then slowly subsided. On Reddit, the study found, the Russians used far more toxic language and personal attacks than did genuine threads. The reaction and the buildup of aggressive, angry, and hate-filled dialogue was much faster than on Twitter.

Gallacher and Heerdink wrote, "While it remains to be seen whether these online effects translate into offline actions, there is evidence that

online activities can have substantial effects on real world behaviour ....
Our research also shows that online interaction between groups predicts
offline violence." The pair said their work has demonstrated the risk of
future vulnerabilities in the social media forums used among the North
Atlantic democracies: the ability of hostile actors to create or heighten
social and political divisions is increasing with technological advances
such as machine-generated text that closely resembles human speech. The
creation of deepfake videos — essentially fabricated but genuine-seeming
animations of real people that show influential public figures and politicians
saying or doing things they never actually said or did — could also be a risk.
"If this technology is paired with malicious intent to drive communities
apart using social media platforms, then the volume of content may well
expand and increase the severity of the challenge to detecting inauthentic
content and oppose it," Gallacher and Heerdink concluded.

Under pressure from regulators on both sides of the Atlantic, and facing
the adverse reaction of stock markets, Facebook and Twitter have made
several attempts to prevent misuse of their platforms and to increase their
transparency. Facebook has created a database of all political advertisements
it carries and gives periodic reports on all types of manipulation it detects
and removes. Twitter informed all 1.4 million users who got caught up in
the network of messages and comments spread by the IRA what had happened. The company expressed the hope that this experience will give
them some immunity to similar attacks in the future. Facebook has also
introduced new rules about the type of political advertising it will allow
in the future. Both companies have beefed up the algorithms deployed
to detect automated or manipulated accounts. These measures appear to
have been reasonably successful. Twitter found 232 million accounts that
showed signs of being bots in the first half of 2018 alone. Facebook removed
2.8 billion fake accounts during the period between October 2017 and
November 2018. Facebook has also made changes to reduce the effects
of malicious material on its main platform. This includes fact-checking
suspect material, reducing the image size of questionable posts, and loosing
automated tools to detect headlines whose sole objective is to serve as

clickbait that viewers will be tempted to share. Twitter has made it harder to set up large volumes of fake accounts quickly, and Facebook has created a group whose responsibility is to prevent election interference.

This, however, is a running battle. As the highly respected UK-based global risk assessment company Oxford Analytica — which has been at pains to firmly point out it has no relationship of any kind with Cambridge Analytica — wrote in a May 2019 assessment of election meddling, "These changes may be ineffective in preventing future interference." There are strong indications that Russia's IRA is moving away from what are now traditional and established social media sites like Facebook and Twitter and is following young people and fringe groups to sites such as Instagram, 4chan, and Gab. The Russians expect that "such activity will be harder to detect because it will be spread and shared by genuine users, and so will appear unsuspicious to the newly introduced algorithms and machine-trained classifiers."

The Oxford Analytica paper said it also expects "malicious actors will focus on image and video content" rather than text-based messages as at present. "This will be much harder to monitor due to the great level of nuance that can be included, and also because groups are likely to become more internet-savvy and embed themselves in groups they wish to influence, repurposing the 'memes' they use to communicate." Rapid increases in the evolution of artificial intelligence systems make it possible to produce convincing deepfake videos. There was a small hint of what might come in May 2019, when a US right-wing website slowed down a video of House Speaker Nancy Pelosi speaking and altered the pitch of her voice. The result was that she appeared to be slurring her words as though drunk or suffering a medical condition. This fake video was tweeted by Trump and attracted millions of views. There was another political victim of a purposefully doctored video in the November 2019 election campaign for the Parliament of the United Kingdom. Video of an interview with a senior opposition Labour Party figure, Sir Keir Starmer, was cut so that it appeared he refused to answer some key campaign questions and was then posted online. In May 2018, a left-wing political party in Belgium re-edited a video of Donald Trump to make it appear as though he was specifically criticizing Belgium for upholding the Paris climate agreement. The party acknowledged what it had done and said it was only trying to draw attention to the issue.

NOT ALL DISINFORMATION on the Internet is aimed directly at political targets or at sowing social strife, but it achieves serious social consequences nonetheless. Human society has always had a propensity for blaming unexpected or inexplicable events on unseen forces with dominant powers. Sometimes these anxieties have been codified into religion. On other occasions, these fears appear as conspiracy theories that fester and mutate as they worm their way through society. The Internet has provided a superhighway for conspiracy theories to travel and gather acolytes as they spread. Three current issues attracting conspiracy theories are vaccinations, climate change, and the 5G network spreading the COVID-19 virus.

The World Health Organization said in August 2019 that reported cases of measles "are the highest they have been in any year since 2006." In the United Kingdom, there were 989 cases of measles in 2018, up from just 91 in 2015. There was a similar dramatic rise in the United States, where the Centers for Disease Control reported 1,249 cases in the first nine months of 2019, up from 375 cases for the whole of 2018. This outbreak of a very serious and sometimes deadly illness is being blamed on parents not getting their babies inoculated with the measles, mumps, and rubella (MMR) vaccine. Many parents were convinced to avoid the vaccine by a study published in the UK medical journal *The Lancet* in 1998 linking the MMR vaccine with autism. The article and the claim were withdrawn in the face of criticism of the lack of scientific evidence. A host of studies since have clearly shown the MMR vaccine has nothing to do with children becoming autistic. But fear among parents continued to be stoked online by groups of militant opponents of any vaccinations for children. In response, public health officials throughout Europe and North America have launched an information counterattack, with significant success. But this clear example of the social consequences of widely disseminated misinformation is a warning that other aspects of medical advice available online need to be looked at closely for its origins and veracity.

One of the immediate repercussions of the COVID-19 pandemic in 2020 was an accelerated drop in the number of children being inoculated against measles. However, this was because of people observing home isolation instructions and the national medical systems focusing on combating the coronavirus. Some public health officials in North America and Europe expressed the hope that experience of the reality of a pandemic, which would continue to be a threat to daily life until a vaccine was developed, might persuade misguided parents of the value of the measles inoculation.

The increasingly common habit by people who feel unwell of consulting "Doctor Google" before seeing a medical professional has the potential to become a serious problem. There are already many examples of the Internet providing a happy hunting ground for quackery and the sale of questionable potions and wonder treatments being marketed as remedies for all manner of illnesses and diseases. In response, health authorities in Europe and North America have found it necessary to deploy their own social media teams to try to counter the falsehoods and fanciful claims being made online by ignorant activists and greedy snake oil merchants.

Climate change — and human culpability for it — is an issue that touches a multitude of political, financial, and other interests. Among scientists, there is no doubt that global warming is caused by pollution created by human beings. That's the judgment expressed in 97 percent of papers on the subject published by accredited scientists. But a surprising number of people prefer not to believe the scientists. The problem is especially acute in the US, where less than 50 percent of adults believe climate change is the result of human activity, and, even worse, fewer than 40 percent think scientists can be trusted on the issue. There are many reasons for this reluctance to see the obvious. In the US, religious fundamentalism is undoubtedly a factor. The results of polls differ depending how the question is asked, but between 30 and 40 percent of Americans reject Charles Darwin's theory of evolution and the understanding of human and global natural history that has flowed from it. They believe, often with utter certainty, that human beings were created between six and seven and a half thousand years ago, exactly as described in the Bible. With that view of society goes a reluctance to accept the word of scientists on many topics, of which climate change is but one. This has provided a willing audience for conservative think tanks, populist politicians, amateur bloggers, a few contrary scientists enjoying unwarranted and unexpected limelight, and some fake grassroots campaigns of unknown origin. It may be that the Russian IRA trolls and bots have latched on to climate change as an issue where it is profitable to sow discord in Western democracies. There is some evidence of that, but the Russian enthusiasm to milk this topic is not as evident as it is on others.

For some players in this drama, there is a financial motive. In 2017, a group of Harvard academics published the results of a survey they had done on the causes of climate change as described in external and internal communications at the ExxonMobil energy company. The study examined messages going back to 1977 and found that 80 percent of ExxonMobil's internal documents on the subject acknowledged that climate change is the result of human activity. However, the numbers were reversed when ExxonMobil spoke in public. Then, 81 percent of the company's pronouncements voiced doubt about human activity affecting climate change.

A major element in the opposition to the concept of anthropogenic climate change is the rejection of the expensive and culturally disruptive measures being advocated to try to reverse the course of events. Opposition is mounting to the carbon tax, a common remedy being promoted by many European and North American governments at the urging of economic advisers. The object of the tax is to reduce carbon emissions by making it more expensive to use fuels that emit airborne pollutants. This is seen as a visceral threat in some communities that are economically reliant on carbon fuel production or where the ownership of and freedom to use petroleum-driven cars, trucks, and motorbikes has become a defining cultural expression.

As the evidence builds that human-created climate change is happening now and is not just a worry for the future, this opposition is unlikely to change. What these opponents are likely to do is shift their targets to try to discredit individuals who promote actions designed to counter climate change. This is already on record in assaults on the young Swedish climate change activist Greta Thunberg and former US Vice President Al Gore, whose campaign to educate people about global warming was described in the 2006 documentary film *An Inconvenient Truth*. Personal attacks will intensify the bitterness of an already rancorous debate. The polarization will be fed by gyrations in weather such as those that caused the massive bushfires in Australia over the height of the austral summer in 2019–2020. This is also a time when the lack of clear political leadership on climate change in many democracies suggests confusion and conflicts to come. Donald Trump's withdrawal of the US from the 2015 Paris Agreement to set goals for bringing down greenhouse gas emissions has taken the wind out of the whole international effort to reduce air pollution. Yet climate change is only one issue where it is legitimate to ask whether the current political systems among North Atlantic democracies are fit to enable citizens to engage in effective debate and resolve the great social and economic issues looming on the horizon.

Again, the COVID-19 experience may influence this debate. The closing down of much of the world's industries and air and sea transportation had a profoundly positive effect on global air quality and the level of pollution. "After Europe ground to a coronavirus-enforced halt, images captured by one of the European Space Agency's (ESA) Copernicus satellites showed huge reductions in nitrogen dioxide concentrations over Paris, Madrid, and Rome from 14–25 March, compared to the same week in 2019," the online journal ScienceBusiness reported in early April 2020. "The same is true for China, where the Copernicus satellite recorded a dramatic fall in NO2 released by power stations, factories and vehicles in all major Chinese cities between late January and February. ESA also observed a decrease of around 20–30 percent in fine particulate matter, one of the most important air pollutants, in February 2020 compared to the previous three years," they wrote.

THE REAL DANGER of invasions of democratic elections through hacking or malevolent manipulation of social media is not that they will determine the outcome. It is that they will cause so much confusion and disruption that voters become distrustful of and disenchanted with the process. Donald Trump's chief strategist Steve Bannon crisply described this approach in 2018. "The Democrats don't matter," Bannon said in an interview with author Michael Lewis. "The real opposition is the media. And the way to deal with them is to flood the zone with shit." Ensuring that citizens will have confidence in the political information they receive from the Internet, especially through their social media networks, requires action on two main fronts. The first is to promote a skeptical approach and critical thinking toward all information that arrives by the World Wide Web. The second is to require online companies such as Google, Facebook, Twitter, YouTube, and the rest to acknowledge that they are publishers that must take responsibility for the material they put out. They are not, as many companies using the web try to argue, simply information highways with no involvement in the affairs of the people who use them.

Judgment, critical thinking, and the ability to weigh the relative value of events that affect daily life are the objectives of education, or they ought to be. At the heart of democracy is the freedom for citizens to make personal, social, and political choices. To that end, a fundamental objective of education is and always has been to impart critical thinking skills and the ability to weigh the relative value of events that affect daily life. The desired outcome is children who are able to discern what is true and what is not, what is important and what can be ignored. Dealing with distorted or malignant information on the Internet is essentially no different from the pitfalls people have faced throughout the ages. There are particular disciplines needed to categorize and tame the cacophony that spews endlessly from social media. Several countries have recognized that children need new skills for a new and rapidly evolving technology, but Finland is the leader. Finland is blessed with what is often judged to be the world's best education system, and it is a largely homogeneous society. Finns are certain of their own identity and nationhood. This is an important advantage when confronting online attacks from Russian trolls. It makes malevolent, socially disruptive disinformation easier to spot.

Finland has been a target of Vladimir Putin's troll campaigns to destabilize Russia's neighbouring Baltic states since the mid-2000s. The Finnish government launched its anti-disinformation program in 2014, with the aim of ensuring citizens, students, journalists, and politicians have community college programs available to show them how to identify and counter messages designed to create discord.

That's a valid response to a present danger, and several other countries are looking to the Finnish example of how to win the war against misinformation. For the future, Finland is taking the view that the first line of defence against false information is what is taught in kindergarten. A core element running through the education system is a critical thinking curriculum that provides students with the key elements of digital literacy and the skills to fact-check the information they are receiving, especially if they consider sharing it with others in their network.

⸻

THE INTERNET AND social media promised to be aids that would simplify life and enhance an individual's community involvement, so it is dispiriting to discover that the social network can be as poisonous as rumour mongering around the village well and that fact-checking is just as much of a chore as it was when the trustworthy reference material was books. The growing gap between the promise and reality of the Internet has Sir Tim Berners-Lee, the inventor of the World Wide Web, tearing his hair. At the end of 2019, he warned in a speech that the Internet threatened to become a "digital dystopia" because governments, corporations, and individuals are failing in what he sees as their duty to make the web accessible and positive. Berners-Lee produced what he calls the "Contract for the Web," which, while non-binding on its signatories, he expects will provide a blueprint to safeguard the best qualities of the web. By the end of 2019, more than 150 organizations and companies had signed up to his initiative, including major players Google, Microsoft,

Twitter, and Facebook, as well as interest groups like Reporters Without Borders and the Electronic Frontier Foundation.

Berners-Lee's contract contains nine principles and seventy-six different clauses that he believes governments, corporations, and individuals should follow. He believes access to the Internet is now a basic human right for all citizens, and this should be guaranteed by governments. At the same time, governments must respect online privacy and the personal data rights of their citizens. The EU has produced regulations in this area, and at the beginning of 2020 the US state of California began framing similar legislation.

Berners-Lee is perhaps straying into wishful thinking when his contract says the Internet should be available to all citizens at all times. Governments must not shut down access, the contract says, in order to frustrate opponents of the administration, as has happened in several countries to prevent the organization of anti-government street protests. All governments, even the most democratic ones with the greatest respect for human rights, have contingency plans for disaster scenarios. Taking direct control of all means of communication has always been among measures that can be taken in a crisis.

Corporations must make access to the Internet affordable for everyone, says the contract. This should include offering special pricing for deprived members of society. Again, corporations like governments must respect users' privacy and personal data. This principle is another area where Berners-Lee is pushing against commercial reality, because so much of the money that tech giants make out of the web comes from selling users' data to marketers.

His contract calls on individual web users to act with respect for civil discourse and human dignity. Individually and collectively they also have a duty, he says, to hold governments and corporations accountable for ensuring open access to the web.

The contract has some strong elements, but it is infused with the idealism tinged with naïveté that allowed the Internet to race beyond the control of its creator to begin with.

At one end of the spectrum, Finland's education program provides a practical response for individuals to spot the flaws in the web. At the other end of the spectrum, the NATO Strategic Communications Centre report provides suggestions for what governments might do.

"Identifying the impact of information operations is only the first step in creating counter measures. Evidence suggests that organized attempts to challenge the veracity of disinformation on Twitter are generally ineffective, while spontaneous fact-checking on Facebook is rare and generally unsuccessful. Other technical solutions should therefore focus on the early detection of artificial content before it can manipulate online conversations, or educational methods which may mitigate the effects of disinformation through inoculation of citizens," the report says in a terse postscript. "Structured changes to social media platforms promoting positive exposure to members of opposing groups will also likely reduce and dilute the impact of efforts to divide these same groups through negative contents injections. Addressing the challenge of disinformation is so broad that designing effective interventions will require interdisciplinary efforts at multiple levels of analysis."

When Berners-Lee created the World Wide Web, he produced an attractive and compelling but unruly child that is going to be a worry for a long time. But there are already signs of parental control and the promise that eventually it will become manageable.

CHAPTER TWELVE

—

Twilight of
the Demagogues

ALL OVER THE world in 2019, tens of thousands and sometimes millions of people took to the streets to bellow rage at their governments. The events that triggered this global outpouring were often minor. In Sudan, in January, the cause was an increase of a few cents on the price of bread. In Iran, in November, it was a four-cent-a-litre hike in gasoline prices. It was an increase in subway prices in Chile in October that set off protests there. In Lebanon, also in October, it was a tax on using the cell phone communications app WhatsApp.

On multiple occasions, the issues that incited riots were more substantial. New citizenship laws and refugee regulations in India, perceived as discriminating against Muslims and other non-Hindus, fuelled protests and riots across the country. These persisted and then intensified in response to harsh police methods. The introduction of legislation in Hong Kong in March to allow extradition to mainland China of people accused of crimes reawakened suspicion of Beijing that had simmered since the handover in 1997 from British colonial occupation. The extradition bill was seen by millions of Hongkongers as the latest in a succession of efforts by the Chinese Communist Party to curb freedom of speech, association, and dissent in the territory, despite promises before the handover that civic freedoms would be untouched. Public suspicion about Beijing's intentions spilled out onto the streets in June and rapidly became a mass protest in favour of fundamental political reform. On at least one occasion, two million people mounted a peaceful protest march, but there were also many violent incidents between pro-democracy activists and an increasingly impatient and aggressive police force. Seven months later, as 2020 dawned, the protests continued and the core issues were still unresolved.

The fingers of blame pointing from the streets wagged just as fiercely at the leaders of democratic governments as they did at autocrats. The global protests of 2019 were an indiscriminate outpouring of public disillusionment and frustration. The sparks that ignited the protests may have been inconsequential in many cases, but once on the streets, the protesters from Paris to Prague, London to La Paz, and Manila to Moscow voiced a common message: their governments were out of touch with the lives of quiet desperation lived by most ordinary citizens. The establishment classes, many demonstrators charged, had become corrupt, self-perpetuating aristocracies. The protests of 2019 brought down some autocrats, such as Bakhytzhan Sagintayev in Kazakhstan in February, Abdelaziz Bouteflika in Algeria in April, and Omar al-Bashir of Sudan later the same month. The street protests also felled leaders whose original democratic credentials had strayed into questionable political legitimacy. These included Lebanon's Saad Hariri in October, Bolivia's Evo Morales in November, and Iraq's Adil Abdul-Mahdi in December. Mass protests following the assassination of crusading Maltese journalist Daphne Caruana Galizia brought down Maltese Prime Minister Joseph Muscat.

Among the democracies of Europe and North America, the most persistent and violent of the 2019 protests were in France. The *mouvement des gilets jaunes* — the yellow vest movement — was named for the high-visibility vests French drivers are required to carry in their vehicles in case of emergency. The movement sprang out of opposition to increased fuel prices and the high cost of living. It became, however, a textbook example of the failure of a modern democratic government to understand and respond to underlying anger and anxieties among its citizenry. By the time 2019 ticked into 2020, the yellow vest movement was one part of widespread strikes and demonstrations across France protesting plans by the administration of President Emmanuel Macron to reform the national pension scheme.

Macron was elected in 2017 on an anti-establishment ticket with the promise of modernizing France's governmental and business cultures. He was aware from the start that he would face some popular opposition and that this would probably be expressed in protests on the streets, which is a more normal part of the political discourse in France than in other European countries. It became evident quite quickly, however, that the protesters' outrage was more intense than anticipated and went well beyond just an objection to Macron's attempts to rationalize contradictions in fuel pricing. But by that time, ten people had died in the weekly protests, and both sides were firmly dug in. More than that, the yellow vest movement had become something of a poster child elsewhere for demonstrating popular discontent with what was perceived as an inattentive, uncaring, and dismissive government. The yellow vest was adopted as a symbol by protesters in twenty-seven countries around the world, championing a wide variety of causes flowing from the French demonstrations. None of these copycat protests achieved the intensity of the French fountainhead, but anxiety about them in some countries with recent histories of popular uprisings, such as Egypt, prompted their governments to restrict the sale of yellow vests.

In most other parts of Europe, large segments of the populations felt the same fears and anxieties as the French. The difference was that they did not take to the streets in the same numbers or with the same persistence as the French. A study published by Oxford Analytica in early December 2019 warned that governments across Western Europe faced the possibility of protests and social unrest. Real and perceived losses in standards of living and deep-seated fears that the future was bleak had increased the sense of social anxiety across the continent. This had created a political environment in Europe, stated the report, that "is more favourable to fringe parties and populists today than at any time since the Second World War."

Oxford Analytica observed that unless tackled carefully, this trend would get worse. It pointed to three pitfalls. Nationalist parties would feed on native populations' antipathy to rising numbers of immigrants and refugees. Yet any attempt to curb the activities or political participation of extreme fringe parties of left or right that attempted to take advantage of people's anxieties would probably backfire and exacerbate the situation. Opposition to multinational free trade deals, which in many people's minds are the face of globalization and the door through which jobs disappear into the Third World, may increase and pose a threat to economic growth.

The report looked at France, the Netherlands, Belgium, and Germany and concluded, "Significant groups of voters across the four countries are concerned about the rising cost of living, combined with lower incomes and job security, stagnant social mobility and a perceived loss of control. Many fear that future generations will struggle to afford housing and health care, to raise a family or enjoy a financially secure retirement." The analysis was assembled from published public opinion polls, and some of the results were stark. Across the four countries, from 30 percent of the workforce in France to 56 percent in Germany feared losing their jobs because of automation and not having the skills to find new employment. In Germany, 27 percent feared poverty in old age. In France, that figure was 68 percent, spurred by Macron's plans for pension reform. The French were equally pessimistic about the prospects for their country in general, with 72 percent seeing a dark future. Germans were slightly more cheery, with about half optimistic and half pessimistic. Inevitably, this gloom was linked to a wider sense of political mistrust. Germans' confidence in their political system had slipped from 76 percent in 2017 to 69 percent in 2018. In France, 39 percent said they distrusted politics. In the Netherlands, only 42 percent said they had confidence in their politicians. In Belgium, the home of the European Union bureaucracy, it was worse still: only 27 percent of those polled said they had faith in their political parties, while 73 percent did not.

THE OXFORD ANALYTICA compilation throws an interesting light on the debate over whether proportional representation (PR) or first-past-the-post electoral systems produce the most effective and representative legislatures.

A central argument for PR is that legislatures created by this system faithfully mirror the proportion of votes cast for each party, including minor parties. And, goes the argument, although elections under the PR system seldom produce a majority government, this is a virtue because it forces political parties to listen to one another, make compromises, and consider the views of minorities. In contrast, supporters of winner-take-all systems say victorious parties may have only a minority of the popular vote, but a clear winner allows for decisive and responsive government. PR, say the system's detractors, all too often produces a legislative body — and sometimes it can't even do that — that is hobbled from the start by the long, tedious, and regularly inconclusive business of policy negotiation. More than that, because candidates under the most popular PR systems are assigned based on their party affiliation rather than their community, this separates the politicians from the people they are meant to represent. Over time, this tends to reinforce the picture of politicians as a distinct and separate class of people.

In Europe, including those countries outside the twenty-seven members of the EU, all countries except France and the United Kingdom use variations of PR. Within North Atlantic culture, both Canada and the United States use first-past-the-post systems. A valid interpretation of the Oxford Analytica reports of disaffection with government across Europe suggests that PR systems do little or nothing to put the public and politicians more in tune with each other.

A regular argument for first-past-the-post is that in times of need, it can produce governments that are strong enough in Parliament to be able to confidently tackle serious social, economic, or other problems as well as long-simmering contentious issues that might otherwise be avoided. Supporters point to Margaret Thatcher's tackling of trade union power in the UK in the 1980s and her legislative moves to impose a reasonable level of democracy on union organizations. Similarly, in the 1990s, UK Prime Minister Tony Blair was able to reform and modernize social services because he had a secure parliamentary majority. In the US, President Lyndon Johnson in the 1960s was able to push through his Civil Rights Act and his anti-poverty vision, called "the Great Society." Equally, Canadian Prime Minister Pierre Trudeau was able, after winning a clear majority in the 1980 election, to press ahead with the contentious issue of patriating the Canadian Constitution from the UK, with the addition of a Charter of Rights and Freedoms. This was an issue that successive Canadian governments had avoided since 1931. From this point of view, it can be argued that France in 2017 needed a leader with the electoral authority to tackle the multiple distortions and inequities that had built up over decades.

A good deal of political opportunism brought Macron to power in 2017 as, at age thirty-nine, the youngest French president ever and the youngest leader since Napoleon Bonaparte. Macron's education and early career had followed the classic path for a French establishment figure through the study of philosophy at Paris Nanterre University, a master's degree in public affairs at Sciences Po, and graduation from École nationale d'administration in 2004. He first worked as a senior civil servant at the Inspectorate General of Finances and later became an investment banker at Rothschild & Co., where he made a lot of money. Socialist French President François Hollande made Macron one of his senior advisers in May 2012, and the young whiz kid went on to become the minister of the economy and industry in August 2014.

On the surface, Macron was a socialist member of a socialist government, but that seems to have been a garb of convenience while he served in the Hollande government. He discarded that cloak after Hollande decided his popularity was too low for him to have a hope of winning another five-year term in the 2017 elections. Macron emerged in a new political uniform as a centrist but pro-business candidate for the presidency with his own political party, En Marche ("Forward"). He led the first round of voting in

April with 24.01 percent of the vote, a short lead in front of Marine Le Pen of the right-wing National Rally, who got 21.30 percent. This wiped out the socialist and left-of-centre candidates. In the second round in May, most of the left-wing votes, 18 million of them, went to Macron, who won 66.1 percent of the ballots cast, while Le Pen picked up only an extra 3 million votes and ended up with 33.9 percent of the total.

Legislative elections were held on June 11 and 18, 2017, to elect the 577 members of the National Assembly. Macron's party, renamed La République En Marche! (LREM), led an alliance with the centrist Democratic Movement. Together, the two parties won 350 of the 577 seats in the National Assembly, including an outright majority of 308 seats for LREM. The Socialist Party was reduced to 30 seats and the Republicans to 112 seats. These were the lowest number of seats won by the centre-left and centre-right parties in the Fifth Republic's legislative elections. Macron's sweeping capture of both the presidency and the National Assembly, together with his uncompromising dedication to his agenda, left the feeling that opposition to his policies by legitimate political means would be ineffective and futile. What is difficult to quantify is to what extent popular opposition to Macron was driven by the belief that the National Assembly was impotent and how much was just an example of the time-honoured French political cultural expression of people taking to the streets when outraged.

For a while after the 2017 elections, a mood of optimism dominated and it seemed as though France was entering a new and vibrant age. Among the leaders of the major North Atlantic democracies, Macron, with his youth, wit, and sharp intellect, and his wife, Brigitte, almost twenty-five years his senior, who had once been his high school teacher, stood out. In the United States, the rigged political system had just produced President Donald Trump, a seventy-year-old TV game show personality with a record of unethical business dealings, an even more sullied history of sexual relationships, and a talent for self-promotion. The UK was in the throes of the Brexit referendum hangover. Prime Minister Theresa May was trying unsuccessfully to find a route out of EU membership that anyone would agree to. In Germany, Chancellor Angela Merkel remained the pillar around which the rest of Europe had revolved for over a decade, but clearly her sell-by date was at hand, and it seemed unlikely that her replacement would inspire the same widespread confidence. Only Canada's newly elected Prime Minister Justin Trudeau was of the same generation and on the same wavelength as Macron. However, the worst curse that can befall a new leader coming into office is unrealistically high expectations. Macron's promise of a new era in France quickly became a bitter replay of old arguments. His fall from grace was accelerated by a succession of public incidents in which Macron emerged as an intellectually arrogant personality, with no rapport with ordinary citizens and very little understanding of the way they lived their lives.

Macron had come to office with pledges to reform France's contorted and convoluted labour and economic practices, which strangled productivity and enterprise. From the start, there were questions on all sides of French society about who would benefit from Macron's revolution. Early in his administration, Macron launched into an austerity program to cut the budget deficit. He accompanied this with attempts to either simplify or destroy the mounds of special economic arrangements and convoluted rules and regulations that had grown up over the years to deal with momentary and passing problems. This plethora of patchwork instant solutions to long-forgotten problems made daily functioning as a French citizen a complex and frustrating matter even at the best of times.

Macron's lack of patience and intolerance for roadblocks turned the public against him and made his reform program an uphill fight. After fewer than six months in office, his popularity had sunk to 47 percent, down from 66 percent at the time of the election. By November 2018, when the yellow vest movement began, Macron's popularity was at only 25 percent, and he had become known as *le président des très riches* ("president of the very rich").

It takes years (and more likely decades) of unbalanced decisions or lack of attention by politicians and administrators to engender uprisings like the yellow vest movement. And seldom is there one issue that brings people out on to the streets. In the case of the yellow vest movement, however, the initial cause can be traced back to French transportation policy in the decades after the Second World War. Successive governments prioritized encouraging private car ownership for daily commuting and other transportation, with cheap diesel as the fuel. By 2015, the cost of diesel fuel was dramatically lower than gasoline, and two-thirds of all cars on French roads were diesel-powered. As Macron came to office, that advantage was changing. This was partly due to market conditions that narrowed the gap between the prices of diesel and gasoline, but also because of his policies to combat climate change by hiking the cost of running personal vehicles to reduce the use of air-polluting carbon fuels. In the twelve months running up to October 2018, the price of diesel fuel at the pump rose 23 percent, making it as expensive as gasoline. Within that increase, taxes on diesel accounted for 14 percent. This came from a policy decision to bring the carbon tax component on diesel up to the same level as that on gasoline. This was a red flag for those who had not bought into the logic between carbon taxes and combating climate change. On top of that was a 2017 decision by the Macron administration to lower the rural speed limit from ninety kilometres per hour to eighty kilometres per hour. The aims were to cut the death toll on rural roads caused by speeding and to bolster the climate change agenda by lowering fuel consumption.

There were widespread feelings that these tax and price increases fell disproportionately on rural people and the urban poor. An online petition opposing the hikes was started in May 2018, and by mid-October it had almost a million signatures. The following month, a Facebook page on the issue was launched with calls for protesters to "block all roads" on November 17. The appeal went viral. Somewhere in the traffic of Facebook messages, someone suggested demonstrators wear the yellow vests all motorists are required to keep in their vehicles for emergencies. Well over three hundred thousand people turned out for the protests, blocking roads, especially entrances to fuel depots, across France. But even this first day of protest reached into French cities with a broader message of outrage at government austerity policies. It even reached the French southern Indian Ocean island of Réunion — which by some sleight of hand of geography is considered part of metropolitan France — where there were riots and looting.

The second yellow vest protest came the following weekend, November 24, when the focus began to shift to demonstrations in towns and cities across France. That remained the forum right into 2020, as the protests continue with tens of thousands and sometimes hundreds of thousands of people taking to the streets every weekend. They have gone through periods of intense violence, with protesters being confronted by riot squads, water cannons, and tear gas. In 2019, the government went as far as to call out the military to support the police. At the same time, the target of the demonstrators' outrage has changed from disgust at diesel tax increases to a broader criticism that Macron's reform agenda is falling unequally on the poor and the urban working class. By the end of 2019, the yellow vest movement had been joined on the streets by striking trade unionists and many others concerned about Macron's plans for the national pension scheme. Two key concerns prompted the strikes and protests. One was a planned increase in the age for full retirement benefits from sixty-two to sixty-four. The other was the prospect of reduction in pensions by as much as US$1,000 a month. Polls showed that about 58 percent of French people supported the strikers and protesters. In January 2020, Macron backed down on the planned increase to raise the age of retirement on full benefits.

After well over a year of trying to swim against an unforgiving tide of discontent, it is understandable that in November 2019, Macron vented his frustration at what he saw as the fount of disillusionment among European voters. In an interview with *The Economist*, Macron said Europe was "on the edge of a precipice." Unless it woke up, "we will no longer be in control of our own destiny." Unless European leaders realized the risks they faced, he said, there was a good chance the European Union would disappear. "I don't think I'm being either pessimistic or painting an overly gloomy picture when I say that," Macron told his interviewer. Too many EU leaders and governments see the union as merely an integrated market and not a political bloc, he said, touching on the issue that inflamed nationalism across Europe. Macron proclaimed himself a staunch believer in political integration. He said EU member states must press ahead with political union and develop common policies on technology, industrial strategy, and climate change.

Macron put some of his comments in the context of his observation that the United States is no longer as interested in or supportive of the EU as the essential framework for the continent's security and prosperity. The US will stay on this track of decreasing support for EU affairs with or without Donald Trump in the White House, he said. Trump had loudly supported Brexit, given many indications he regarded the EU as a competitor rather than a friend, and given inconsistent views of his support for the North Atlantic Treaty Organization. Macron's interview came soon after Trump had ordered US troops out of Syria, resulting in the abandonment of Syrian Kurds who had been US allies and the front-line troops in the battles against the Islamic State. "Strategically and politically," Macron said, "we need to recognize that we have a problem." He went on to propound his proposal for an integrated European military force, but there is no unanimity on this issue among the twenty-seven post-Brexit EU members. Some are actively opposed to military solutions to international problems under any circumstances, while others, especially those bordering Russia, are alarmed at any suggestion that the security offered by the US military umbrella may be drawing to a close.

MACRON'S OUTBURST CAME just as a new generation of EU political and bureaucratic leaders were easing into office after the May 2019 parliamentary elections. In those elections, traditional centrist parties suffered significant losses, right-wing parties did worse than expected, and outliers, especially Green parties, did well. Sixty percent of the elected members of the European Parliament were new to the job, and most came knowing that the time when the contradictions and incongruities in the EU could be ignored or finessed was rapidly coming to an end. Indeed, a two-year Conference on the Future of Europe was slated to start in 2020 with the aim of charting a new path forward. There are two fundamental issues this conference planned to address. The first is what the European Union is meant to be. Some, such as the departing United Kingdom, want it to be no more than a free trade area, while others, such as Macron and Merkel, see political union as the only secure objective. Those two visions headline a long list of sub-issues, such as the character of the common currency — the euro — used by only nineteen of the EU members. Then there's the difficulty, some say futility, of trying to formulate and administer common foreign and defence policies for an association of countries with such different prerogatives and perceptions. The EU is an agglomeration of countries with individual geographies, cultures, histories, and ethnic backgrounds divided roughly into northern, southern, eastern, and western quadrants.

The second issue is the clear lack of democracy in the way the political and administrative leadership of the EU is chosen. That major flaw welled to the surface once again as the EU set about choosing a new European Commission president after the May 2019 parliamentary elections. A process has evolved, known by its German name, *Spitzenkandidat* ("lead candidate"), which requires each of the political party groupings in the European Parliament to put forward a candidate. This shortlist then goes to the European Council, which is made up of the heads of government of all member states. They vote on the new president from among the candidates, usually nominating the candidate of the leading party. In 2019, however, the system imploded. If the Parliament had been able to agree on one or two candidates, the system might have worked. But they couldn't agree, and none of the *Spitzenkandidaten* commanded a majority in Parliament. Subsequently, the issue was sent to the European Council to sort out. The council couldn't agree on any of the three candidates either, so they reached outside the whole process, which they were legally entitled to do, and picked German Defence Minister Ursula von der Leyen. When her name went back to Parliament for ratification, she was able to win only 383 votes — nine more than the minimum required to be given the job. She took the reins of the EU at a crucial time in its history with shallow political legitimacy. This prompted her to prioritize popular issues, such as a Green agenda to turn the EU into a carbon-neutral economy, rather than some of the more difficult but imperative questions of the organization's survival.

What von der Leyen promised would be "a new push for European democracy" is scheduled to be handled by the Conference on the Future of Europe. That agenda and von der Leyen's priorities were jettisoned with the arrival of the coronavirus early in 2020. It is unclear when the conference will be able to take up its task. The conference consists of representatives of the European Parliament, the European Council, and the EU's administrative commission, and it has been given two years to plan what it wants to do, the issues it wants to tackle, and the outcome it is aiming at. There are expected to be at least six citizens' assemblies involved, as well as assigned roles for representative young people, civil society organizations, and European institutions.

The *Spitzenkandidat* system is one that the Conference on the Future of Europe will need to tackle, though there is little room for radical change. There is room, however, for a good deal more transparency and predictability to ensure that even when the European Council feels it has to reach beyond the Parliament's candidates, there is an open and deliberate process involved.

On another issue of democracy, the departure of the UK is offering an opportunity. For a time, there has been discussion about having some directly elected members of the European Parliament who are not based in any particular country but who are selected by voters from a list of transnational candidates. The idea is that this would bring to Parliament and its debates people whose vision on issues stretches beyond the interests of individual member states and focuses on the EU as a whole. With the departure of the UK, there are now twenty-seven seats vacant in Parliament, and this offers an opportunity to give the idea of transnational members a trial run.

There are many other issues that need to be addressed, and the Conference on the Future of Europe will take on its own momentum as it proceeds. But the success of the project will depend on whether public confidence in EU institutions can be restored by bridging the substantial divide that now exists between the people of the member states and the bureaucrats in Brussels. As the conference makes its arrangements at the start of 2020, all over Europe and beyond, think tanks, institutes, political parties, and individuals are drawing up recommendations for actions the EU might take to build bonds of involvement and ownership of the pan-European system among the region's citizens. Some are practical. Some are fanciful. Some are brutally pragmatic. Others are naive in the extreme.

The EU has a record of muddling through political problems, and this is the most likely outcome of the planned two years of consultation, but the union is approaching the time when muddling through and failing to confront problems head-on could well be the cause of its dissolution. The conference must make an effort to deal with the democratic deficit, but it may be less inclined to confront the problem of whether the EU is simply a trade pact or a federation under construction. Under that scenario, the already established "two-speed EU" is likely to expand into shifting patterns of co-operation among various states on specific issues. It is easy to envisage Germany and France being more proactive than others, especially the Mediterranean littoral members, on immigration and refugees. The Baltic states have already forged links among themselves on providing digital services, and that is likely to continue. France and Italy have shown that they are more prepared than others to participate in military peacemaking interventions, with or without NATO. They will probably also try to promote the objective of a pan-European military force outside the North Atlantic alliance.

Observers with experience of the EU expect a fudge. In 2004, a new and far-reaching constitution for the EU was constructed after much discussion and negotiation. But the project fell apart when Dutch and French voters rejected it. Five years later, in late 2009, something of that effort was salvaged and set out in the Treaty of Lisbon. This, though, rang alarm bells about political integration among Euroskeptics in the UK. That in turn started putting pressure on UK Prime Minister David Cameron's

Tory backbenchers to demand a referendum on EU membership. As they begin a new round of reform exploration in 2020, those involved in the Conference for the Future of Europe will have Brexit very much in mind. There is clear determination not to allow the UK to be the first in a cascade of countries quitting the EU. This should force the realization that, as Macron has said, they are on the edge of a precipice and need to act seriously and firmly to repair the defects in the union.

Another looming problem for Europe is a crisis in leadership. Germany's Angela Merkel is on the way out. She hoped to ensure a smooth transfer to a successor that would guarantee Germany remained at the hub of Europe. She resigned the leadership of her Christian Democratic Union (CDU) in 2018, and Minister of Defence Annegret Kramp-Karrenbauer, usually known as AKK, took her place. The intention was that AKK would succeed Merkel as Germany's chancellor when the time came. But a scandal in early February 2020 threw those cards in the air and raised the prospect of political upheaval and realignment in Germany that could leave a gap in EU leadership when it is needed most. The scandal happened in the eastern state of Thuringia, when the CDU took over the regional government only because it won the support of the neo-Nazi Alternative for Germany (AfD). There was outrage throughout the CDU, which regards any formal or informal dealings with the AfD as taboo. Merkel fired one of her ministers who congratulated the Thuringian leader and called the whole situation "unforgivable." The Thuringian CDU leader resigned the next day after calling new elections, but the shrapnel from the affair continued to ricochet around the corridors of power in Berlin. There was ever-louder talk that the affair showed that AKK didn't have the ability to command authority in the party. Her departure opened the door for a hotly contested CDU party leadership with the prospect of succeeding Merkel as the gold ring. But that ring may turn out to be brass. The CDU and other mainstream parties have not found any formula for winning back the support of anti-immigrant voters in eastern Germany who have been lured by the AfD. Meanwhile, in the west of the country, voters are turning more and more toward the Greens as an alternative to the traditional political fare. Since the Second World War, the accord between Germany and France has kept the European community afloat. Without a shared agenda and the personalities to drive it in Berlin and Paris, the EU will sputter and stall.

—

FORMAL DISCUSSION AND debate about improving the level of democracy within the EU and its institutions came to a screeching halt with the arrival of the coronavirus early in 2020. As COVID-19 settled in northern Italy and Spain, in particular, all European member states abandoned the organization's principle of open borders, shut out visitors, and put their economies into hibernation.

The pandemic worked at the fault lines of the EU, and the coming months and years, as the union emerges from the period of lockdown, may well further irritate the established tensions among member countries and between some of them and Brussels. Economic reconstruction is the priority, and other issues that had appeared to be major concerns in January moved well down the list by the end of February. A foretaste of the sort of difficulties that will arise was evident as the EU finance ministers worked to agree on a financial package to protect workers, businesses, and the national treasuries of the countries worst affected by the disease. Those negotiations quickly became a replay of past financial crises and boiled down to a lack of trust in northern Europe, led by Germany and the Netherlands, over how the countries of the south — primarily Italy and Spain, worst hit by the pandemic — would repay their debts. A compromise was cobbled together, but other clouds churned on the horizon. In mid-April, the European Commission was forced to postpone publication of an exit strategy for countries to restart their economies as the COVID-19 pandemic waned. While there had been substantial agreement among EU members on the necessity of confronting the coronavirus with economic hibernation and requiring citizens to stay at home, there was a wide divergence of views about the right exit strategy from the shutdown. Those countries that had been most orderly in confronting and containing the effects of the virus — Germany, Austria, Denmark, and the Czech Republic — wanted to start lifting restrictions beginning in the middle of April to get their economies operating as soon as possible. Meanwhile, the worst affected countries, Italy and Spain, whose health systems were still overwhelmed by the number of cases, resisted an early lifting of restraints. The Spanish and Italian governments feared that an uncoordinated opening up of Europe would lead to a second wave of infection and would also leave them at a distinct economic and business disadvantage if other members got an early start.

In addition to these deep-rooted mutual suspicions between the north and south of Europe, COVID-19 exacerbated the east-west tensions. As has already been described, leaders in both Hungary and Poland used the application of states of emergency to address the pandemic as opportunities to enhance their own authority in other areas, such as power over the judiciary, the media, and lower levels of government.

—

ON BALANCE, EVEN with the challenges added by the coronavirus pandemic, reviving democracy in Europe, where many countries have well-established representative and accountable political systems on which to build, is a more realistic project than the problems facing the United States. The US was constructed as a republic to be governed by members of an enlightened upper class. Democracy was an afterthought adopted with hesitation, which never received full commitment and which has never fitted comfortably into the structure created by the Founding Fathers. Moreover, it is a structure that subsequent generations have shrunk from reconstructing in any meaningful way to adapt to changing times. Library shelves sag under the weight of books analyzing what has gone wrong with the American model. No one viewpoint can reveal the panorama of such an involved and complex topic, but historian and political scientist Francis Fukuyama took a good stab at it in his August 2014 essay in *Foreign Affairs*, "America in Decay." Fukuyama's treatise predates the arrival of Donald Trump on the political scene and puts that event in its proper context as an effect, not a cause, of a process of decay already well underway.

"A combination of intellectual rigidity and the power of entrenched political actors is preventing its [political] institutions from being reformed. And there is no guarantee that the situation will change much without a major shock to the political order," Fukuyama wrote.

The Constitution of the United States was built around revulsion at the despotism of European monarchs, exemplified by George III. To that end, it is a maze of checks and balances — more properly described as vetoes, perhaps — against the functioning of government. While democracy in the parliamentary system and in Europe more generally has grown up around governmental administration at the core, with the law and the representative legislature evolving around it, the American model is almost the reverse. Fukuyama, drawing on the work of fellow historians, argues that the US started as system of law courts and political legislatures, the responsibilities of which were to veto or usurp the activities of government and of each other. He cites, for example, numerous times when the US courts, by ruling on issues such as civil rights and segregation, have performed functions that under the parliamentary system are the responsibility of the legislature or government.

"The story of the courts is one of the steady judicialization of the functions that in other developed democracies are handled by administrative bureaucracies, leading to an explosion of costly litigation, slowness of decision-making, and highly inconsistent enforcement laws," Fukuyama wrote. "In the United States today, instead of being constraints on government, courts have become alternative instruments for the expansion of government."

Fukuyama doesn't say so, but the picture he paints explains why one of the greatest imperatives for a political party in the US once it has gained a majority in the Senate is to pack the courts with like-minded judges. This process was well underway before Trump became president in 2017. The Republican majority leader in the Senate, Mitch McConnell, used his position during the last two years of Barack Obama's presidency, 2015–16, to block the confirmation of judges to fill 103 vacancies. With this inheritance from the previous administration, by early May 2020, the Republicans had overseen the appointment of 193 judges. Of these, 2 were Supreme Court justices, 51 were circuit court judges, 138 were district court judges, and 2 were US Court of International Trade judges. The common characteristic of these appointments is that they are dominated by young, highly conservative white men. Often their political loyalty is more impressive than their judicial experience. A typical example is Justin Walker, thirty-seven years old and less than ten years out of law school at the time of his appointment in April 2020 to the court of appeals for the District of Columbia. This is one of the second-highest courts in the US, yet Walker had never tried a case nor served as counsel during a trial. Walker was, however, a clerk to Brett Kavanaugh, Trump's second appointment to the Supreme Court. When Kavanaugh's appointment was mired in allegations of sexual misconduct, Walker went on Fox News, the Trump supporters' network, to defend his former boss. McConnell can still oversee the appointment of at least two dozen more conservative-minded judges before the end of Trump's four-year term. In an interview with conservative radio talk show host Hugh Hewitt in April 2020, McConnell said, "My motto for the rest of the year is to leave no vacancy behind." There are even reports that McConnell has been urging elderly judges to retire promptly so that young conservatives with decades of judging ahead of them can be appointed. In an interview in late April 2020, Laurence Tribe, a constitutional law professor at Harvard University, told *The Guardian*, "The transformation of the federal judiciary into a series of puppets for a very right-wing ideology will have a lasting impact for decades." The price of the evangelicals' support for Trump and the Republicans is the revisiting and reversal of the landmark 1973 Supreme Court decision that gave pregnant women the right to choose to have an abortion without restrictions from government. Other highly divisive social issues that will almost certainly find their way to McConnell's courts in coming years are environmental regulations, immigration rules, access to health care, and gun control.

Bribery of legislators and public officials, once an inescapable feature of American public life, has now mutated into something slightly different.

Special interest groups now exert influence through lobbyists or political donations in an electoral system that gives the advantage to big-spending candidates. Fukuyama notes that in 1971 there were only 175 registered lobbyists in Washington, but there were 2,500 a decade later, and 13,700 in 2009. Since Fukuyama's essay, figures show the number has dropped slightly to 11,586 registered lobbyists in 2018. But several analysts say that is not the true picture and that many lobbying operations aimed at influencing members of Congress have found ways of obscuring their activities. There is an increasingly widespread view that because of the prevalence of lobbying and the money involved in both influence peddling and corporate-funded political action committees at campaign time, the US should properly be described as an oligarchy. "These interest groups exercise influence way out of proportion to their place in society, distort both taxes and spending, and raise overall deficit levels by their ability to manipulate the budget in their favor," said Fukuyama. "Both phenomena — the judicialization of administration and the spread of interest-group influence — tend to undermine the trust that people have in government. Distrust of government then perpetuates and feeds on itself. The result is a crisis of representation, which ordinary citizens feel that their supposedly democratic government no longer truly reflects their interests and is under the control of a variety of shadowy elites."

The grim irony, of course, is that a system designed expressly to keep despots at bay has brought about the reverse. Because the system has undermined public confidence in itself, it has left the citizenry vulnerable to the blandishments of a populist, a would-be despot who has promised to "drain the swamp." The atmosphere in the US political forum is now so polarized it is hard to envisage a way out that does not first involve passage through a time of extreme crisis. If the polarization were limited to the political classes, there might be more cause for optimism. But in the US, the polarization runs throughout society, and the currency of the populist is the spreading of hatred and fear of outsiders and opponents.

Those divisions are especially troubling in respect to the Second Amendment to the Constitution, ratified in December 1791, which drew a legal framework for the keeping of guns by ordinary citizens. The original idea, in the eighteenth century, was to have at hand men who could quickly form a militia. This was at a time when the country had little in the way of a standing army and was trying to survive and thrive in a tough neighbourhood with potential enemies all around — the British Empire to the north and the Spanish Empire to the south. That practical idea has been reinterpreted, reimagined, and glorified as a view of Americans as, essentially, a society of free anarchists whose communal dealings are driven by an unshakable Christian moral compass. Sadly, though, as much as most Americans would like to believe the images promoted by their popular culture, few Americans measure up to Gary Cooper as Marshal Will Kane in *High Noon*. This idealized vision has become corrupted, inevitably, even among its most staunch believers. It has degraded into a fixation among large segments of American society that no one is to be trusted: not government, not neighbours, and certainly not strangers. American citizens must be armed because they are under constant threat from everyone around them.

An extraordinary and telling sight as the COVID-19 virus struck in early 2020 was that while Europeans and Canadians rushed to the supermarkets to stock up on essential supplies for a period of quarantine at home, millions of Americans went to their gun stores to get weapons and ammunition. Figures gathered by the FBI showed that Americans bought over 2 million guns in March, 1.1 million more than were purchased in the same month in 2019. Illinois led with the sale of nearly half a million guns, followed by Texas, Kentucky, Florida, and California. The BBC quoted Georgia State University law professor Timothy Lytton as saying he suspected people feared the pandemic would provoke a breakdown in law and order and felt that having a gun was a "self-help survival tool."

"Some people," Lytton said, "are worried about the fact that government's falling apart and won't protect them, and other people are worried that the government is getting too strong and is going to limit their freedom." There was an indication of the brink on which the US is poised on April 15, when thousands of people, some of them armed, demonstrated outside the Michigan State Capitol in Lansing, demanding that the pandemic lockdown be lifted. The state's Democratic Governor Gretchen Whitmer, who had imposed the restrictions to halt the spread of the virus, was the target of demonstrators, who adopted the Donald Trump 2016 campaign slogan "Lock her up." Some carried signs saying, "Gov Whitmer We Are Not Prisoners," and others voiced support for Trump's position that the restrictions should be lifted even if the pandemic is not over. On April 30, groups of heavily armed men entered the capitol building and posed for photographs. When questioned by reporters about the invasion, Trump said they were "very good people." Trump had repeatedly attacked Whitmer when she requested emergency medical supplies from the federal government. She remained highly popular in her state, and the armed demonstrators were clearly a small minority. Yet the readiness with which some factions within the US will reach for guns to bolster political arguments underlines a deep-seated malaise. This social culture of fear and suspicion of neighbours and fellow countrymen is not one with which any community can function or survive.

ON THE SURFACE, there are similarities between the rise of Donald Trump in the US and Boris Johnson in the UK. But after examination of the social and political upheavals that have propelled Johnson and Brexit, the similarities quickly disappear. A major difference is that through-out the turmoil in the UK leading to the decision to leave the EU, the democratic institutions in the UK have continued to function and to determine the outcome.

There are flaws in that system, of course. In the December 2019 election, Johnson and the Tories won a clear majority of seats in the House of Commons and a mandate to "Get Brexit Done" on January 31, 2020. That is despite the fact that a majority of voters — 52 percent — voted for parties with policies to remain in the EU. Even as the vote count was being confirmed, groups were forming to advocate for the UK's re-entry into the European Union. After a breathing space of a few years, when the reality of the UK's lone status has become apparent, these campaigns for re-entry may well get some wind beneath their wings. In the interim, the big fight is going to be the survival of the UK as a federation of England, Scotland, Wales, and Northern Ireland.

In the December election, the Scottish Nationalist Party won most seats in Scotland. Its leader, Nicola Sturgeon, who heads the SNP government of what is, in effect, the UK province of Scotland, immediately asked Johnson to allow another referendum in Scotland on independence. In the last referendum, in 2014, the "No" vote won with 55.3 percent of the votes against 44.7 for independence. The voter turnout was over 84 percent, a record. Sturgeon's argument is that most Scots showed in the 2016 Brexit referendum that they want to stay in the EU and that the UK leaving the group has fundamentally changed the equation. Johnson's response was to refuse to give legal authority for a new referendum. The next Scottish regional elections are due in May 2021. If, as is likely, the SNP again wins a substantial majority, the moral imperative for another referendum will be hard for Johnson to refuse.

The picture in Wales is not as clear as it is in Scotland. A majority of Welsh voters — 52.5 percent — opted for Brexit in 2016. But in the 2019 election, 40.9 percent voted for the pro-EU Labour Party, while 36.1 percent supported Johnson's Tories. Support for both parties was down from the last election, and the only party to increase its vote was the nationalist Plaid Cymru (PC). But PC's support was only 9 percent, still a long way from the influential level achieved by the SNP in Scotland.

The situation is different again in Northern Ireland, but the centrifugal forces toward the breakup of the UK are just as strong. After Brexit, the border between Northern Ireland and Eire is the only land link between the UK and the EU. In theory, this means the re-establishment of a hard border once the free movement of trade and people ends. But that open border is a key element in the 1998 Good Friday Agreement, which ended thirty years of civil war between the conservative Protestant unionists intent on keeping the province as part of the United Kingdom on one side and the Catholic Irish Republican Army (IRA), with its political wing Sinn Féin, who wanted unification with the Irish republic, on the other.

After Theresa May lost her majority in Parliament in 2017, the survival of her government became dependent on the support of the ten Democratic Unionist Party members of Parliament. Thus the whole Brexit project became dependent on what happened at the Irish border. Johnson's election victory swept that issue away. He was able to ignore the Unionists and make an agreement with Brussels that fudges the issue of the border. But in that election, Irish nationalists, led by Sinn Féin, for the first time won a majority of the seats in Northern Ireland. This reflects a demographic shift driven by a relative increase in the republican population. This clearly portends ever-mounting pressure for Northern Ireland to end its status as part of the UK and to become part of the Irish Republic. That prospect became more likely in mid-February 2020, when national elections in the Irish Republic saw Sinn Féin come out marginally ahead of the main traditional parties, the centrist Fianna Fáil party and the centre-right Fine Gael. Both these parties have vowed not to make political alliances with Sinn Féin because of its association with the terrorist IRA. Clearly, a realignment in Irish politics is underway, as it is in so many countries of the North Atlantic.

There is no question that the social divisions caused by the long and drawn-out debate on the UK's membership in the EU were just as heated and traumatic as the political turmoil in the US. But what happened in the UK never reached anywhere near the levels of hatred and violence experienced in the US. There was that strange period between the referendum in 2016 and the 2019 election, when the whole project stalled and no one was able to find a formula to get the process out of the doldrums. But throughout that period, everyone stuck to the principle that somewhere there was a parliamentary solution to the problem. On a couple of occasions, the courts were involved, but throughout the process, the supremacy of Parliament was maintained. Unlike in the US, the instruments of democracy were preserved and used to end the stalemate.

What happens next is pretty much impossible to predict. Johnson has an electoral mandate strong enough to keep him and the Conservatives in government for five years. In the process, he has changed the face of the

Conservative party, which now holds northern blue-collar constituencies it has not held since the forming of the Labour Party early last century. Johnson seems determined to honour that confidence. One of the first Cabinet meetings of 2020 was held in Sutherland, the first constituency to vote for Brexit in the 2016 referendum and previously a Labour stronghold for generations. But to succeed in changing the course of UK politics, Johnson will have to overcome a personal history of betraying almost everyone who has ever put faith in him.

Johnson's mandate allows him to play a firm hand in negotiations with the EU over new commercial, technical, and other administrative arrangements sovereign entities must agree to allow for a functioning relationship. Johnson says he wants that agreement achieved by the end of 2020. That was an unrealistic deadline from the start, and the arrival of COVID-19 made it impossible. But lurking behind Johnson's enthusiasm for leaving the EU is a sense — one much more pronounced among some of his extremist followers — that he would be quite happy if there were no deal at all; the yearning for a hard Brexit, for the ability to raise a contemptuous V sign at Brussels and all its works, is evident among many of them.

Whatever the outcome, there has been an inevitability about Brexit since the 1980s, when the European project began to move beyond a free trade agreement onto the road toward political union. Margaret Thatcher rejected those moves from the start, and her successor, John Major, faced a backbench revolt when faced with signing the Maastricht Treaty that created the European Union in 1992, ending the trade-focused European Economic Community and moving significant political authority to Brussels. The UK's demand for exceptions continued through the creation of the common currency, the euro, and through the 2009 Lisbon Treaty, which also introduced such changes as decision by majority vote rather than consensus among the council of European leaders and the European Parliament.

There will be an important catharsis for the UK in leaving the EU. England, in particular, may find exactly what Johnson and the Praetorian Brexiteers have promised, a new Elizabethan Age that calls from the horizon. Or England may find, especially if pressure builds in Scotland and Northern Ireland to leave the UK and remain with the EU, that the world today is a far more intimidating place than it was in the late sixteenth century. Buccaneering entrepreneurship is no longer a sound basis on which to run a country — not a diverse and heavily populated one, at any rate. It is not beyond imagining that down the road the UK, or what remains of it, will seek to rejoin Europe, especially if by that time the EU has overcome the democratic deficits that now stain its image.

DEMAGOGUES – POPULISTS – ARE hyperactive because, like sharks, to be still is fatal. If the public has a chance to take a clear look at them, the magic of the multicoloured cloak falls away. Robbed of the ability to constantly divert public attention by pointing to some new wonder or outrage, populists are seen for what they are: rather sad and empty show-men. COVID-19 was the agent that stopped both Trump and Johnson in their tracks and gave US and UK citizens clear views of the essences of the men who had been elected to lead them. Intuitively, Johnson and Trump knew their political lives were in danger when the prospect of COVID-19 as a pandemic came into focus in February 2020. They knew that as devastating a global event as the spread of the coronavirus promised to be would rob them of control of the daily news agenda. It would also throw to the wind the hopes Johnson had of maintaining UK economic stability through the Brexit process. For Trump, the head of steam for re-election he had stoked with massive tax reductions for the rich, record levels of employment built on the work of the Obama administration, and a stock market bubble that appealed to a man for whom ratings are the only measure of success vanished overnight.

The first reaction of both Trump and Johnson to persistent warnings from epidemiologists and their own security analysts was to deny the threat. Both men dismissed the coronavirus as nothing more than a bad case of influenza, and Johnson adopted a strategy of herd immunity that said the epidemic should be allowed to run its course. It was only after he was shown a study by Imperial College epidemiologists demonstrating that this would mean the death of up to a quarter of a million people that Johnson changed his tune. Belatedly, he ordered people to stay home unless absolutely necessary, but the virus had already taken hold, especially in the more densely populated parts of the UK. At the beginning of May, 207,000 people in the UK were confirmed to have been infected by COVID-19 and 30,615 had died, the largest number of any European country.

In April, COVID-19 got a grip on Johnson himself. After two weeks of working in isolation through video links to his ministers, Johnson's condition deteriorated, and he was taken to hospital, where he spent two days in intensive care and came, by his own account, close to death. Those weeks while Johnson was out of circulation were highly instructive for the public. Daily televised updates on the course of the pandemic were given by a rotating roster of ministers, accompanied by public health experts. It was readily apparent that Johnson's government was made up of a singularly weak body of men and women lacking in intellect and experience. With one or two exceptions, their performances were woefully inept or crudely defensive. It took no wit to see that Johnson had surrounded himself with people whose essential qualities were an ideological fixation on Brexit and loyalty to their prime minister. In a rough way, Johnson had shown he regarded them as nothing more than a supporting chorus for his starring arias. In January, Johnson had forced the resignation of his finance minister, Chancellor of the Exchequer Sajid Javid, shortly before the new government's first budget was due to be presented. Johnson had ordered Javid to fire all his advisers and replace them with people appointed by Johnson's own chief policy guru, the Machiavellian and ruthless Dominic Cummings. Javid, perhaps the most able of Johnson's ministers, quit rather than submit, and the incident warned the lesser mortals in the government that they were totally disposable.

The message from the weeks of Johnson's absence was that this was a government built exclusively to bang the drum for Brexit. It did not have the fleetness of foot or soundness of breath to deal with the unexpected events that wise prime ministers fear most. On top of that, the necessity of closing down the UK in order to try to contain the spread of COVID-19 means that the country will go into life outside the protective canopy of the EU with an economy that is only a fraction of its former self. The consistent predictions from economists and bankers were that even at the best of times, Brexit was going to cut up to 2.5 percent off the UK's gross domestic product and cause a real decline in people's living standards. COVID-19 is ensuring that UK citizens are going to have to pay a good deal more than that as the price of supposedly regaining their national sovereignty from Brussels.

As soon as COVID-19 began making itself known as a national disaster in the US by spreading swiftly across the country from its first appearance in Washington State on January 21, 2020, Trump was caught in a trap of his own making. His populism was built on railing against experts and the media, both of which institutions were now essential to overcoming COVID-19 and informing the public about how to do it. More than that, Trump had hobbled himself in the early months of his administration in his enthusiasm to dismantle government and "drain the swamp" of skilled people. He'd disbanded the task force on pandemics attached to his National Security Council and left unfilled hundreds of vacant posts at the Centers for Disease Control. Like Johnson, it was stark estimates from epidemiologists that doing nothing would cost the lives of hundreds of thousands and perhaps millions of people that finally forced Trump to act. But even then, he did as little as possible and explicitly renounced any personal responsibility for the anti-coronavirus campaign. He even denounced the closing down of economic activity and requirement for people to stay home as a cure that was worse than the disease. He rein-forced his stance that on this occasion the buck does not stop at the desk in the Oval Office by handing responsibility for combating COVID-19 to the state governors. The US is fortunate that with the Commander in Chief gone AWOL, the state governors for the most part took respon-sibility for dealing with the epidemic in their own jurisdictions. New York State was especially hard hit, with over 320,000 people with confirmed infections and over 20,000 deaths by the end of the first week in May, but it would have been worse without the firm hand and straight-talking manner of Governor Andrew Cuomo. From Washington and New York States, the infection spread with awful inevitability throughout the US, finding fertile ground among the country's poorest and therefore most unhealthy communities. A survey of victims in Chicago in April found that 70 percent were African-American.

Despite his denial of responsibility, Trump tried to insert himself into the centre of the pandemic by seeking to control the distribution of personal protective and other medical equipment to states in need. He attempted to force governors to shower him with compliments as the price of receiving aid from Washington. That did not work. So Trump took to staging his own daily televised briefings, some of which rambled on for well over an hour. And as he verbally abused reporters for asking him nasty questions, he chided them for not being more grateful that his performances were delivering them massive audience ratings. These increasingly bizarre demonstrations of the warped presidential mentality came to an end when in late April Trump suggested that injections of chlorine or finding a way to internally zap COVID-19 patients with ultraviolet light would end the pandemic. Seeing his prospects for re-election drifting away, Trump finally found a target he knew he could sell to the American people. In early May, Trump and Secretary of State Mike Pompeo began making charges that COVID-19 had been created in a Chinese virus research laboratory in Wuhan. They claimed to have evidence that the virus had escaped from this laboratory but did not present said evidence, leaving the idea floating that the Chinese Communist Party had let COVID-19 loose purposefully as a weapon of biological warfare. None of this was supported by US intelligence reports or analysis by epidemiologists, who insisted all the scientific evidence was that the coronavirus was a natural phenomenon engendered in horseshoe bats sold for food in the Wuhan wet market. But with the death toll reaching over seventy thousand and outstripping in three months the number of Americans killed in the twenty years of the Vietnam War, Trump needed to divert attention from his massive failure of leadership. By the end of the first week in May, he had fixed on China. Speaking to reporters in the Oval Office of the White House on May 6, President Trump said, "We went through the worst attack we've ever had on our country, this is really the worst attack we've ever had. This is worse than Pearl Harbor, this is worse than the World Trade Center. There's never been an attack like this. And it should have never happened. Could've been stopped at the source. Could've been stopped in China. It should've been stopped right at the source. And it wasn't."

This is a dangerous tack that can easily lead to mistakes or miscalculations. Where it leads will depend to a degree on how fixated Trump is on getting re-elected at any cost. Against that may be ranged the number of Republican senators and members of Congress who see little hope of re-election if led by Trump in his current state of mind.

CHAPTER THIRTEEN

—

Restoring
Democracy

VIEWED FROM THE jet stream above the mid-Atlantic, Canada looks like a bastion of democratic calm and stability in a turbulent neighbourhood. That picture is not wrong, but it is not complete. Even though Canada has avoided much of the social upheaval and fear-mongering politics that have plagued much of Europe and the United States for over a decade, there are clear indications of voter exasperation, weakness before the temptations of populism, and a willingness to be caught up in the politics of hate. This public antipathy stems from structural fatigue in some aspects of the Canadian political system and the divide that has grown between the country's establishment and its voters. These weaknesses require addressing with some urgency, as the balance of global power is shifting with the relative decline of the US and the growing economic, political, and military influence of China, India, and others. Very soon, Canada is going to be on its own in the world as it has not been before.

For the first half of its life as an independent nation, Canada was the eldest lion cub of the British Empire, a role that demanded huge sacrifices without expectation of recompense. For the second half of its life, Canada has been drawn into the US national cordon of economic and strategic security. Neither of these relationships has been even-handed. In both, more was expected and taken from Canada than was given. But one of the benefits of that imbalance is that Canadian diplomacy, as it evolved after the Second World War, included the development of essential survival skills to surreptitiously promote and achieve Canadian objectives. Canadian diplomats tend to be masters of proceeding by indirection. And, to be fair, both London and Washington have often recognized Canada's contribution to joint security by giving support for Ottawa's particular foreign policy objectives. However, neither of those old allies now see Canada as an essential strategic partner, and both are entering periods where old alliances and friendships count for little. The vision for the UK of Boris Johnson and the Brexiteers appears to be a European version of Singapore or Hong Kong, a financial and trading centre with elements of Taiwan's supremacy as a hub of technical innovation. It is a bold venture, but it is self-absorbed. The quest for self-sufficiency is even more pronounced in the US, a country that has regularly gone through periods of isolationist introspection.

A POTENT EXAMPLE of the changing times is the Huawei affair. On December 1, 2018, Canadian border officials at Vancouver International Airport arrested Meng Wanzhou, the chief financial officer of the Chinese communications technology giant Huawei Technologies. The previous August, the US Department of Justice had issued an international warrant for her arrest and deportation to the US on charges of fraud and circumventing Washington's sanctions against Iran. On December 10, 2018, Chinese officials took into custody two Canadians in China, former diplomat Michael Kovrig and businessman Michael Spavor. It is hard not to interpret these subsequent arrests as retaliation and to consider the "two Michaels," as they have come to be known in the popular press, as hostages of the regime in Beijing. At the time of writing in May 2020, the two Michaels face charges of threatening the security of the People's Republic of China; they have been denied access to Canadian diplomats since January, ostensibly because of the COVID-19 pandemic. Meng is living in one of her two Vancouver mansions and is still waiting for her day in court, which has been delayed, also because of the coronavirus. The Huawei affair has become a subplot in the growing contest for power, authority, and economic supremacy between Washington and Beijing. For Canada, which was only abiding by its commitment to the rule of law and respect for the international treaties it has signed, this affair has shown how impotent Ottawa is in this fast-changing international order. The Trump regime has done nothing to help Canada secure the release of the two Michaels or resolve the impasse, and Beijing has responded to Ottawa's attempts to find a diplomatic solution with scorn and contempt.

This is a vision of the future.

Canada could be sent no clearer message that it needs to find a new circle of friends and allies among middle powers with shared civic, strategic, and international values and interests. For that purpose, Canada's democratic institutions must be fit for a rough passage in the coming decades. It is not at all certain that in the challenging years ahead, the way Canadian democracy currently works will be able to achieve a consensus view of the country's national interests, keep voter confidence in the political system, and sustain good and equitable government in a vastly diverse country. And building a circle of dependable friends among middle-power democracies will not be a breeze. Despite what many Canadians like to think, this country is not universally envied or admired, even by friends and allies. Canadians often display an unattractive propensity for self-satisfaction and an irritating refusal to admit there are flaws in their own national culture, let alone a willingness to address those flaws with energy and urgency. The word that comes most persistently to foreign critics' lips when describing Canada's most unattractive characteristics is "supercilious." Canadians can often be haughty and scornful, with an air of superiority.

As in other North Atlantic nations, a serious democratic deficit has metastasized through the Canadian body politic in recent decades. At the core of the disease are defects that were built into Canada as its creation was negotiated in the 1860s and brought to fruition in 1867. Canada is still hobbled by political and administrative institutions that were imported from Britain — a small, unitary state — and applied, largely unaltered, to the huge new confederation of geographically and culturally diverse regions that make up this country. Managing federal-provincial relations is a massive bureaucratic industry of muddle and compromise, conducted largely away from public view because efforts at reformation have usually brought national crises of confidence.

The lack of a clear-cut relationship between the provinces and Ottawa has often made the Supreme Court the arbiter of disputes. This has added to the political function of the court inherent in the 1982 Charter of Rights and Freedoms. There is a perception among a majority of the Canadian public that it is the Supreme Court that makes the rules on many questions about the values and mores that govern daily life in Canada. There are a few examples to support this view, but when push comes to shove, Parliament remains supreme. The problem is that many Canadians do not see Parliament as leading on social issues. They see the court as the place where liberal and progressive interpretations of the Charter are made. There is a vocal minority of social conservatives, of course, who see the same thing and find it absolutely abhorrent.

The influence of members of Parliament and Cabinet ministers has also been diminished by the effects of popular culture and the belief among campaign managers and party officials that pollsters know more about voters' attitudes than their elected representatives. The dominance of screen culture as the dictator of public perception has turned politics into a game of branding. The winner in Canadian politics is no longer the party whose policies the voters find most convincing and desirable but the party whose leader the screen audience finds most compelling. As a result, Canada's Parliament and its ten provincial and three territorial legislatures have become little more than backdrops for the stage on which the government leaders perform.

Under the constant assault of cultural demands to conform to the dictates of screen culture, the media too has largely abandoned its traditional role as the Fourth Estate, or has taken up that duty only as an afterthought. The responsibility of holding government to account is no longer the central driving force of media. Newspapers, magazines, radio, and television have become an amorphous hybrid of news and entertainment that gives what amounts to never-ending reviews of the performances of government leaders. Too often, the media no longer sees its duty as telling its audience what happened, when, why, how, and by whom. Its drive has become to amass an online following by appealing to the preconceptions of particular audiences. The mission is no longer to broaden people's knowledge and understanding but to present them with a narrow vision of the world that panders to their prejudices. This trend is not as pronounced in Canada as elsewhere, especially the US and the UK, but Canadian media is running mindlessly into that looming storm.

A DEFINITIVE CRITIQUE of the state of Canadian democracy — its ills and the remedies that should be pursued — was published in 2019 by the Olympian analyst of Canada's political and administrative mechanism Donald Savoie, the Canada Research Chair at the Université de Moncton in New Brunswick. Savoie describes his book, *Democracy in Canada: The Disintegration of Our Institutions*, as his magnum opus, and it does indeed float on the scholarship of his forty-five previous books examining all aspects of Canadian public life.

Savoie readily admits to approaching his vision of Canada past and present from the vantage point of one of the poorer and least politically influential provinces, the cultural heritage of which is less well defined than those of Ontario or Quebec. There's no harm in that. He portrays the rush to put Canada together in 1867 as a muddle born out of the uprisings in Upper and Lower Canada in 1837, the stalemate that had developed in the subsequent union of those two colonies, and the threat from the south posed by the American Civil War. It was felt that the friction between Upper and Lower Canada could be moderated by the creation of a confederation with Britain's seaboard colonies, and this would have the added virtue of presenting a firm face to the US. Sir John A. Macdonald, Upper Canada's leader and one of the principal architects of Confederation, along with George-Étienne Cartier, George Brown, and Alexander Galt, viewed the process with what is now thought of as a central Canadian bias. Macdonald especially wanted Canada to be a unitary state, and to that end he and the others decided to import unaltered the political and administrative institutions that functioned in Great Britain. Leaders from the Maritime colonies, such as Albert Smith from New Brunswick and Joseph Howe and William Annand from Nova Scotia, wanted a federation. They understood better than Macdonald that this would require homegrown systems to be built into the structure of the new country to accommodate the inevitable push and pull of conflicting regional needs and aspirations. They, together with Lower Canada, forced Macdonald to agree to a federation, but at his insistence that came with the political and administrative institutions designed to run a unitary state. Savoie concludes that the British North America Act founding Canada was "deeply flawed." He wrote, "For one thing, it lacked a fundamental requirement: an amending formula. For another, it made no provision for counterbalancing representation by population with a voice for the regions within national political institutions."

Savoie believes that a Senate with an equal number of senators from each province, following the example of the US, should have embodied that regional representation and influence in Ottawa. Instead, the role of advocate for the regions has fallen by default to the provinces. They loom much larger than the marginally embellished municipal governments that Macdonald envisaged. But without a constitutional template geared to reality, federal-provincial relations are a daily drama performed largely offstage and by troupes of unaccountable bureaucrats. The result is that a sense of regional grievance — a belief that every other part of Canada is dining on cream — has become embedded among Canadians in all provinces and regions. A 1990 paper by Richard French, "The Future of Federal-Provincial Relations ... If Any," states, "Sixty-four percent of Canadians feel their province gets back less in federal spending than the taxes sent to Ottawa. Nearly three-quarters of Canadians feel that the federal government favours one region of Canada over the others, and very few feel that their region is the one favoured."

The founding notion that collectively the Maritime provinces would act as a counterbalance and, on occasion, arbitrator between Ontario and Quebec never gained traction. Had they been amalgamated into one province, the outcome would have been different. And as the country expanded westwards, the two central provinces successfully maintained their hegemony by arguing against the creation of one prairie province that would threaten the dominance of the centre. As a result, comments Savoie, "there is no capacity in Canada's national political institutions to bring regional circumstances to light when shaping national policies."

There is a widespread belief in Canada that the constitutional entrenchment of the Charter of Rights and Freedoms by the government of Pierre Trudeau in 1982 handed what should rightly have been parliamentary power to the Supreme Court. Savoie points out, however, that this process of judges making decisions on political matters has a long history. It began with the founding of the country, because of the failure to properly define Canada as a confederation. Until 1949, the Judicial Committee of the Privy Council — five thousand kilometres away in London — served as Canada's Court of Appeal. During the years from Confederation in 1867 until 1949, it heard 173 cases where it was required to interpret the British North America Act. The decisions of the British judges played a pivotal role in revising and reshaping the Canadian federation, frequently in favour of the provinces. Savoie concludes that the system has become so convoluted that Canada no longer meets one of the fundamental requirements of democracy: that a voter can easily see which politician or authority is responsible for a policy with which he or she disagrees.

"Canadian federalism has become a potpourri of federal-provincial agreements, federal-provincial policies, federal-provincial measures, federal-provincial initiatives, and federal-provincial regulations. It has given rise to a multitude of federal-provincial committees managing a myriad of shared-cost programs. All federations have different forms of collaborative agreements between levels of government, but no other federation has taken the matter as far as Canada," he wrote.

"The result is that politicians and public servants from eleven governments have become the constitutional decision-makers for Canada. They operate behind closed doors, and when agreements are struck, it is difficult to discern who proposed what, who opposed what, and how the consensus was struck."

Looked at from a constitutional, legal, and administrative point of view, Savoie is right. But there are political and cultural aspects to the way the relationship between the provincial, territorial, and central governments have evolved that argue that the situation is not as dire as he suggests. Canada's provinces do not have the independent power possessed by states in the US. Their powers are bestowed by the Crown in the shape of Ottawa. But each provincial and territorial government has its own democratic legitimacy, and Ottawa abuses that at its peril. Canadian voters, especially in Quebec, Ontario, and British Columbia, have become adept at intuitively voting for one party in federal elections and another in provincial ballots. As a result, Canada's most populous and economically diverse provinces provide a counterweight to the federal government in national political life. The effectiveness of this voter sleight of hand is most evident when there is a weak opposition or overriding government majority in Ottawa. The provincial governments then slip seamlessly into their roles as the country's alternative democratic opposition.

Some analysts contend another institutional opposition has come into play with the passage of the Charter of Rights and Freedoms as part of the package patriating the Canadian Constitution from Britain in 1982. F.L Morton and Rainer Knopff, in their 2000 book *The Charter Revolution and the Court Party*, contend that Pierre Trudeau's insistence on this way of embedding rights created "judicial supremacy." They argue it ended the tradition of parliamentary supremacy over all manner of social issues, especially those affecting distinct groups such as Indigenous peoples, those seeking support for same-sex marriage, and linguistic minorities. Outflanking the innate social conservatism of Parliament was one of Pierre

Trudeau's aims, but it also made the Supreme Court judges, in Morton and Knopff's view, "active players in the political process" and encouraged them to abandon the "deference and self restraint that characterised their pre-Charter jurisprudence." The position of the court as a political actor in contest with Parliament came to a head during the Conservative government of Stephen Harper from 2006 to 2015. Emmett Macfarlane noted in a 2018 issue of the *Canadian Journal of Political Science* that the Harper administration "is the only Charter period government to have policies specifically outlined in its electoral platform invalidated [by the court]." In other words, the Supreme Court overruled the decision of the Canadian voters when they elected a Tory government. "Harper became convinced that the Court had set itself up as the unofficial opposition," Macfarlane wrote.

There is support for that judgment. For Canadians who for one reason or another could not get their concerns addressed fairly by Parliament, the legislatures, or the political establishment, the Supreme Court became the natural last resort in the hunt for justice or resolution. It is evident, though, that this a result of the failure of government and the political system at all levels to meet the needs of significant sections of Canadian society rather than of judicial assertiveness. The ascendancy of the court was evident in a 2015 survey done by the Angus Reid polling company. The survey found that 61 percent of Canadians expressed confidence in the Supreme Court, while only 25 percent had similar faith in Parliament. The numbers got worse when people in the sample were questioned in more detail. Only 13 percent of Canadians trusted political parties, and only 12 percent had confidence in politicians as a tribe.

Even so, there are good reasons to question whether the court has handled its stardom with respect for the proper balance between the executive, legislative, and judicial pillars of government. From some perspectives, it has set itself up as the most explicit example of populism in Canada. The Supreme Court is, after all, an unelected and unaccountable body, responsible to no one but itself. It blocks inquiries under access to information legislation into the expenses of judges. It recently ruled that notes and other documents from its deliberations that led to judgments must be kept secret for fifty years. The normal period in government for keeping sensitive documents secret is thirty years. And yet the court produces a steady stream of judgments that have far-reaching effects on all aspects of Canadian life. It has taken to doing this without having any responsibility to manage the effects of its rulings. One particularly questionable aspect of the Supreme Court's overreach in recent years have been the occasions when it has dictated to elected governments what should be done, sometimes in contradiction of the policies and decisions of those governments. In New Brunswick in 2008, the government decided to eliminate its early French immersion school program as part of a broadbased austerity budget. Parents challenged the policy and took the case to court, which decided the Fredericton government had not violated the parents' Charter rights. But the court did rule that the government had not given enough time for debate on the issue. On this basis, the court decided the move by the Ministry of Education was "unfair and unreasonable" and quashed it. The New Brunswick government decided not to appeal the decision, instead returning to the consultation process and eventually revising its plans for early French immersion classes. This example can best be described as the court going on a nitpicking exercise, instructing a democratically elected government on how it should conduct its relationship with its citizens.

Another example of the apparent insouciance of the Supreme Court about the practical problems raised by its judgments is a decision from 2012 that governments and school boards could not use budget constraints or other arguments to justify limiting programs for students with special needs. Justice Rosalie Abella wrote, "Adequate special education is not a dispensable luxury." Critics said it was unacceptable for the court to single out one area of provinces' education budgets as inviolable without taking any responsibility or offering any advice on how the shortfall was to be met.

There is no question that on occasion, armed with the Charter of Rights and Freedoms, the Supreme Court and other senior provincial courts have exceeded their proper role in Canadian public life. It is important to recognize, however, that that is because of a failure of Canadian political life, not a coup by the judges. By assuming the role of defenders of individual rights and aspirations, they have filled a vacuum created by a deficient political system. The response, then, must not be to try to constrain the forum in which the courts operate — which would be a political impossibility anyway — but to revive and restore the purpose of Canada's political institutions.

THE DEGRADATION OF Canada's democracy and political system has been sneaking up for decades. There is much that can be done to reinvigorate Canadian democracy at a time when it is becoming more important than at almost any other time in the country's history. The country needs to be able to forge national self-confidence and purpose in an era when old alliances and securities are falling away.

As in other North Atlantic democracies, the demand for public services of a multitude of kinds has led to the creation of countless boards, commissions, and authorities at federal, provincial, and municipal levels whose deliberations have direct effects on the daily lives of Canadians. Yet these bodies are often unaccountable and sometimes almost invisible. To be fair, the problem of democratically deficient bodies is not as pervasive in Canada as it is in some other North Atlantic countries — the UK, for example — but there is still room to clarify and perhaps add to the responsibility of these agencies to report to Parliament and provincial legislatures.

For the legislative assemblies themselves, in Ottawa and the provincial capitals, interconnected problems have degraded the currency of Canadian democracy over the last fifty years.

Pierre Trudeau's remark in Parliament on July 25, 1969, about his fellow MPs is often cited as a mark of his intellectual arrogance. "When they get home, when they get out of Parliament, when they are fifty yards from Parliament Hill, they are no longer honourable members — they are just nobodies, Mr. Speaker," he said. Never mind that the full context of what he said gives a rather different meaning to the remark, a major problem now with Canadian democracy is that MPs are nobodies even when they are in the House of Commons (or when their provincial counterparts are in their legislatures). To a dangerous degree, all legislative assemblies across Canada are spinning toward irrelevance. All governments are on the verge of becoming bodies where all authority, both political and legislative, is in the hands of the prime minister or the premier. In a ministerial system, the level of collegial work and respect always depends on the personalities involved. Some political leaders bestride their worlds; others are happiest as team captains. There are signs in Canada, however, that the supremacy of the government leader is becoming institutionalized. In many cases, even Cabinet ministers have ceased to be political restraints on or sources of alternative policy choices to the leader. Instead, as Savoie put it, they have become merely "a focus group" against which the prime minister or premier tests his or her intentions.

The erosion of collegial government and the rise to almost presidential or head of state status of premiers and the prime minister is a relatively recent phenomenon born of two broad but interlocking developments. One is apparent improvement in the methods of public opinion polling that have been going on since the 1970s. The second is the media's increasing fixation with celebrity. This has created a potpourri of public figures ranging from political leaders to influencers of popular taste, all of whose performances are judged by startlingly similar standards.

That said, it is astonishing how often pollsters miss major shifts in public thoughts and attitudes. The election of Donald Trump and the referendum vote for the UK to leave the EU are glaring examples. Those outcomes, largely unforeseen by pollsters, are a reminder that any poll is only as good as the design of the questions that are asked. But political party managers have come to believe that polls tell them all they need to know about the frame of mind of the public in order to construct an election campaign. And, they believe, where there are distinct regional differences in attitudes, the polls will pick up the nuances so that campaign messages can be tweaked to respond to local views. One of the appeals of poll-led campaigns is that they are easy and appear to provide a clear framework on which to construct the drive for election. It does away with the often troublesome business of a government leader having to appoint to Cabinet knowledgeable and powerful regional political figures — often ones who have their own ambitions. Trust in opinion polls is a lot less murky than the time-consuming business of mounting major canvassing campaigns, which often produce no clear picture of what the voters want or how the candidate is doing. In the event of voting day disasters, it is easier to blame polls that got it wrong than to accept misreading what voters were saying on the doorstep.

Reliance on public opinion polls as the templates for election campaigns radically alters the nature of the democratic exercise. The first impact is to enhance the importance of the national campaign designed in the party's central office and to place less weight on the local knowledge or standing of the individual candidates. That in turn inflates the importance of the party leader and his or her national vision as the points on which the election will turn. The branding and marketing of the leader, rather than policies or political ideologies, has become the determining factor in the outcomes of Canadian elections. This trend has been propelled by the changing nature of media and how it is used. An effect of the continuing intensification of screen culture is the now near complete dominance of image over content as the basis for the choices put before the public on which to judge public figures. With this has come the erasure of lines between the worlds of politics and entertainment, celebrity and accomplishment, reality and fantasy. Now, more than ever in the past, it is the image of the party leaders on which the outcome of elections turn.

Journalism, unforgivably, has allowed itself to be carried along on this wave. Televised leaders' debates have become the signal events where elections are decided. The lust is for the "gotcha" moment when one leader or another delivers a devastating quip that seals the election. The most decisive of these moments in Canadian electoral history is Conservative Brian Mulroney's "You could have said 'no'" to John Turner in the leaders' debate in 1984, when Turner tried to justify patronage appointments he had made as the unelected Liberal prime minister. But the emphasis on leaders' debates denigrates election campaigns to the level of TV game shows. Television networks like the debates because the game show format appeals to a wide audience. Having one of their star presenters acting as umpire in a verbal brawl between the leaders is a lot easier than having to prepare a skilled interviewer to confront the leaders in one-on-one discussions.

Writing in *Policy Options* in May 2007, pollster David Herle described how the leader's brand has come to overtake policies, ideologies, and the stature of individual constituency candidates in Canadian politics. "Parties don't run on what their members think and can't if they want to be successful. They run on what will get them the most votes. It is a strategic marketing exercise rather than a genuine contest of ideas."

The dominance of the leader's image, adjusted and directed by the polling results flowing into the prime minister's or premier's office in this age of year-round election campaigns, is having just as much effect on Parliament and government as it does on elections. It used to be that an essential element in stable and successful federal governments was the appointment of ministers well versed in the issues and sensitivities of their home regions to act as advocates for their provinces in Cabinet debates. One of the first acts of Justin Trudeau after he was elected in 2015 was to do away with this system. One reason was his priority to appoint a Cabinet that was 50 percent women. Another was that he didn't have the heart to make difficult choices between the surfeit of powerful regional members the election had given him. A third reason was that believing the increasing sophistication of polls, he and his political advisers didn't feel they needed regional barons who could become lightning rods for dissent within Cabinet.

Just as the electoral process has become more and more dominated by the brand image of the party leaders and the legislative process less and less influenced by ministers and MPs, so the role of political parties has diminished too. In his 2007 essay, "Policy Study and Development in

Canada's Political Parties," Carleton University political science professor William Cross wrote, "Canadian political parties are not effective vehicles for policy study and development. They neither offer voters meaningful opportunity for involvement in the policy making process, nor do they regularly generate policy alternatives for consideration and examination by those in elected office or in the senior bureaucracy."

Because of this, he continued, party membership continues to drop and people committed to exploring policy alternatives for Canada tend to gravitate toward special interest groups or non-governmental organizations that use lobbying techniques to influence government. A result of the abandonment by political parties of their role as forums for the evolution of policy ideas is that they have become truculent last bastions of partisan ideological purity and exponents of the view that in politics, winning is the only objective. David McLaughlin wrote in *The Globe and Mail* in 2013, "Faithful to the partisan glue binding them to their parties, our political class is doing everything possible to diminish, demean, and destroy the precious commodity they actually hold in common: their own political integrity. In their relentless attacks on everything and everyone on the opposite political divide, they continue to devalue the basic political currency — trust — essential between electors and elected in democracy. We, the voters, are the losers."

IT IS HARD to find anyone, especially among those directly involved, who is happy with the way the Canadian political system is working today. And there is no shortage of politicians, partisans, academics, and others who have written books, essays, and reports brimming with ideas for remedies. The problem is the simple and perennial one in these kinds of circumstances: who has the political will to rise to the occasion and confront the challenges the country faces?

To this end, there may prove to be a lasting benefit from the COVID-19 pandemic. The enormity of its assault on all aspects of Canadian life has provoked a readiness to examine national values, constraints, and balances of power. It is possible that the coronavirus will inspire action on some fundamental rethinking on political, democratic, economic, and cultural priorities.

Until then, government leaders have little interest in promoting the authority and influence of Parliament over legislative affairs. That will only make life more difficult for the prime minister or premier in a world already kept constantly off balance by the twenty-four-hour news cycle and the increasingly potent vexations of social media.

In the same vein, Justin Trudeau came to office in 2015 promising that the election just fought would be the last first-past-the-post ballot and that the next election would be under some form of proportional representation that ensured that "every vote counted." It didn't happen, and in retrospect it was a foolish promise to make without careful consideration of the implications. Once in government, the Liberals didn't take up their pledge because there is no consensus among Canadians that a proportional representation system would produce a Parliament that genuinely represents the country and — perhaps even more important — is able to create governing coalitions that actually function. The experience of European democracies was also considered. Proportional representation has allowed extremist, anti-democratic parties, mostly of the right, to get legislative seats and, with that, political legitimacy. In some cases, these parties have even become members of governing coalitions. There is a profound difference between having an inclusive legislative assembly and giving a platform to purveyors of hate, division, and tyranny.

Another, more visceral question that any Canadian prime minister who has just won a significant majority under the first-past-the-post system must inevitably ask is: Why would I give up this in favour of a system where I can expect to run only a minority government at best?

The danger for Canada is that its democratic deficit will get worse and potentially become fatal unless it is addressed and remedied. The politics of fear and hatred are already well established in several parts of the country, most notably Ontario, Quebec, and the West, and those infections are being fed by unscrupulous partisans. Meanwhile, there is the proliferation of social media as the medium that brings most Canadians their news and which for commercial purposes tries to ensure the news they are sent reinforces what they already believe. This is a recipe for polarization of society, as is all too evident in the US. Left unreformed, large segments of the Canadian voting public will soon be fixed in extreme views and beyond the reach of centrist political influence.

Environmental policy and the foreseeable end of Canada's oil and gas industries present an immediate challenge to Canadian provincial and federal political leaders to show they have learned the lessons of the last thirty years. COVID-19 and the shutdown of the Canadian economy has, ironically, given a significant boost to the environmental movement by showing how quickly nature can rebound when the daily outpouring of human-created air pollution and other waste is lessened. This experience will underline the inevitable truth that the oil and gas industries centred in British Columbia, Alberta, Saskatchewan, and Newfoundland and Labrador are well into their twilight years. But instead of working to develop a national campaign to manage the winding up of this industry, with emphasis on offering retraining and opportunities in new energy industries to employees, political leaders in Ottawa and the affected provinces are bickering over pipelines, market access, and subsidies. As a result, the federal-provincial dialogue has become increasingly bitter and polarized. That rancour has infected the electorate, and Canada is at risk of being infected with the same kind of irrational, hate-filled social divide that is killing the US.

The future of Canada's oil and gas industry is probably the greatest immediate challenge to the country's democracy and to public confidence in the efficacy of the system. Canadian political leaders need to get right their approach to this divisive issue. If they don't, the damage to the country's political cohesion could last generations. In a broader context, the end of the COVID-19 pandemic is going to present national governments with a scarred economic landscape on which many industries and businesses have died or been mortally wounded. The streets are going to be full of people whose jobs have disappeared and may never return. Federal and provincial governments must grasp that handouts and subsidies are a temporary measure and will not suffice for the long term. A major program of reconstruction and retraining is necessary, or else these victims of the consequences of the coronavirus will be a ready-made audience for populists.

Before they attempt to regain the confidence of the Canadian people, the country's political classes need to get their own houses in order, and this applies to the provinces just as much as to Parliament in Ottawa. In the current context, a good place to start would be to revive the status of Parliament and the legislatures as the stages on which issues of the day are debated and resolved. Governments across Canada have got into the habit of avoiding, overriding, minimizing, or otherwise degrading the opportunity for reasonable debate and consideration of legislation and policies. The format of the omnibus bill — in which governments mash together a whole host of incompatible objectives, swamping the opposition and their own members with a tidal wave of indigestible information — is the most egregious example of suppressing informed debate. This practice is little short of contemptuous for the institution of Parliament and begs the question: If governments show such disdain for Parliament and its members, why shouldn't the public feel likewise?

As well as having their role in assessing legislation revived, it would be a great help if the balance of power between party leaders — the prime minister and premiers in particular — and their caucuses were changed. To that end, political parties should make their leaders far more dependent on the support of caucus members than they are at the moment. Clearly, a party leader whose position flows from the support of his caucus is far more likely to use his MPs intelligently and promote their involvement than one whose job is at the bequest of party members in convention or a gamble on whose supporters bought the most memberships online.

Canadian parties, by and large, have adopted systems under which the leader is selected by the party membership as a whole. This sounds wonderfully democratic, but it is not always sensible. On several occasions in recent years, tub-thumping party conventions have thrown up leaders with little or no experience of elected office, or ones who have been anathema to the members of the caucus they have been selected to lead. There are ways of dealing with this. One of the most useful models to consider comes from the unlikely source of the British Conservative Party. There, members of caucus go through several rounds of voting for the prospective candidates until there are two left. Then those two names are put to the party members at large to pick the winner. The system has the advantage of usually producing a new leader who has the support of the bulk of caucus, has experience in Parliament, and is not a rank outsider. Excessive caucus control over the tenure of the leader is not to be encouraged either. Most Australian political parties follow a system known in the local jargon as a "spill." This involves the caucus removing its leader by a vote among members. Traditionally, it has taken only a simple majority, though some parties are moving to require a two-thirds vote in favour of an ouster. Tightening up the rules flows from the popularity of removing the leader on a Monday morning if the poll results reported in the weekend newspapers have looked bad. There were seventy-two spills among Australian political parties between 1970 and 2015, and thirty-one between 2000 and 2015. One of the recent victims was Prime Minister Malcolm Turnbull, who was removed in a caucus spill in August 2018.

There is, however, another aspect of Australian politics that Canada would do well to follow. Since 1924, it has been compulsory for adult Australians to register and to vote in national elections, by-elections, and national referenda. Those who don't turn out to cast a ballot face a small fine of $80, which is added to their tax return accounts if unpaid. For many Australians, however, the carrots are more attractive than the stick. Elections are always held on Saturdays, and voting day has become akin to a public holiday when democracy is celebrated with barbecues and parties. As a result, the turnout in Australian national elections is consistently over 90 percent. The turnout in Canada's October 2019 election was under 66 percent of registered voters — but the number of registered voters in Canada does not represent all Canadians who are eligible to vote, though the gap is much narrower than in other North Atlantic democracies. Registering to vote and voting on election day is relatively easy, when compared with the patchwork of regulations in US states and other democracies in Europe.

———

IN CANADA, THE resources of the Prime Minister's Office and the Privy Council Office have grown significantly in the last four decades. With the growth of policy and administrative capacity available directly to the prime minister has gone a diminution of the role and influence of ministers, both singly and collectively, in Cabinet. On top of that, since Jean Chrétien was prime minister in the 1990s, political appointments to the staff of ministers have been made by the PMO. This practice has continued and by some accounts was intensified during the Conservative administration of Stephen Harper. There's a glaring lack of trust in the ministers if the prime minister feels it necessary to have his own political watchdogs in every ministerial office. Another area of over-politicization is the relationship between the political parties and the senior ranks of the civil service.

For generations, the Liberals, as Canada's natural party of power since the Great Depression, have directly appointed senior civil servants, especially deputy ministers and the heads of extra-governmental boards and commissions. This practice has led to great suspicion on the occasions when Canada has had Conservative governments. Tory governments have always harboured the belief that most senior civil servants are Liberals under the skin and bent on frustrating their agendas. That view has sometimes been right. When Brian Mulroney came to office in 1984, he tried to thwart any Liberal prejudice at the senior levels of the civil service by appointing conservative-minded deputy ministers to key departments. Harper, when he became prime minister in 2006, had a fixation with the Ministry of Foreign Affairs. He saw the department as not only a bastion of Liberalism but also an institution that appeared to believe that no politician of any stripe could interpret and administer an appropriate foreign policy for Canada as well as the professionals in the Lester B.

Pearson Building. Harper went so far as to require all senior ambassadors and other Foreign Affairs officials to submit to the PMO for vetting the drafts of any public speeches they intended to make. Some senior diplomats found it humiliating that the prime minister did not trust them out in public without oversight, and there was an exodus from the senior and middle levels of the department during the Harper years.

Ottawa should adopt a variation of the systems of seniority and meritocracy used by most parliamentary democracies in their senior civil service appointments. In Alberta, candidates for the position of deputy minister are interviewed by a committee of current deputy ministers chaired by the clerk of the Privy Council. The committee then makes a recommendation to the minister of the department involved, and the minister takes that advice to Cabinet for ratification. The premier still has a veto, as is proper, but clearly only serious misgivings would justify turning thumbs down on a recommendation made by a non-partisan committee of the candidate's peers.

PATRONAGE IS ONE of the original sins of Canadian politics. Canadian political history is richly punctuated by examples of politicians using their power to make appointments for personal or party benefit. The Pacific Scandal of 1873, the Beauharnois Scandal of 1930–32, and the Sponsorship Scandal of the 1990s and 2000s stand out, but those affairs don't begin to describe the extent of Canadian political corruption. Much has been done in recent decades by both Conservative and Liberal governments to introduce necessary levels of transparency and meritocracy into the appointments of countless federal and provincial boards and commissions. But patronage is a persistent vice, and there remains much that could be done to assure the voting public that politics and government do not still float on a buoyant sea of cronyism.

Trust is the essential factor in the working of a representative democratic system. In the 1970s in Canada, there was a brief fascination with participatory democracy, which worked on the idea that more ordinary citizens should get directly involved in government and the policies that drive it. It is an idea, of course, that harks back to the Athenian practice of allowing all adult male citizens to take part in the process of government. As appealing as it may sound, participatory democracy is neither practical nor desirable in this day and age. Voters select representatives to go to Parliament because they have neither the time nor the inclination to do the job themselves. Also, any constituency-based advisory committees would clearly be vulnerable to domination by special interest factions of one sort or another. This is already a problem of varying intensity among municipal governments in Canada. What is needed is recognition by elected members and political parties at both the federal and provincial levels that the democratic deficiency in Canada has been created in large part by the public's lack of trust in them and their methods. They need to look to the US, the UK, and Europe to see that if they don't grasp the problem and lead a campaign from the top to rebuild trust, it will be imposed on them from below. And in the end no one — not the voters nor the political and government establishments — will like the way that solution plays out.

Epilogue

AS I COMPLETED the first draft of this book in mid-February 2020, it was becoming apparent that the epidemic of the new coronavirus that had forced the Chinese authorities to close down the central city of Wuhan was about to become a pandemic. From the start, it was obvious that the disease known as COVID-19 was going to have profound effects on several of the themes that I had tackled in this book. One was the rush to security among EU states and the closing of national borders in defiance of international agreements on the free movement of people. Soon after, Canada and the nations of Europe issued mandatory stay-at-home orders, effectively closing their societies and shutting down their economies. This was done to try to stop the human-to-human spread of COVID-19, preventing further contagion.

The short-, medium-, and even long-term implications of this strategy are profound.

They could also become central factors in the trials and tribulations facing the North Atlantic democracies. This is especially pointed as two of the populists in power — Boris Johnson and Donald Trump — were evidently taken off guard by the pandemic and didn't know how to respond. They realized that the pandemic threatened to sweep away their own political agendas, so their first reactions were to deny the seriousness of the virus and its threat to their people. This put the populists in a head-to-head contest with scientists, whose advice and judgments they — Trump in particular — had dismissed as elitist mumbo jumbo in their thrusts for power.

The message of the pandemic for all but those irretrievably addicted to the ideology of minimal government was a reminder of the importance of having a representative, effective, trusted, and well-funded administration for times when disaster strikes.

As soon as the extent of the pandemic became evident, I started going back through my manuscript, making inserts and adjustments to the text to take COVID-19 into account. The question then became to try to identify the lasting implications of the coronavirus for the North Atlantic democracies and their places in the world, especially alongside China. I am writing this epilogue in mid-May 2020, at what looks to be the peak of the infection around the North Atlantic countries. How COVID-19 will affect Africa, South Asia, the Middle East, and Latin America is still to be seen; thus, making forecasts about the lasting effects of the pandemic is a perilous business. But I think one can say with confidence that there are going to be lasting economic, political, and social effects. How deep those effects run and how long they last are beyond predicting, and their course and impact will undoubtedly be changed by subsequent events. But on the economic side, I think the effects of the coronavirus have bolstered the argument that unbridled capitalism is destructive of democracy. The immediate impact of the shutdown of North Atlantic economies was to present the public with a stark picture that it is the essential workers in their societies who make it work day to day, not the captains of industry and commerce. The people who enabled health and security services to function and ordinary citizens to self-isolate in their homes were society's most poorly paid, such as food store workers, transport drivers, homecare employees, cleaning staff, and agricultural workers. That vivid picture may propel arguments to restructure tax regimes in order to reduce disparity. It might encourage a more diligent examination of the virtues of establishing a universal basic income as a much more economic, positive, and productive approach to empowering low-paid or unemployed citizens than the current dog's breakfast of social security payments. In Canada, the universal basic income is being promoted with eloquence and persistence by former Progressive Conservative Senator Hugh Segal. The response of most North Atlantic governments to COVID-19 has added power to his argument. In the rush to shut down their economies, almost all governments handed out large payments to the millions of people put out of work by the closures. If universal basic incomes had been in place, the system would have almost automatically moved to protect the most vulnerable. Spain, one of the countries hit hardest by the coronavirus, began very soon after the virus struck to take steps to introduce a universal basic income.

Very quickly, after it moved from being an epidemic in China to becoming a worldwide pandemic, COVID-19 appeared to present a massive threat to the survival of globalization and the network of multinational supply chains for goods and services that have dominated international commerce for the last three decades. Many of the North Atlantic countries quickly discovered they had become reliant on foreign suppliers for a multitude of products and that cutting those supply chains presented huge dangers. Questions about the efficacy of unlimited globalization will undoubtedly survive the end of the pandemic. It seems unlikely that globalization is dead, as some have predicted. But it is certain that many countries will take a broader look at what constitute strategic products necessary for the country's security. As I write, most North Atlantic countries have already restarted medical equipment and pharmaceutical industries that had migrated to China, India, and other low-cost production centres. Those revived domestic production facilities will probably stay in place after COVID-19 has been overcome and may be joined by the revival of other strategic industries, with domestic food production perhaps high on the list. Too many epidemiologists are warning that people and governments must be prepared for pandemics to become a regular part of human life for anyone to feel comfortable, even when COVID-19 is overcome.

Another aspect of globalization thrust to the fore by the pandemic is the ease and popularity of international air travel and tourism, including the proliferation of cruise lines. It was people travelling on planes and ships for pleasure or business who were the vectors that took COVID-19 around the world in a matter of days. As a result, governments shut down not only the tourism industry but much of the world's air transport network as well. When the pandemic is over, tourism will revive, but it will take time, and it may not in the foreseeable future attain the level it had before the coronavirus outbreak. Quite apart from a heightened reluctance among many people to expose themselves to infection while travelling and subject themselves to a required fourteen-day quarantine when they arrive, industry analysts are warning that the era of cheap flights is probably over for several years. People living in many favourite tourist destinations will breathe a sigh of relief. Amsterdam, Rome, Paris, and Venice, among other favourite tourist destinations, were already leading a widening campaign to restrict visitors' access to their cities, which are on the verge of becoming unlivable.

Some of the most poignant horror stories of the first weeks of the pandemic were cruise ships with hundreds of infected people among thousands of passengers and crews. Some of these ships were held in quarantine in ports, with healthy passengers becoming more and more anxious as the virus spread. Other cruise ships, carrying infected passengers and crews, found themselves refused access to port after port and roamed the seas for weeks, seeking somewhere — anywhere — to land. Cruise ships have always been petri dishes for disease. The industry will have to examine its health protocols and mount a major public relations offensive to make it viable again.

The closing down of air travel also reinforced the already evident truth that business meetings can be conducted just as easily, and perhaps even more productively, online. This was already known, but the habit of calling people in from far-flung outposts to head office for gatherings of one sort or another was hard to break. Collegial bonding in person is comforting for both managers and staff. But COVID-19 reaffirmed the utility of video conferencing software, whose popularity exploded over the course of the pandemic — and not just for businesses. Book clubs, school lessons, university lectures, family dinners, cocktail parties, discussion groups, and a host of other social gatherings gravitated to video conferencing programs. Thanks to COVID-19, these have become an established part of communal life. People will revert to the joys of proper human contact once the restrictions are loosened or lifted, but the business sector will latch on to the utility and economy of video links and working from home where feasible. They will discover, however, that there are dangers in this, especially in trying to retain a stout corporate culture among a disparate workforce of people beavering away in their home offices. As someone who has spent most of his career working alone and usually in distant office outposts, I know very well the importance of the cultural infusion and inspiration that one can only get from association with colleagues. Having too many people working from home is likely to lead to a dangerous stultification of corporate imagination.

In politics, the pandemic is testing the relationship between the rulers and the ruled. Throughout this book, I have pointed to the mistrust for authority that has gathered among many citizens as one of the most serious threats to democracy. In response to the pandemic, most North Atlantic governments started by setting out the arguments for self-isolation to halt the spread of the virus. In most cases, they then asked rather than compelled citizens to follow this advice, though some did enforce lockdowns and curfews. For the most part, citizens responded positively to the appeals to behave safely and sensibly. In Canada, the annual Trust Barometer published in mid-May by global communication company Edelman found that 70 percent of Canadians said they trusted the government's handling of the outbreak, compared with the 50 percent of Canadians who said they trusted government in the 2019 survey. In most cases, the heightened trust was because political leaders were wise enough to base their actions on the advice of public health officials and scientists and to let those officials make the case to the public. Wise political leaders will recognize that the public's response to COVID-19 has given them an opportunity to examine what has gone wrong in the relationship between the governing and the governed and what needs to be done to make the reconciliation permanent.

This call for self-discipline also provided an important moment when experts, in this case scientists and doctors knowledgeable in the ways of epidemics, could demonstrate to the public the value of facts and experience. The only part of the North Atlantic region where this did not happen was in the US — more particularly, from the federal government. There, Donald Trump and his team continued to pander to their supporters by downplaying and sometimes deliberately belittling the advice of public health officials, promoting quack remedies, and attempting to use the pandemic for political advantage.

In some cases, such as Italy, Spain, the UK, and France, the pandemic tested national health systems to the breaking point. There will undoubtedly be public pressure for greater investment in health care systems, which some political leaders will follow, at least for a while. One of the great weaknesses revealed in some countries was not in the national health systems but in homes for the elderly who are no longer able to live independently or with relatives. The proportion of victims of COVID-19 on both sides of the Atlantic who contracted the virus in these homes and who died there or in hospital without being able to see their closest relatives was very high. In Canada at the end of the second week in May, 82 percent of all COVID-19–related deaths were in long-term care homes. In the US, the percentage of COVID-19 deaths in long-term care homes was 35 percent. In England and Wales, 22.5 percent of all COVID-19 deaths were in care homes, but it was 40 percent in Scotland. In Italy, Spain, France, Ireland, and Belgium, between 42 and 57 percent of deaths from the virus were in care homes. It is an unforgiveable indictment of the degree to which the elderly had been abandoned to profitable and often unaccountable long-term care businesses, some of which abused the trust that had been placed in them.

COVID-19 will present a major test for democracy as the pandemic is contained and the time comes to consider lifting the restrictions put in place to halt the spread of the virus. I have described how some leaders with despotic ambitions introduced emergency measures that go well beyond what can be justified as public health measures. But even in the more vibrant and dedicated democracies, some of the measures employed raise questions about respect for civil liberties. In Canada, people were fined for sitting on park benches or standing too close to other people with whom they were talking. These kinds of incidents raise questions about whether even the most democratic governments will entirely lift the emergency restrictions once the emergency is over. History says that once governments have adopted emergency powers, they are reluctant to remove them, sometimes keeping selected powers even when the main restraints have been lifted. Nearly twenty years after the 9/11 attacks on New York and Washington, significant elements of the anti-terrorism regulations imposed at the time are still in force despite the killing of Osama bin Laden, the effective dismantling of his al Qaeda terrorist group, and the destruction of other terrorist organizations such as the Islamic State.

Civil and human rights organizations began raising questions and warnings about the emergency measures even as they were being imposed. The clamour for a full lifting of the restrictions will continue, and in the end it will be successful in deep-rooted North Atlantic democracies. There are already signs that getting authorities in fledgling democracies and populist outposts such as Hungary and Poland to lift the restrictions on challenges to their rule is going to be a more difficult proposition.

There are other questions that the COVID-19 pandemic raises about technological surveillance and what citizens in democracies are willing to put up with in the interests of security. Taiwan and South Korea are credited with exemplary responses to the outbreak. Taiwan, despite being just off the coast of China and having significant two-way business traffic, in the first hundred days of the pandemic had only 376 confirmed cases and 5 deaths. South Korea got off to bad start when a religious gathering became the vector for widespread infection. By late February, more than 10,000 people had been infected and 192 had died. But six weeks later, the daily increases in the number of infections were down to single figures. While both countries, and especially Taiwan, learned much from the

SARS epidemic at the beginning of the century and had potent response mechanisms in place, both also used contact tracing apps in cell phones to establish where infected people had been and whom they had met. Other countries, including Canada, examined the success of the contact tracing programs with future pandemics in mind. Contact tracing apps open to governments raise many more questions about the right to privacy and to what other purposes police and security organizations might put the records of people's movements. A host of questions about rights to privacy and the information platform companies sell to marketers have come into sharper focus.

The COVID-19 pandemic has provided timely intervention for North Atlantic peoples to examine their societies and their lives at a moment when many aspects appear to be careering down a road to destruction. Looking at the story of the last forty years in Europe and North America, there has been a clear loss of balance on both the left and right of the political spectrum. Driven by hard-line right-of-centre economic ideologies, disparity between a tiny global oligarchy of the super rich and the rest of humankind has reached levels that threaten social stability. Governing elites have pursued liberal democratic goals and postures of political correctness that are sometimes out of touch with the beliefs and attitudes of the majority of their countries' populations. Mass migrations in search of wealth or safety have unsettled ethnically homogenous societies and excited dangerous levels of xenophobia and rampant nationalism. These upheavals in democratic societies have presented a golden opportunity to post-communist totalitarian leaders in Russia and China. They are using every tool that comes to hand to undermine confidence in the system among citizens of democracies.

This can all look terribly forbidding and ominous. And yet, so far, no democratic government among the countries of North Atlantic culture on which this book focuses have been elbowed into autocracy, though men like the United States' Donald Trump, Hungary's Viktor Orbán, and Poland's Jarosław Kaczyński are doing their best to take their countries over that line. That is true also of democratic countries further afield where populists have taken power, such as Turkey, Brazil, the Philippines, and India. That being said, some Western democracies are close to being oligarchies. The US is well along the road to that transition, and from some perspectives it has already arrived.

⸻

WHILE DEMOCRACY IS tougher and more resilient than it may appear, the assaults from within and without are dangerous to its survival as a relevant and sustainable form of government. Democracy's victory cannot be taken for granted. Help and attention are needed to confront the imbalances within democratic societies that have thrown them out of kilter. I have chosen the unconscionable level of economic disparity as the most pressing problem that needs addressing to begin restoring balance to the democratic nations. I would go further. I find convincing the argument that measuring the health of nations by their annual increases in wealth — growth in the Gross Domestic Product (GDP) — is not a proper or viable way of assessing the well-being of their populations. Measuring the mere growth or shrinkage of the economy doesn't say anything useful about the nature and value of the society.

Indeed, from an ecological point of view, growth is a vice, not a virtue.

However, I'm not convinced by the Bhutanese system of measuring the success of its government on the basis of Gross National Happiness. Happiness is a nondescript state that can mean anything or nothing. It can even be a vice if one person's happiness is the cause of another person's anguish. Witness the silliness of Americans' constitutional right to the "pursuit of happiness." Personal happiness comes in many forms, and many of them are anti-social for the rest of the community.

I prefer the far more rigorous assessments that go into judging Gross National Well-being (GNW). New Zealand adopted GNW over GDP in 2019 as the annual assessment of the country's stature based on sixty-one criteria. Scotland did the same early in 2020. These criteria paint an overall picture of the state of nation under seven headings assessing mental, physical, workplace, social, economic, environmental, and political well-being. Several other countries are looking to make the same change. The Organisation for Economic Co-operation and Development started publishing tallies of GNW in 2011. Its 2017 report lists the top ten countries for national well-being: Norway, Australia, Iceland, Canada, Denmark, Switzerland, the Netherlands, Sweden, Finland, and the United States. Other more recent reports using similar criteria have the same Nordic and northern European countries plus Canada, New Zealand, and Australia at the top of the list, but the US more often falls into the lower twenties in the rankings. I referred earlier to the dramatic and troubling increase in the proportion of less well educated young white men in the US who are dying by their own hands or because of the abuse of drugs or alcohol. That is only part of the story of the lack of well-being in the US. Studies published by the *American Journal of Psychiatry* show that levels of clinical depression doubled over the decade from the early 1990s to the early 2000s. Subsequent studies suggest the situation is getting worse; for example, doctors feel it necessary to prescribe antidepressants to children and adolescents in ever-increasing numbers.

An important factor in the change from GDP to GNW is a change of perspective on human life on planet Earth. With 7.7 billion people on the planet in 2019 (and the population projected to reach 10 billion by 2050 and 11 billion by 2100), the end to feasible growth is in sight. The Earth is already showing clear signs of rebelling against what looks from its point of view like an increasingly irritating skin disease. Earth has rid itself of infestations in the past and is quite capable of doing so again. As COVID-19 has demonstrated, human developments in transportation have created the perfect system for creating pandemics. The closing down of economies and global transportation also showed how swiftly the Earth's atmosphere can recover when relieved of human pollution. It is time humankind established a sustainable, symbiotic relationship with its host. Turning away from a fixation on growth and beginning to judge political and social actions by their broad contribution to the people of the planet would be a major advance.

In democracies, the ultimate choice for the direction a country should take is in the hands of the voters. But to a disturbing degree, the voters don't control the choices that they are offered. They are presented with visions of their own societies — their hopes and fears, benefits and perils — based on pictures conjured up by establishment elites. There may be a core of reality behind those pictures, but all too often the political messages are exaggerated, self-serving, and designed to keep the populace subservient or scared just enough to support the political leadership. That is what happened with the election of Donald Trump to the presidency in the United States and the votes to leave the European Union in the United Kingdom.

Throughout the process of putting this book together, I have been struck by the failure of political parties across the North Atlantic region to recognize and adjust to what has actually concerned mainstream voters in the last four decades. I found this failure even more striking because I lived through and reported for newspapers on many of the events dealt with in this book. I didn't see the broader context at the time any better than anyone else. Yet looking back over the lessons of the last forty years, it is obvious that far too many political parties are out of touch with their constituents. More than that, they have been hijacked by a culture of political gamesmanship in which the voters are almost an afterthought. When asked about their responsibilities to democracy, far too many political operatives say their only duty is to win an election. The nurturing of democratic culture in their home countries is nothing to do with them. It is this virulent "winners and losers" attitude that has polarized and poisoned party politics; this is especially true in the US, but the symptoms are visible in other North Atlantic democracies, including Canada.

For decades, there has been an affinity between how politics and sports are played. Just as sports have largely abandoned sportsmanship and tipped into a culture where it is not enough to win a game, one must humiliate the opponent, so it is with politics.

As they scan the state of democracy in Europe and North America, political parties should recognize that they need to go through a serious process of self-examination. Central to that should be consideration of their relationships with voters, the degree to which they listen and are driven by voters' concerns, and what they do — or neglect to do — to provide political solutions to what ails their constituents. I have also come to believe that political parties have a responsibility to promote voter participation in the democratic process as a whole. Where parties do approach voters, it is usually in the hunt for committed members, though even this is far less common than it used to be. That is not enough. If parties don't seek to promote democracy as well as their own platforms, voters will continue to do what they are doing now, and with greater fervour. They will run to increasingly politicized courts, or they will gather around the first glib anti-establishment salesman who climbs on a soapbox and beguiles them with a simple remedy for their problems. Build a wall. Expel foreigners. Regain sovereignty. Lock up the opposition. Blame the media.

Similar off-balance distortions have overcome the corporate world. Whatever the endeavour, customers and employees have lost out to senior management and stockholders as the beneficiaries of the enterprise. This has created an unhealthy and ultimately destructive model of customers and employees as commodities in the transaction, undoubtedly influenced by the eruption of digital commerce, where the customers themselves are often the only commodity. Levelling the taxation rates for earned and unearned income, along with critically examining the remuneration given to senior corporate managers, can partially redress the inequality of relationships in the business quadrangle. There may also be some benefits from the pandemic. COVID-19 and the shutting down of national economies has hit consumer retail and service businesses much harder than enterprises such as agriculture that are central to human survival. While in self-isolation, millions of people have seen how much of their lifestyle is essential to their well-being and how much is frippery. There are undoubtedly many people who yearn for the return of the pleasures of self-indulgence. But the evidence of social media, radio phone-in shows, and such is that many others are using the enforced discipline of isolation and limited access to necessities to review their consumerism. Business organizations and individual entrepreneurs are already predicting that many retail and service outlets will not survive the pandemic. The survivors may well find that they have to pay far more attention to their customers than in the past. And the likelihood that physical distancing requirements are going to be in place for some time to lessen the risks of infection will make the safety and well-being of employees a more pressing issue than in the past.

The broader aspect of consumer and popular culture recalls the phrase the "froth of expectation." This description is fifty years old now. It was coined by journalist and author Christopher Booker in his 1969 book *The Neophiliacs: The Revolution in English Life in the Fifties and Sixties*. Booker examined the way accelerated technological change in Britain in the 1950s and 1960s had created fanciful and grossly self-indulgent attitudes toward the political and social life of those decades. Nothing much has changed in half a century. Life for many people is driven by neophilia — love of the new — with little consideration of its implications. The froth of expectation that goes with the gleaming paint on the new toy, fresh out of the box, is part of the growth of the culture of celebrity. With that has come a crash in the ability to measure the relative value of things. These days, political leaders, public intellectuals, television presenters, sports stars, and pop idols all come out of the same chocolate factory. Their views on the issues of the day are now given equal weight; they are interchangeable. Political and other opinion leaders now adopt the manners and mores of popular culture in order to float on the froth of expectation. That is not a recipe for the survival of democracy.

Earlier in this book, I quoted Francis Fukuyama from his 2018 book, *Identity: The Demand for Dignity and the Politics of Resentment*, when he wrote, "Successful democracy depends not on optimization of the ideals, but balance: a balance between individual freedom and political equality, and between a capable state exercising legitimate power and the institutions of law and accountability that seek to constrain it."

That is as good a remedy as any for fixing what is wrong now and for sustaining democracy in the future.

Acknowledgments

IT USUALLY TAKES me at least five years to decompress after the mental isolation of writing a book. So I was hesitant when my editor and publisher at Cormorant Books, Marc Côté, urged me in the summer of 2019 to follow up on *Claws of the Panda: Beijing's Campaign of Influence and Intimidation in Canada*, which had only been out for six months. But I'm glad he did. It has been both a chilling and rewarding exercise to retrace much of my career as a political reporter and foreign correspondent over the last thirty years. It has been chilling because I can now see all the hints and clues I and many others missed at the time, and rewarding because I and others didn't miss all of them.

As well as Marc, the managing director at Cormorant Books, Sarah Cooper, production manager Barry Jowett, and designer Tannice Goddard there are a few other people whose help and support over the research and writing of this book I must acknowledge. My good friend Graham Hutchings played his now well-established role whenever I set out on one of these journeys of authorship. He read the first draft chapters for me, red crayoned the nonsense bits, and pulled me back on to the track when I dived down enticing but dead-end rabbit holes. I must also thank Dennis Madden, the former Controller of the Inter-American Bank in Washington, DC, and a former senior executive of the Bank of Montreal and the

Royal Trust. Dennis was also president of the Society for International Development in Washington, DC. He has recently spent some time thinking and writing about populism and was kind enough to allow me to read his files on the topic.

As always, my biggest debt is to Petrina, who for months carries on regardless that the mind of the man with whom she shares light housekeeping duties was somewhere else entirely.

Victoria, British Columbia, May 2020

Index

We acknowledge the sacred land on which Cormorant Books operates. It has been a site of human activity for 15,000 years. This land is the territory of the Huron-Wendat and Petun First Nations, the Seneca, and most recently, the Mississaugas of the Credit River. The territory was the subject of the Dish With One Spoon Wampum Belt Covenant, an agreement between the Iroquois Confederacy and Confederacy of the Ojibway and allied nations to peaceably share and steward the resources around the Great Lakes. Today, the meeting place of Toronto is still home to many Indigenous people from across Turtle Island. We are grateful to have the opportunity to work in the community, on this territory.

We are also mindful of broken covenants and the need to strive to make right with all our relations.